Spirituality

WILEY-BLACKWELL BRIEF HISTORIES OF RELIGION SERIES

This series offers brief, accessible, and lively accounts of key topics within theology and religion. Each volume presents both academic and general readers with a selected history of topics which have had a profound effect on religious and cultural life. The word "history" is, therefore, understood in its broadest cultural and social sense. The volumes are based on serious scholarship but they are written engagingly and in terms readily understood by general readers.

Other topics in the series:

Published

Heaven	Alister E. McGrath
Heresy	G. R. Evans
Death	Douglas J. Davies
Saints	Lawrence S. Cunningham
Christianity	Carter Lindberg
Dante	Peter S. Hawkins
Cults and New Religions	Douglas E. Cowan and David G. Bromley
Love	Carter Lindberg
Christian Mission	Dana L. Robert
Christian Ethics	Michael Banner
Jesus	W. Barnes Tatum
Shinto	John Breen and Mark Teeuwen
Paul	Robert Paul Seesengood
Apocalypse	Martha Himmelfarb
Islam, 2nd edition	Tamara Sonn
The Reformation	Kenneth G. Appold
Utopias	Howard P. Segal

Spirituality
A Brief History

Second Edition

Philip Sheldrake

WILEY-BLACKWELL

A John Wiley & Sons, Ltd., Publication

This second edition first published 2013
© 2013 John Wiley & Sons, Ltd
Edition history: Blackwell Publishing Ltd (1e, 2007)

Wiley-Blackwell is an imprint of John Wiley & Sons, formed by the merger of Wiley's global Scientific, Technical and Medical business with Blackwell Publishing.

Registered Office
John Wiley & Sons, Ltd, The Atrium, Southern Gate, Chichester, West Sussex, PO19 8SQ, UK

Editorial Offices
350 Main Street, Malden, MA 02148-5020, USA
9600 Garsington Road, Oxford, OX4 2DQ, UK
The Atrium, Southern Gate, Chichester, West Sussex, PO19 8SQ, UK

For details of our global editorial offices, for customer services, and for information about how to apply for permission to reuse the copyright material in this book please see our website at www.wiley.com/wiley-blackwell.

The right of Philip Sheldrake to be identified as the author of this work has been asserted in accordance with the UK Copyright, Designs and Patents Act 1988.

Library of Congress Cataloging-in-Publication Data

Sheldrake, Philip.
  Spirituality: a brief history / Philip Sheldrake. – 2nd ed.
    p. cm.
  Includes bibliographical references and index.
  ISBN 978-0-470-67352-2 (cloth) – ISBN 978-1-118-47235-4 (pbk.)
1. Spirituality–History. 2. Church history. I. Title.
  BV4501.3.S532 2013
  248.09–dc23
                                                    2012043026

A catalogue record for this book is available from the British Library.

Cover image: Snape Maltings, Suffolk. © Susie Hayward
Cover design by www.simonlevyassociates.co.uk

Set in 9/11.5pt Meridien by SPi Publisher Services, Pondicherry, India
Printed in Singapore by Ho Printing Singapore Pte Ltd

1 2013

To Susie

Contents

Preface

I am grateful to Rebecca Harkin of Wiley-Blackwell for proposing a revised and expanded edition of this Brief History, originally published in 2007, and to the publisher's readers for their thoughtful suggestions. The subject of spirituality is now an important academic field, not least in the English-speaking world. Equally, in so many ways, "spirituality" is a word that defines our era. The growing interest in the subject is one of the most striking aspects of contemporary Western culture, paradoxically set alongside a decline in traditional religious membership.

When the original edition of this book was first discussed, it was agreed that it would be too complicated to attempt a brief history of spirituality in general. While there are commonalities between the spiritualities of the major world faiths, they also differ from each other in significant ways. Equally, the concept of "spirituality" is now employed outside religion by an increasing range of intellectual and professional fields. For this reason, it was decided to limit the scope of the book specifically to Christian spirituality. However, this does not imply any sense of exclusivity. It was simply an attempt to control a vast subject by setting clear limits.

Even so, to write a brief yet reliable history of Christian spirituality is risky – particularly for a single author. How do you encapsulate two thousand years in a short space without reducing matters to names, dates, and superficial generalizations? The only realistic answer is to be relatively selective in terms of personalities, traditions, and themes. My choices are inevitably subjective, but I hope they are also reasonably balanced. The book follows a broadly chronological framework blended with thematic elements that are highlighted as particularly characteristic of an age. In recent years, for teaching purposes I have also found it helpful to identify four major "types" of Christian spirituality. I call these "the ascetical-monastic type," "the mystical type," "the active-practical type," and "the prophetic-critical type." These are identified in the pages that follow.

There are a number of significant changes in this revised and expanded edition. Timelines related to each chapter have been provided and there is now a Select Glossary of key words at the end of the book. There are also two major structural alterations. What was the Introduction has been substantially expanded into a new Chapter 1 and subsequent chapters have been renumbered accordingly. Second, the brief Epilogue has become a full-scale final Chapter 8, which explores twenty-first century trajectories. The new Chapter 1 defines "spirituality" in more detail, expands the section on the contemporary meaning of the term and its popularity, defines the relationship between "spirituality" and "mysticism" and how they are to be distinguished, analyzes briefly the current debate about the academic study of spirituality, discusses the use of "types" as a tool for describing the history of spirituality, and, finally, provides some criteria of judgment to apply to the wide range of movements, writings, and practices that have been labelled "spirituality." The final Chapter 8 asks whether Christian spiritual traditions will survive in the new world of multiple spiritualities. The chapter then briefly surveys the current "spirituality" versus "religion" debate, places contemporary Christian spirituality in a fully globalized context, briefly introduces some new spiritual movements, discusses the role of spirituality in inter-religious dialogue, outlines the impact on spirituality of the Internet, and finally relates the Christian spiritual tradition to a selection of the ways spirituality is appearing in non-religious fields such as business and economics, healthcare, and the meaning and future of cities.

Most of the remaining chapters have also had additions made to them. Chapter 2 "Foundations: Scriptures and Early Church" has new material on shrines, pilgrimage, and the development of devotion to saints. In Chapter 3, "Monastic Spirtualities," I have updated the textual edition used for the quotations from the early desert tradition and have also added material on desert spiritual practices. Additional references have been made to Gregory the Great, Anselm, and Hildegard of Bingen. The section on "The Spiritual Values of Monasticism" now ends with a brief summary of the practice of scriptural meditation known as lectio divina. The section on "Spirituality in the East" has new material on the practice of the Jesus Prayer, and the chapter ends by noting the early expansion of Christian spirituality into Asia, particularly India and China. Chapter 4, "Spirituality in the City," has an entirely new section on "Apocalyptic Movements" including Joachim of Fiore. The short note on Julian of Norwich has become a separate and expanded section. Finally, there is now an additional section on the early influences of Islam on Christian spirituality, notably in medieval Spain. The section in Chapter 5,

"Spiritualities in the Age of Reformations," on "The Radical Reformation: Anabaptist Spirituality" has been expanded into a broader treatment of the Radical Reformation. There is new material on Thomas Müntzer and Hans Hut as well as reference to the open attitude of some Anabaptists such as Müntzer to Islam and Judaism. The chapter also has a new and expanded section on George Herbert to illustrate key aspects of Anglican spirituality. The section on "Ignatius Loyola and Early Ignatian Spirituality" has also been enhanced with new material on discernment and on Ignatian practices of prayer. There are wholly new sections, first, on the spread of Christian spirituality beyond Europe, particularly in India and in Central and Latin America, and, second, on the birth of a distinctive Russian spirituality with two diverging styles of monasticism and spirituality. In Chapter 6, "Spirituality in an Age of Reason," there is new material in the section on "The Oxford Movement" on the social spirituality of key figures in late-nineteenth and early-twentieth century Anglo-Catholicism. Finally, in Chapter 7, "Modernity to Postmodernity," there are new sections on the spirituality of Charles de Foucauld and on twentieth-century Eastern Orthodox spirituality. Finally, the section on "Making Spirituality Democratic: Pentecostal and Charismatic Spirituality" has been expanded to embrace material on the origins of Pentecostalism.

As I mentioned in the Preface to the first edition, I have taught spirituality for thirty years to students on both sides of the Atlantic. This revised and expanded edition is a distillation of these experiences. So, once again, I want to thank all the students I have taught for the stimulation they provide. My own researches have been greatly helped by thought-provoking conversations with friends in the international Society for the Study of Christian Spirituality. Warm thanks are also due to my present colleagues at Westcott House in the Cambridge Theological Federation for providing a friendly working environment and particularly to Dr Will Lamb for reviewing some of the material. Once again, this new edition is dedicated to Susie whose partnership, love, and conversation have been the greatest stimulation of all.

Chapter 1

What is Spirituality?

In her classic book, *Mysticism: The Nature and Development of Human Consciousness*, Evelyn Underhill suggests that human beings are vision-creating beings rather than merely tool-making animals.[1] In other words, they are driven by goals that are more than mere physical perfection or intellectual supremacy. Humans desire what might be called spiritual fulfillment. For this reason, an enduring interest in spirituality should not surprise us.

This book is intended to be a guide for the historical study of Christian spirituality. However, at the outset this raises a basic question about what exactly we intend to explore. If the history of "spirituality" is not simply coterminous with general religious or cultural history, what does it cover? Clearly, "spirituality" is an influential category within the overall history of a religion such as Christianity and, indeed, of wider culture. It both has an impact on culture and is also influenced by it. However, even if the concept of "spirituality" is not entirely free-standing, it still needs to be distinguished from broad historical studies of Christianity. These will discuss religious institutions such as the papacy, or movements such as the Reformation, or the interaction between the Church and political or social events (e.g. the role of the Church in the medieval crusades or nineteenth-century social reform movements), or the overall impact of Christianity on wider culture (e.g. its relationship to the arts).

With these exclusions in mind, a history of Christian "spirituality" is likely to cover those people, movements, texts, or artifacts as well as practices that relate directly to the promotion of wisdom about how to lead a "spiritual life." This history will cover both how such a

Spirituality: A Brief History, Second Edition. Philip Sheldrake.
© 2013 John Wiley & Sons, Ltd. Published 2013 by John Wiley & Sons, Ltd.

life has been understood and also how it has been practiced at different times and in different places.

Origins of the Word "Spirituality"

The origins of the word "spirituality" lie in the Latin noun *spiritualitas* associated with the adjective *spiritualis* (spiritual). These ultimately derive from the Greek noun *pneuma*, spirit, and the adjective *pneumatikos* as they appear in St Paul's letters in the New Testament. It is important to note that, in this context, "spirit" and "spiritual" are not the opposite of "physical" or "material" (Greek *soma*, Latin *corpus*) but of "flesh" (Greek *sarx*, Latin *caro*), which refers to everything that is contrary to the Spirit of God. The intended contrast is not therefore between body and soul but between two vastly different attitudes to life. Thus, a "spiritual person" (see 1 Cor 2, 14–15) was simply someone within whom the Spirit of God dwelt or who lived under the influence of the Spirit of God.

This Pauline moral sense of "spiritual," meaning "life in the Spirit," remained in constant use in the West until the twelfth century. At that time, under the influence of the "new theology" of scholasticism, influenced by Greek philosophy, the concept of "spiritual" began to be used as a way of distinguishing intelligent humanity from non-rational creation. Yet, the Pauline moral sense and the supra-material sense of "spiritual" continued side by side in the thirteenth-century writings of a theologian like St Thomas Aquinas. Interestingly, the noun "spirituality" (*spiritualitas*) during the Middle Ages most frequently referred to the clerical state. So "the spirituality" was "the clergy." The noun only became established in reference to "the spiritual life" in seventeenth-century France – sometimes in a pejorative sense. It then disappeared from theological circles until the end of the nineteenth and the beginning of the twentieth centuries when it again appeared in French in positive references to the "spiritual life" as the heart of Christian existence. It then passed into English via translations of French writings.

The use of the word "spirituality" as an area of Christian study gradually re-emerged during the twentieth century, but it was only after the Second Vatican Council in the early 1960s that it began to dominate and to replace older terms such as ascetical theology or mystical theology. The emergence of "spirituality" as the preferred term to describe studies of the Christian life increased after the Council until it was the dominant term from the 1970s onwards. This expressed an implicit shift in values.

First, it countered older distinctions between a supernatural, spiritual life and our purely natural, everyday one. Second, it recovered a sense that "the spiritual life" was collective in nature rather than predominantly individual. Third, it was not limited to personal interiority but integrated all aspects of human experience. Fourth, it re-engaged with mainstream theology, not least biblical studies. Finally, it became an area of reflection that crossed the boundaries between different Christian traditions and was often a medium for ecumenical growth. By the end of the twentieth century, this had extended further into the wider ecumenism of interfaith dialogue.

Contemporary Meaning

"Spirituality" is a word that defines our era. A fascination with "spirituality," often contrasted favorably with "religion," is a striking feature of our times and is presumed to be open to everyone. So, in broad terms, how is "spirituality" defined today? The answer is not simple because the word is used in such a wide range of different contexts. However, contemporary literature on "spirituality" regularly includes some or all of the following approaches.

First, spirituality concerns what is holistic – that is, a fully integrated approach to life. The basis for this lies in the fact that historically the concept of "the spiritual" relates to another concept, "the holy." This translates the Old English *hālig*, "whole" or "complete," and is also related to the ancient Greek *holos*. In this sense, "spirituality" is best understood not so much as one element among many in human existence but as the integrating factor in life – attending to "life-as-a-whole." Second, in contemporary understanding, spirituality is also engaged with a quest for the "sacred." The "sacred" in religious spiritualities such as Christianity is closely related to beliefs about God but in wider culture also nowadays refers to rather broad understandings of the numinous (sometimes embodied in nature or in the arts), the undefined depths of human existence or to the boundless mysteries of the cosmos. Third, spirituality is frequently understood to involve a quest for meaning, including the purpose of life, and for a sense of life direction. This association with meaning and purpose is in many ways a response to the decline of traditional religious or social authorities, particularly in Western cultures. Because of its association with meaning, contemporary spirituality implicitly suggests an understanding of human identity and of personality development. An interesting example of the way this has been applied was the concept of "spiritual development" in some 2004 documentation for English secondary schools produced by the UK Office for Standards in Education. In this context, "spirituality" is defined as "the development of the non-material element of a human being, which animates and sustains us." The purpose of including this in the school curriculum is: "…about the development of a sense of identity, self-worth, personal insight, meaning and purpose. It is about the development of a pupil's 'spirit'."[2] "Spirituality" is also regularly linked to the concept of "thriving" – what it means for humans to thrive and how we come to thrive. Finally, contemporary definitions of spirituality often relate it to the quest for ultimate values in contrast to an instrumentalized or purely materialistic approach to life. Thus, "spirituality" not only suggests a self-reflective life rather than an unexamined life but also overlaps in significant ways with ethics and moral vision.

These contemporary approaches to spirituality provoke some critical questions. First of all, is spirituality essentially a personal or even an individualistic matter or is it also inherently social? Interestingly, on the Web, the majority of available definitions of spirituality emphasize inner experience, introspection, a subjective journey, personal well-being, inner harmony or happiness. Here, spirituality does not connect strongly with our social existence. This also provokes another question as to whether spirituality is more than another useful form of therapy – concerned with promoting everything that is comforting and consoling. In other words, can there be such a thing as "tough" spirituality and is spirituality capable of confronting the destructive side of human existence?

Some critical commentators on the contemporary phenomenon of spirituality, such as Jeremy Carrette, are deeply skeptical about these developments, suggesting that the current enthusiasm for "spirituality" is nothing more than another off-shoot of consumerism.[3] There is considerable justification for this assertion in consumerist "lifestyle spirituality" that promotes fitness, healthy living and holistic well-being. However, at the beginning of the new millennium there are also signs that the word "spirituality" is expanding beyond an individualistic quest for self-realization. It increasingly appears in debates about public values, the further development of professional fields, or the transformation of social structures – for example, in reference to healthcare, education, business and economics, the arts and more recently the re-enchantment of cities and urban life, and even the need to recover a sense of the "spiritual" in politics. Academically, "spirituality" has now begun to appear in disciplines well beyond the confines of theology or religious studies such as philosophy, psychology, and the social sciences.[4] This means that even a specialist area of study such as Christian spirituality must take note of many disciplines, methodologies, and domains of practice.[5]

The contemporary interest in spirituality is part of a broader process of cultural change during the late twentieth century. For a range of reasons, inherited religious and social identities or value-systems were seriously questioned. As a result, many people no longer see traditional religion as an adequate channel for their spiritual quest and look for new sources of self-orientation. Thus, "spirituality" has become an alternative way of exploring the deepest self and the ultimate purpose of life. Overall, the spiritual quest has increasingly moved away from outer-directed authority to inner-directed experience which is seen as more reliable. This subjective turn in Western culture has created a diverse approach to spiritual experience and practice. Nowadays, spirituality frequently draws from different religious traditions as well as from popular psychology.

People who no longer call themselves "religious" often wish to describe themselves as "spiritual." They express this in the values they espouse and the practices they undertake to pursue a meaningful life. Two British examples illustrate this. A major survey by David Hay, an academic scientist with a long-standing interest in spiritual experience, covered the period from 1987 to 2000. It showed that the proportion of people who did not attend a place of worship yet believed in a "spiritual reality" increased from 29% to 55%. Some years later, sociologists Paul Heelas and Linda Woodhead researched contemporary religious and spiritual attitudes in North West England. They concluded that what they called "holistic spirituality" was gradually replacing religion in an evolutionary development because it was a better fit with contemporary needs. The problem with this developmental interpretation is that it operates within very specific boundaries. If the study of history teaches us anything, it is that making such assumptions about a complete rupture with the past, in this case a religious past, is a risky move. Even the ways we perceive the present moment are ambiguous. While, in terms of Western societies, it may be true that increasing numbers of people in non-traditional settings explore a diversity of spiritual theories, experiences, and practices, it is also true that other often young and intelligent people are converting to very conservative forms of Christianity or Islam as their answer to the problem of ultimate meaning in what they feel to be a confusing and dangerous world. If we move beyond Western cultures to take into account Asia, Africa, and Latin America, assessments of the definitive death of conventional religion are even more questionable.

When we turn to people in Western countries who continue to identify with Christianity, we see that they too increasingly adopt a mixture of spiritual genres and borrow from across the boundaries not only of spiritual traditions but also of religious faiths. For example, the Dutch social anthropologist Peter Versteeg has analyzed the current work of Roman Catholic spirituality centers in the Netherlands. These have created an interesting place for themselves on the religious-spiritual landscape, positioned somewhere between the institutional Church and the world of alternative spiritualities. The qualifying adjective "Christian" may only refer to the fact that such centers have a Christian origin. However, what is on offer is frequently identified simply as "spirituality" without any explicit reference to Christian beliefs.[6] A similar eclecticism may be detected in the programmes of many Christian retreat houses and spirituality centers throughout the Western world.

This approach to spirituality among contemporary Christians raises complex questions about how we understand the way a religious tradition such as Christianity functions in radically plural contexts. The French social scientist and expert on Islam, Olivier Roy, borrows the word *formatage* or "formatting" from computer language in his analysis of the process whereby religions and their spiritual traditions are "reformatted" to fit the norms of the different cultures within which they exist.[7] This "reformatting" may occasionally be "from above" when religious authorities consciously seek to adapt to new cultural-social realities. However, "reformatting" is more frequently "from below." Here, in informal and less theoretical ways, and sometimes in contrast to the attitudes of religious authorities, classic themes are reformulated, spiritual practices are adapted, or new ways of life are adopted to re-express a tradition. Something crucial remains identifiably "Catholic" or "Protestant," "Carmelite" or "Ignatian." Yet, at the same time, fundamental ways of understanding such designations and their expressions change in significant ways.

What is Christian Spirituality?

In the twenty-first century, we exist in a globalized and radically plural world. In such a context, Christian spirituality is nowadays situated explicitly in a world of many cultures and many religions. Of course the origins of Christianity lie in the Middle East and in Judaism even if later on European perspectives came to predominate. In the contemporary context, Christian spirituality is an important part of the critical dialogue between faiths. This process will be discussed in more detail in Chapter 8.

However, the contemporary taste for eclecticism raises some new questions about the uniqueness or otherwise of Christian spirituality. There are clearly overlaps between the values and concerns of religious spiritualities. All of them are based on a framework of transcendent beliefs, whether these are explicitly God-related (as in the Abrahamic family of faiths) or not (as in Buddhism). Religious spiritualities also share other characteristics such as foundational scriptures, some visible structures, sacred spaces, and spiritual practices. Yet, each religious tradition is clearly distinguishable from the others.

Thus, we shall discover throughout this book that while Christian spirituality has Jewish origins, it soon developed a distinctive flavor and content. Indeed, as we have already noted, Christianity is the original source of the word "spirituality," although it has now passed into other faith traditions, not least Eastern religions such as Buddhism and Hinduism.[8] In Christian terms, spirituality refers to the way our fundamental values, lifestyles, and spiritual practices reflect particular understandings of God, human identity, and the material world as the context for human transformation. In Chapter 2, we shall examine the foundations of Christian spirituality and what the key overall features of Christian spirituality are. We shall see that all Christian spiritual traditions are rooted in the Hebrew and Christian scriptures, particularly in the gospels, and in the life and teachings of Jesus Christ. Christian spirituality is fundamentally concerned with following the way of Jesus Christ. However, the varied spiritual traditions throughout history are also attempts to reinterpret these scriptural values and teachings within specific contexts and cultural circumstances.

Spirituality and Mysticism

One particular question that frequently arises in the contemporary study of spirituality is the relationship between "spirituality" and "mysticism." In broad terms, many contemporary Western approaches frequently treat "spirituality" and "mysticism" as virtually synonymous. "Spirituality" implies an exploration of the depths of human existence and the ultimate purpose of life and a quest for deeper wisdom. The notion of "mysticism" additionally suggests that we may have immediate encounters with and perhaps an experiential "knowledge" of the mystery of God or the Absolute.

For some Christians, the idea of mysticism is more problematic than spirituality. Until recently, most writing concentrated on it as a category of intense religious *experience*. This results in several problems. First, it separates mysticism from theology – the ways we seek to speak about God. Second, it removes mysticism from the public world into the realm of private inwardness. Third, it concentrates on states of mind and emotions experienced by a limited number of people as a result of intensive meditative practice or ascetical discipline. This tends to separate "mysticism" from the Christian life in general.

In its origins, the noun "mysticism" is relatively modern – first appearing in France in the seventeenth century (*la mystique*). The adjective "mystical," from the Greek *mystikos*, is more ancient as a description of the deeper dimensions of Christian practice and theology. To grossly oversimplify, from the second century CE onwards the word began to be adopted by Christians to signify the hidden realities of the Christian life – whether the deeper spiritual meanings of the Bible or the inner power of Christian rituals and sacraments. As we shall see in Chapter 2, around the beginning of the sixth century an anonymous Syrian, known as Pseudo-Dionysius, adopted the term "mystical theology" to indicate also an engagement with the mystery of God. However, the main point is that, in Christian terms, "mysticism" is rooted in the call of all Christians in their baptism to enter deeply into the "mystery" of God through exposure to the scriptures and liturgy. Equally, mysticism is a *gift* from God rather than something achieved through human effort.

Bernard McGinn, an important contemporary writer on Christian mysticism, notes that "mysticism" takes many different forms, but he attempts a working definition. Mysticism refers to "those elements in Christian belief and practice that concern the preparation for, the consciousness of, and the effects attendant upon a heightened awareness of God's immediate and transforming presence."[9] Mystics are simply those people who believe in and practice their Christian faith with particular intensity. The great mystical writers are adamant that they are describing a *process of life* not altered states of consciousness.

In summary, therefore, spirituality is best understood as the broader concept. Mysticism is merely one aspect of Christian spirituality – a kind of intensification of the Christian spiritual path. It is important to note that the historic role of spirituality and mysticism within Christianity is ambiguous. Many Christian traditions such as Western Catholic and Eastern Orthodox value both. However, some Protestant Christians remain deeply suspicious of mysticism partly because it seems to overemphasize the importance and power of the experiential in our relationship with God. However, as we shall see in Chapter 4, writings on Christian mysticism from the medieval period onwards are *not* purely experiential. They also question the adequacy of conventional theological *language* about God. Thus, the great German mystic, Meister Eckhart, loved to cite St Augustine on speech about God: "If I have spoken of it, I have not spoken, for it is ineffable." Christian mysticism underlines that the truth of "God" (the "God beyond God" as Eckhart suggested) is ultimately beyond all theological categories and doctrinal definitions.

The Study of Spirituality

Nowadays, the study of Christian spirituality has established itself as an interdisciplinary field rather than merely a subset of Christian doctrine or of Church history. Indeed, the role of interdisciplinary study has become a central methodological principle of spirituality.[10]

The criticism used to be leveled at spirituality that it sought to use as many methods and tools as possible only because there was no adequate sense of disciplinary identity. There is certainly a "cheap" interdisciplinarity that merely plunders the language of different disciplines without a real literacy in those disciplines. However, at its best, interdisciplinary study is not a matter of expediency but is a principled position. Late modern or postmodern theory promotes the breakdown of closed systems of analysis, based on a post-Enlightenment mechanization of knowledge. This demanded that academic disciplines be clearly separated, autonomous, free-standing, and pure. This recent breakdown of closed systems of thought has also underlined that the ways we think are necessarily bound up with power issues. Thus, in this context, interdisciplinary study is not merely a potential enrichment of the ways we approach what we study, for example, spiritual classics, but is also a discipline (*áskēsis*) of learning to live with what is multi-dimensional rather than simple and relatively easy to control.

Because Christian spirituality engages with the traditions of a specific faith community, certain disciplines are necessarily involved in its study. Sandra Schneiders, one of the key figures in the modern development of Christian spirituality, describes these disciplines as "constitutive," that is, inherently associated with the Christian nature of what is being studied. She identifies the "constitutive disciplines" as the history of Christianity and scripture. In addition to these, there are what she calls "problematic disciplines." These are those disciplines that allow access to the particular theme or problem that is being studied. Schneiders identifies the leading "problematic disciplines" in the study of spirituality, depending on the context, as psychology, the social sciences, literature, and the sciences. Schneiders is also clear that the study of spirituality is not purely intellectual or abstract. It is also self-implicating and therefore transformative. On her reading, theology as a discipline lies somewhere in between the two categories. However, my own view is that while it is important to move away from thinking of Christian spirituality as derived in some simple way from religious doctrines and their first principles, it is nevertheless impossible to detach a wider understanding of theology from the study of Christian spirituality at any point.[11] Equally, the self-implicating nature of the study of spirituality may act as a subversive reform movement within the wider field of theology by reminding it of its fundamental transformative purpose and resisting the temptation to reduce theology to a purely objective-scientific method.

One specific area where there is a fruitful dialogue between theology and spirituality is the interrelationship between spirituality and Christian ethics (or moral theology). This is paradoxical given that in classic Roman Catholic theology the predecessors of spirituality, ascetical and mystical theology, used to be considered merely as dependent subdivisions of moral theology. Indeed, it could be argued that traditional approaches to ethics or moral theology helped to reinforce the split between theology and spirituality. Both moral theology and ascetical theology were preoccupied with sinfulness and the enfeebled nature of the human condition. This overpowered any deeper theological consideration of Christian understandings of human existence or of the quest for holiness and gave the impression that ascetical theology had very little if anything to say theologically in its own right. It appeared to deal merely with some subsidiary (even optional) aspects of the moral life which was itself derived from dogmatic theology.

Nowadays, however, Christian ethics is no longer focused primarily on the rightness or wrongness of particular actions. There has been a shift from abstract actions to the human agent. Here, spirituality and ethics find a common language in a renewed theology of the human person (anthropology) and of grace (God's action in and for the world). There is an increasing awareness of the basic unity between the ethical life and the spiritual life. Among the themes that focus on the joint task of contemporary spirituality and Christian ethics are how we understand "virtue" (i.e. what enables a person to become fully human aided by God's action or "grace") and "character" or what we should aim to *be*, rather than merely do, if we are to become fully human persons. Christian ethicists increasingly emphasize that our ultimate guide to goodness is not abstract codes of behavior or moral rule books but the presence within us of God's Spirit. This indwelling of God grounds the recovery of a fruitful relationship between ethics and spirituality. Yet, these are not wholly synonymous. Spirituality in its fullest sense includes the whole of a person's or a group's spiritual orientation. In that sense, spirituality overlaps with ethics but cannot be reduced to it.[12]

Spirituality and History

If we now return to the history of Christian spirituality, it is important to underline the degree to which Christianity is explicitly a historical religion. Crucially, the central Christian doctrine of the Incarnation, that God took on a human existence in the person of Jesus of Nazareth, situates the divine at the very heart of human history.

> By affirming that all "meaning," every assertion about the significance of life and reality, must be judged by reference to a brief succession of contingent events in Palestine, Christianity – almost without realizing it – closed off the path to "timeless truth."[13]

Thus, Christian spirituality affirms "history" as the context for spiritual transformation. Even Augustine's future-orientated theology of history, one of the most influential Christian historical theories, did not render contingent history meaningless, even if it distinguished between sacred and secular "history." While he rejected a progress model of history and believed that no age could be closer to God than any other, the thread of sacred history ran through human history, and every moment was therefore equally significant.[14]

In approaching the relationship of spirituality and history, a fundamental factor is how we view the importance of history itself. Western cultures these days sometimes appear weary with the notion of being involved in a stream of tradition through time. It is not uncommon these days for people to believe that history signifies only the past – something interesting but not critical to our future. "Tradition" is perceived by some people as a conservative force from which we need to break free if we are to live a more rational existence. The desire for immediacy encouraged by consumerism also produces a memory-less culture. Perhaps the most powerful factor during the twentieth century has been the death of a belief in history as a progressive force. This evaporated in the face of two world wars, mid-century totalitarianism, and the horrors of the Holocaust and Hiroshima.

Despite contemporary doubts, a historical consciousness is a human necessity. It reminds us of the contextual nature and particularity of spiritual values. Indeed, attention to the complexities of history has been a major development in the study of Christian spirituality over the last thirty years. One reason why the study of Christian spirituality now pays greater attention to the complexity of historical interpretation lies in an important change of language associated with the Second Vatican Council in the early 1960s. The phrase "signs of the times," coined by Pope John XXIII and repeated in the Council documents, effectively recognized that history was not incidental to, but the context for, God's work. Faith is not opposed to history, and no separation is possible between religious history and world history.[15]

Spiritual traditions do not exist on some ideal plane above and beyond history. The origins and development of spiritual traditions reflect the circumstances of time and place as well as the psychological state of the people involved. They consequently embody values that are socially conditioned. For example, the emphasis on radical poverty in the spirituality of the thirteenth-century Franciscan movement was not simply a "naked" scriptural value but a reaction to particular conditions in society and the Church at the time – not least to what were seen as their prevailing sins.[16]

This does not imply that spiritual traditions and texts have no value beyond their original contexts. However, it does mean that to appreciate their riches we must take context seriously. Context has become a primary framework for the study of spiritual traditions. Spirituality is never pure in form. "Context" is not something that may be added to or subtracted from spiritual experiences or traditions but is the very element within which these find expression.[17] This contradicts an older conception of Christian spirituality as a stream of enduring truth in which the same theories or images are simply repeated in different guises.

Interpretation

If we take context seriously, yet also seek to approach spiritual traditions from other times and places for the spiritual wisdom they contain, questions of interpretation arise.[18] We are inevitably aware of different cultural and theological perspectives when we read a text from another time or place. If interpretation is to serve contemporary use, we cannot avoid the question of how far to respect a text's assumptions. Certain responses are naïve. We may ignore the author's intention and the text's structure entirely and simply pick and choose as it suits us. The opposite extreme is to assume that only the author's intention matters. Even assuming that we can accurately reconstruct this, such an approach subordinates our present horizons to the past. Both approaches assume that the "meaning" of a text is simple. A more fruitful, but more complicated, approach to interpretation is to engage in a critical *dialogue* with the text. This allows the wisdom of a text to challenge us, while at the same time it allows our own horizons their proper place. The possibilities of a text, beyond the author's original intention, are evoked in a creative way by the new world in which it finds itself.

The example of music is helpful in understanding this approach. Musicians interpret a score. Performers cannot do simply anything and call it a Beethoven symphony. Although they may be technically faultless in following the composer's instructions, a good performance is *more* than this. It will also be creative because the composer did not merely describe how to produce notes but sought to shape an experience. This image of performance leads us to the heart of the interpretative process. Without ignoring the technicalities of a text, we uncover new and richer meanings every time we read or perform it.

These comments about context in relation to spirituality are now widely accepted. However, a comparison of three classic histories of spirituality written during the twentieth century soon reminds us of how substantial changes have been. P. Pourrat's four-volume *La Spiritualité Chrétienne* was published shortly after the First World War.[19] His unified approach to spiritual doctrine led him to suppose that the same theology of prayer, virtue, or spiritual growth was found in all spiritual traditions. Different approaches to spirituality differed only in presentation. Pourrat also limited his attention to monasticism and mysticism with virtually no reference to lay (or "popular") spirituality.

Louis Bouyer's three-volume (in the English edition) *A History of Christian Spirituality* was published in the early 1960s around the time of the Second Vatican Council.[20] Bouyer was still preoccupied with the essential unity of spirituality and often lacked an awareness of differences between traditions of spirituality. However, in other respects, his approach was a considerable improvement on Pourrat. The cultural perspective was broader, lay spirituality had more substantial treatment, and his third volume offered a relatively sympathetic treatment of Orthodox, Protestant, and Anglican spiritualities. However, women were still largely invisible.

Finally, the three Christian volumes within the Crossroad series, *World Spirituality: An Encyclopedic History of the Religious Quest*, appeared in the late 1980s.[21] These differ vastly from Pourrat and Bouyer, both of whom worked within a Roman Catholic perspective. The *World Spirituality* volumes are ecumenical and international collections of essays by a range of scholars rather than a grand survey by a single author. The history of spiritual traditions is understood as plural, linked to specific contexts. The volumes offer a degree of balance between Eastern and Western Christianity and make other efforts to express the cultural plurality of spirituality. The spirituality of lay Christians and women's perspectives are better represented. Where these volumes are still relatively weak is in their treatment of Christian cultures in Africa, Asia, and Latin America.

Any adequate historical analysis of spiritual traditions must address a number of critical questions.[22] First, in any tradition or text, how was holiness conceived? Which categories of people were thought of as holy? What places or things were deemed to be particularly sacred – and, negatively, who or what was excluded from the category "holy" or "sacred"? For example, close association with sexual activity (marriage) or with the material world (manual labor or commerce) was for many centuries difficult to connect with ideas of holiness. Second, who creates or controls spirituality? For example, to what degree does the language of spirituality reflect the interests and experience of minority groups such as clergy or monastic personnel? Third, what directions were not taken? In other words, to what degree has it been assumed that the choices made were in some absolute way superior to those that were rejected? For example, what were the real motives for the condemnation as heretics of the medieval women's spiritual movement, the Beguines? Was it a genuine concern for the spiritual welfare of laypeople or a suspicion of laypeople not sufficiently under clerical control? Finally, where are the groups that did not fit? For example, why was it that, within the Western Catholic tradition, the experience of lay Christians, particularly of women, was largely ignored until recently in the formulation of spiritual theory?

All historical studies involve choices, and this affects our interpretation of spiritual traditions. First, *time limits* are chosen. In other words, writers decide on the appropriate boundaries within which to date spiritual movements and thus to understand them. For example, our sense of the continuity or discontinuity between the spiritualities of the

Middle Ages and the Reformation may be affected by an apparently simple matter of how and where authors divide a multi-volume history.[23] Second, traditional histories reveal a *geographical bias*. We make assumptions about where "the center" and "the margins" are in the history of spiritual traditions. For example, until recently, the spirituality of Irish Christianity was often treated only in relation to its absorption into a homogenized Latin Christianity around the eleventh and twelfth centuries rather than on its own terms. Third, we choose *certain evidence as significant*. So, for example, if studies of spirituality concentrate exclusively on mystical texts or monastic rules, the impression is given that spirituality is essentially literary, is to be found exclusively in privileged contexts, and may be distinguished from mere devotional or "popular" religion.

Despite the wariness of many people in the contemporary West about institutional religion, the place of history in the study of spirituality is a reminder of the positive power of religious-spiritual tradition. Without some sense of tradition, an interest in spirituality lacks something vital that can only be gained by a renewed attention to historic Christian spiritualities that have had such an influence, explicitly or covertly, on Western culture.

Types of Spirituality

Any attempt to write a history of Christian spirituality confronts the question of how to organize into an intelligible pattern what otherwise may seem to be a series of unrelated themes. First, I have found it helpful to identify four major "types" of Christian spirituality – although, in different ways, these types are present in the spiritualities of all the major world religions. "Types" of spirituality are essentially distinctive styles of wisdom and practice with shared characteristics. It is then possible to develop a comparative framework (what is called a typology) that enables us to compare the four types and to understand the differences between them. However, we need to use typologies with caution. These are useful tools to help us analyze the complexities of spirituality. However, we must remember that they are *interpretations* of reality rather than purely descriptive.

The four types are "ascetical-monastic," "the mystical," "the active-practical," and finally the "prophetic-critical." These types sometimes overlap to some degree. Thus, ascetical forms of spirituality may have mystical elements. Each type tends to be characterized by a broad worldview, based on religious assumptions. The different types of spirituality foster self-transcendence via a movement away from what they see as the "inauthentic" towards what is "authentic." Broadly, in terms of spiritual growth, the inauthentic can be summed up in terms of a sense of limitation or lack of freedom. Each of the four types of spirituality seeks answers to such questions as *where* transformation is thought to take place (context), *how* it takes place (practices and disciplines), and *what* its ultimate purpose or end-point is (destiny or completion).

The "ascetical-monastic" type sometimes prescribes special places such as the wilderness or the monastery. Characteristically, it also describes practices of self-denial, austerity, and abstention from worldly pleasures as the pathway to spiritual growth and moral perfection. The end in view is a condition of detachment from material existence as the pathway to eternal life. This type will be further explained in Chapter 3.

The "mystical type" is associated with the desire for an immediacy of presence to God frequently through contemplative practice. It does not necessarily demand withdrawal from everyday life but suggests that the everyday may be transfigured into something wondrous. The mystical type is often associated with intuitive "knowledge" of God beyond discursive reasoning and analysis. The ultimate purpose is spiritual illumination and a connection to the depths of existence. The mystical type will be developed towards the end of Chapter 4.

The "active-practical type" of spirituality in a variety of ways promotes everyday life as the principal context for the spiritual path and for a quest for authenticity. In this type of spirituality, we do not need to retreat from everyday concerns in order to reach spiritual truth or enlightenment. What is needed for spiritual growth is within our reach. For, in the words of Jesus, "The Kingdom of God is among you." Because it emphasizes finding God in the midst of everyday existence, this type of spirituality is accessible to everyone and not simply to groups dedicated especially to the ascetical life or with the opportunity for extensive contemplative practice. This type of spirituality seeks to find spiritual growth through the medium of ordinary experiences, commitments, and activity, including the service of our fellow humans. It plays a central role in Chapters 5 and 6.

Finally, the "prophetic-critical" type of spirituality goes beyond the simple practical service of other people in the direction of an explicit commitment to social transformation and social justice as a spiritual task. As we shall see in Chapter 7, while it is possible to argue that historic spiritualities have always had prophetic or critical elements, an explicit attention to prophetic-critical spirituality and its development as a clear "type" only really emerged fully during the twentieth century in response to certain critical social and political situations.

Periods and Traditions

Apart from the concept of "types" of spirituality, two of the most common organizing frameworks in histories of spirituality are "periods" and "traditions." Because neither of these are straightforward, they need a brief comment.

"Periods" implies an essentially chronological approach to history.[24] However, choosing particular time boundaries to divide up a history of spirituality is not straightforward but involves choices. For example, in writing a section about "spiritualities of the Reformation" do we emphasize continuities with the Middle Ages or do we emphasize a complete rupture? More generally, do we take a short view of history or the long view both backwards and forwards from the "main events"? Sometimes, our choice of starting dates and ending dates for a spiritual movement or tradition will also depend on whether or not we give exclusive attention to "official" history and on what our geographical focus is.

The other frequently used framework for histories of spirituality is in terms of "traditions." There has been some debate about whether Christian spirituality should be treated as essentially a single reality or as a plurality of different traditions.[25] In fact, the question of unity or plurality is a matter of viewpoint. On the one hand, all Christian spiritualities take the life and teachings of Jesus Christ as their fundamental starting point. On the other hand, different traditions of spirituality emerge precisely when people seek to respond to the gospel of Jesus Christ in the context of their own time and place.

As a fundamental point, a "spiritual tradition" generally implies a great deal more than the practice of a single exercise of piety or devotion. Rather it embodies some substantial spiritual wisdom (usually encapsulated in certain texts or ways of life) which differentiates it from other traditions. However, is it possible to say when a particular form of spirituality has clearly become a *tradition* in the fullest sense rather than simply a passing phase? This is not straightforward particularly when the form of spirituality emerged relatively recently. Some broad guidelines may help us. First, is there clear evidence of the existence of a generation of practitioners that had no first-hand experience of the founder(s) or origins of the tradition? Second, has the tradition established certain classic texts or documentation or structures for the transmission of the tradition? Third, has the spiritual wisdom shown itself clearly capable of moving beyond its own time and place of origin?

Finally, the notion of how a "spiritual tradition" is interpreted and handed on has been further expanded in the movement known as "traditioning" developed by Hispanic Christian theologians in North America. This new approach confronts the complex issue of re-appropriating or even sometimes resisting historic spiritual traditions. The fundamental question is how Christian spirituality transmits itself, and how it is received across cultural boundaries. There is clearly a question of content – that is, something quite specific is handed on or "traditioned." However, "traditioning" focuses far more on the *process* of transmission. There are four key principles. First, we should attend more closely to the process whereby classic traditions, born in one culture and already reshaped by transmission across time through a number of other cultures, now enter a new cultural context. Second, we must value *lo cotidiano* – that is, "the everyday." That is, the authentic re-appropriation of spiritual traditions takes place in relation to the questions and situations of daily life in the local community. Third, there is a need to give a higher valuation to popular religion – a powerful reality in religious cultures originating outside a European-North American hegemony. Approaches to Christian spirituality and to particular spiritual traditions have often been limited by predominantly conceptual or intellectual presuppositions. Popular religion embraces expressions of the spiritual and sacred in rituals, devotions, cultic objects, shrines, and practices such as pilgrimage. Finally, "traditioning" invites us to consider how the transmission of spiritual traditions depends not simply on clergy or technical "experts" but also on a consensus of reception among the rest of the local Christian community who in reality are the "ordinary" transmitters of tradition.[26]

Conclusion: Criteria of Judgment

By way of conclusion, the great variety of personalities, texts, practices, and values that may appear under the heading of "spirituality" underlines the need for clear criteria to evaluate claims to spiritual wisdom. This is illustrated particularly sharply by the quasi-spiritual ceremonial and even quasi-mystical aspirations of Nazism or Italian fascism. These movements have sometimes been described as forms of "spirituality." However, such quasi-spiritual but destructive movements are best described more in terms of anti-spirituality. While this is an extreme case, it seems vitally important to be able to judge the authenticity and adequacy of teachings, practices, and movements with a spiritual flavor or that make apparently spiritual claims. Some Christian thinkers have developed criteria for evaluating religious or spiritual teachings.

The work of the American theologian David Tracy may be taken as an important example. First, it is vital to show that a religious or spiritual tradition meets the basic demands of modern and healthy understandings of human life. Tracy calls this approach "criteria of adequacy." Beyond this basic human level lies a further level concerning issues of faithfulness to a specifically Christian understanding of reality and human existence. Tracy defines this as "criteria of appropriateness."

The application of criteria of adequacy should not be thought of as a reduction of Christian spirituality to purely secular norms. What it implies is that spirituality cannot be innocent of generally accepted developments in human knowledge. Nor can it ignore the ways in which previously over-confident views of human progress have been undermined by the painful historical events of the twentieth century. To put it simply, we have to take into account the new worlds opened up since the nineteenth century by evolutionary theory, psychology, and the social and political sciences, and more recently by cosmology and quantum theory. Equally, our theology and spirituality can never be the same after the horrors of Auschwitz and Hiroshima.

Tracy suggests three broad criteria of adequacy. First, every religious interpretation of experience needs to be humanly meaningful. That is, it must be adequately rooted in common human experience. Second, the religious understanding of experience should be intellectually coherent. Third, any spiritual tradition needs to throw light on the underlying conditions of life. In other words, does it have anything to say about whether our human confidence in life is actually worthwhile?[27]

In relation to Tracy's criteria of appropriateness, in general terms, any spirituality needs to relate us to a God worthy of our loving commitment.[28] Equally, an adequate understanding of Christian spirituality must relate in some way to the classic Christian beliefs. For example, the language of God-as-Trinity and of the Incarnation acts as a critique of distorted spiritualities that are preoccupied, in a narcissistic way, with "self-realization" or self-improvement.[29] Within the limits of legitimate diversity and of valid emphases, healthy spiritualities should generally reflect the _whole_ Christian gospel rather than be selective in an unbalanced way. Certain questions illustrate this point. What models of holiness are presented? Is the view of human nature holistic or is it dualistic with a low theology of human embodiment? Equally, is there a balanced and healthy evaluation of human sexuality? Understandings of prayer and contemplation are central in Christian spirituality. Does a particular spiritual tradition view Christian life as rooted in the vision of a common humanity and in a single vocation based on baptism? Or is it elitist, giving priority to special groups or particular lifestyles? Does a given spirituality promote a balance between contemplation and action? Christian spirituality of its nature cannot avoid the question of tradition. So, in a particular spirituality, what is the role of scripture and of the wider tradition? Finally, an important question is whether a spiritual tradition has a developed sense of ultimate human purpose and destiny (what is known as "eschatology"), and specifically one that encourages an appropriate balance between "the now" and "the not yet."

Notes

1 Evelyn Underhill, *Mysticism: The Nature and Development of Spiritual Consciousness*, Oxford: Oneworld Publications, 1993, pp. 16–17.

2 Office for Standards in Education, *Promoting and Evaluating Pupils' Spiritual, Moral, Social and Cultural Development*, London: OFSTED, 2004, p. 12.

3 Jeremy Carrette and Richard King, *Selling Spirituality: The Silent Takeover of Religion*, London: Routledge, 2004.

4 The magisterial work of Kees Waaijman, *Spirituality: Forms, Foundations, Methods*, Dudley: Leuven: Peeters, 2002, explores the breadth of the new academic field.

5 On the increasing variety of disciplines and definitions in relation to spirituality, see Peter Holmes, "Spirituality: Some disciplinary perspectives" in Kieran Flanagan and Peter Jupp, eds., *A Sociology of Spirituality*, Aldershot/Burlington: Ashgate, 2007, pp. 23–41.

6 Peter Versteeg, "Spirituality on the margins of the Church: Christian spiritual centres in The Netherlands" in Flanagan and Jupp, eds., *A Sociology of Spirituality*, pp. 101–114.

7 See, for example, Oliver Roy, *Secularism Confronts Islam*, New York: Columbia University Press, 2007.

8 For more details on the history of the term "spirituality" and of its equivalents in the history of Christian spirituality, see Philip Sheldrake, "What is spirituality?" in *Spirituality and History: Questions of Interpretation and Method*, revised edition, London: SPCK and New York: Orbis Books, 1995.

9   Bernard McGinn, "Mysticism" in Introductory Essays, Philip
    Sheldrake, ed., *The New SCM Dictionary of Christian Spirituality*, London:
    SCM Press, 2005, pp. 19–25, quote at p. 19 (in North America, *The
    New Westminster Dictionary etc*, Louisville: Westminster-John Knox
    Press). See also B. McGinn, *The Foundations of Mysticism: Origins to
    the Fifth Century*, New York: Crossroad Publishing, 1991, General
    Introduction, pp. xi–xx.

10 On this point, see Sandra Schneiders, "The study of Christian spiritu-
    ality: Contours and dynamics of a discipline" in Elizabeth A. Dreyer and
    Mark S. Burrows, eds., *Minding the Spirit: The Study of Christian Spirituality*,
    Baltimore: Johns Hopkins University Press, 2005, pp. 5–24. Another
    useful essay is Schneiders, "Approaches to the study of Christian spiritu-
    ality" in A. Holder, ed., *The Blackwell Companion to Christian Spirituality*,
    Oxford/Malden: Blackwell Publishing, 2005, pp. 15–33. Both these
    volumes also contain other important essays on the field of Christian
    spirituality and the study of spirituality. Some other significant books on
    the overall field are the magisterial volume by the Dutch scholar
    K. Waaijman, *Spirituality: Forms, Foundations, Methods*, Leuven: Peeters,
    2002; B. Lescher & E. Liebert, eds., *Exploring Christian Spirituality: Essays
    in Honor of Sandra M. Schneiders*, New York: Paulist Press, 2006; D. Perrin,
    Studying Christian Spirituality, London/New York: Routledge, 2007; and
    Agnew, U., Flanagan, B., and Heylin, G., eds., *With Wisdom Seeking God:
    The Academic Study of Spirituality*, Leuven: Peeters, 2008.

11 See Schneiders, "The study of Christian spirituality," 7–8.

12 For explorations of the connection between ethics and spirituality, see
    the collection of essays, *Spirituality and Ethics*, Michael Barnes, ed., *The
    Way Supplement*, 88, Spring 1997. See also Anne E. Patrick, "Ethics and
    spirituality: The social justice connection" *The Way Supplement*, 63, 1988,
    103–116. For a Protestant perspective that reengages spirituality with
    ethics, see James M. Gustafson, "The idea of Christian ethics" in Peter
    Byrne and Leslie Houlden, eds., *Companion Encyclopedia of Theology*,
    London: Routledge, 1995, pp. 691–715. A recent approach within the
    Roman Catholic tradition is William Spohn, *Go and Do Likewise: Jesus and
    Ethics*, New York: Continuum, 2000.

13 R. Williams, *The Wound of Knowledge*, London: Darton Longman & Todd/
    Boston: Cowley Publications, 1990, p. 1.

14 See the classic work on Augustine's theory of history, R.A. Markus,
    Saeculum: History and Society in the Theology of St Augustine, Cambridge:
    Cambridge University Press, 1970, especially Chapter 1 "History: Sacred
    and secular."

15 G. Ruggieri, "Faith and history" in G. Alberigo, J.-P. Jossua, and J.A.
    Komonchak, eds., *The Reception of Vatican II*, Washington DC: The
    Catholic University of America Press, 1987, pp. 92–95.

16   J. Le Goff, "Francis of Assisi between the renewals and restraints of feudal society," *Concilium* 149, 1981 ("Francis of Assisi today"), passim.

17   P. Sheldrake, *Spirituality and History: Questions of Interpretation and Method*, London: SPCK and New York: Orbis Books, 1995, pp. 58, 84–86, 167–168 and M. de Certeau, "Culture and spiritual experience," *Concilium* 19, 1966, 3–31.

18   For a summary of problems associated with interpreting and using texts and traditions from the past, see Sheldrake, *Spirituality and History*, Chapter 7.

19   P. Pourrat, *La spiritualité Chrétienne*, 4 vols., Paris: J. Gabalda, 1918.

20   L. Bouyer, *A History of Christian Spirituality*, 3 vols., London: Burns & Oates, 1968.

21   B. McGinn, J. Meyendorff, and J. Leclercq, eds., *Christian Spirituality: Origins to the Twelfth Century*, New York: Crossroad Publishing, 1985; J. Raitt, ed., *Christian Spirituality: High Middle Ages and Reformation*, New York: Crossroad Publishing, 1987; and L. Dupré and D. Saliers, eds., *Christian Spirituality: Post-Reformation and Modern*, New York: Crossroad Publishing, 1989.

22   Sheldrake 1995, Chapters 3, 4, and 7.

23   Raitt 1987, Introduction.

24   Sheldrake 1995, Chapter 4.

25   For a summary of this debate, see Sheldrake 1995, pp. 196–198.

26   On the principles of "traditioning," see Orlando O. Espin and Gary Macy, eds., *Futuring Our Past: Explorations in the Theology of Tradition*, Maryknoll: Orbis Books, 2006.

27   David Tracy, *Blessed Rage for Order*, New York: The Seabury Press, 1975, pp. 64–71.

28   Tracy, *Blessed Rage for* Order, pp. 72–79.

29   See Catherine LaCugna, "Trinitarian spirituality" in Michael Downey, ed., *New Dictionary of Catholic Spirituality*, Collegeville: The Liturgical Press, 1993, pp. 968–971.

Chapter 2

Foundations: Scriptures and Early Church

c. 4 BCE	Jesus of Nazareth born
c. 30	Death of Jesus
c. 50–c. 64	Pauline epistles written
c. 70	First gospel, the Gospel of Mark written
c. 70–c. 100	Gospels of Matthew and Luke written
c. 90–c. 100	Gospel of John and Book of Revelation written
c. 60–c. 150	Book of Acts written
c. 100	The Didache written
107	Death of Ignatius of Antioch
130–200	Irenaeus of Lyons lives: bishop and theologian
155	Death of Polycarp of Smyrna
170–236	Hippolytus lives: reputed author of *The Apostolic Tradition*
c. 185–c. 254	Origen of Alexandria: mystical theologian
313	Constantine issues Edict of Milan granting toleration to Christians
325	Council of Nicea – formulates Nicene Creed
329–390	Gregory Nazianzen lives: mystical theologian
c. 330–379	Basil the Great lives: monastic founder and mystical theologian
c. 335–395	Gregory of Nyssa lives: mystical theologian
354–430	Augustine of Hippo lives: theologian
381	Council of Constantinople revises Nicene Creed
399	Death of Evagrius Ponticus, monastic writer
451	Council of Chalcedon – defines Christ as both human and divine
c. 500	Pseudo-Dionysius writes *Mystical Theology*

Spirituality: A Brief History, Second Edition. Philip Sheldrake.
© 2013 John Wiley & Sons, Ltd. Published 2013 by John Wiley & Sons, Ltd.

It is important to begin with a framework for understanding the foundations of Christian spirituality and its particular characteristics. Needless to say, the origins of Christian spirituality lie in the scriptures – particularly in the New Testament. However, during the first five centuries of the Christian Church, the specific doctrines about God, the human condition, and the world were also defined more clearly, and from the start these can be understood in relationship to patterns of the Christian life. Drawing upon these two foundations, it will then be possible to conclude with a brief summary of the key features of Christian spirituality in general.

Christian Spirituality and the Scriptures

In one sense, it seems quite straightforward to say that all Christian spiritual traditions are rooted in the scriptures. Yet, such a statement also needs further explanation and expansion. For example, where do we begin? Behind the Christian scriptures (the New Testament) lie the Hebrew or Jewish Scriptures (traditionally called the Old Testament by Christians). Apart from the obvious fact that Jesus and his disciples were Jews, the Christian scriptures refer to and grow out of the Jewish scriptures in many different ways. Equally, the Jewish scriptures have had a significant role in Christian spirituality across two thousand years from the use of the Book of Psalms in liturgy and the Song of Songs in mystical-contemplative writings to the role of the Book of Exodus in late-twentieth century spiritualities of liberation. Sadly, there is no room in a brief history to do justice to this longer story of scriptural origins, and so this chapter will begin with the Christian scriptures in the narrow sense.

A second important question concerns how exactly we approach the scriptures in relation to Christian spirituality. For example, in what sense are they foundational to all spirituality? The logic of the Christian doctrine of the Incarnation – that God entered into human history in the person of Jesus of Nazareth at a particular time (the first century) and in a particular place (Palestine) – is that God's revelation takes place in and through context-bound realities. This implies a tension. On the one hand, Christianity (and Christian spirituality) clearly implies a faithful relationship to the inaugurating events of Jesus Christ. Yet, on the other hand, because historic forms of spirituality are also particular to their own time and place, they cannot be identical repetitions of Jesus' life and are therefore necessarily different from these beginnings.

There is clearly a difference between describing the general scriptural foundations of Christian spirituality and exploring spirituality *in* the New Testament. In the first case, our interest is in general scriptural markers for Christian spirituality as a whole, while trying to avoid unhelpful or inaccurate generalizations. In the second case, our interest is specifically in the distinctive spiritualities of, say, the Gospel of Mark or the letters of Paul. The first part of this chapter will attempt to offer some brief reflections both on general scriptural markers and then on the key elements of spirituality expressed in the main books of the New Testament.

Scriptural Markers

A fundamental scriptural image for Christian spirituality is discipleship. Indeed, during the later history of Christian spirituality across two millennia, the concept of "discipleship" became virtually interchangeable with leading a Christian life. At its most fundamental, spirituality in the Christian sense is reducible neither to devotional practices nor to some abstract framework of beliefs. It is a complete way of life. In other words, to be a Christian is to live in the world in a certain way. Interestingly, this "way" of discipleship is most regularly expressed in the gospels and the Acts of the Apostles by the Greek noun *mathētēs* (a person who learns) which implies not simply a teacher–student relationship between Jesus and the disciple whereby wisdom or teaching is passed on. It also implies that the disciple learns, or more properly absorbs, a way of existence by being alongside the teacher. This links the concept of discipleship to the other important New Testament word, a verb, *akolouthein*, to follow, or follow after.

The notion of discipleship has two related elements. The first is a call to conversion in response to the incoming reign of God. "The time is fulfilled, and the kingdom of God has come near; repent and believe in the good news" (Mk 1, 15). The second dimension of discipleship, of following the way of Jesus, is both to adopt a way of life and to join in the work of building the Kingdom of God. "And Jesus said to them [Simon and his brother Andrew], 'Follow me and I will make you fish for people'" (Mk 1, 17). The same dual call to repentance and discipleship is present at the beginning of Jesus' ministry in the Gospel of Matthew (Mt 4, 17, and 19) and, although expressed differently, is implicit also in the Gospels of Luke and John.

In New Testament terms, to become a disciple is not the same as the modern quest, initiated by seekers, for a wise and reliable spiritual teacher who is then selected by the seeker. Nor is it a matter of choosing to sit at the feet of such a teacher until we have gained enough autonomous wisdom of our own to move on. Jesus is recorded as choosing and then calling his own disciples (Mk 1, 16–20; Mt 4, 18–22; Lk 5, 1–11; Jn 1, 35–42). This involves four things. First, discipleship is not self-chosen but is a response to a call, or, put more theologically, it is a response to God's grace. Second, the identity and title of "disciple" is not given because of social status or because of some kind of religious or moral perfection. Jesus calls tax-collectors (Mt 9, 9) and all kinds of sinners or socially unacceptable people (Mk 2, 15–17). Unusually for the time, there were also women in his immediate circle (Lk 8, 1–3). There is a tension there. On the one hand, Jesus called upon everyone to repent and to welcome the Kingdom of God, yet on the other hand his call to join with him in formal discipleship is only made to some. However, as we shall see this notion of calling or discipleship expands in the post-resurrection period of the early Church. Third, the call to discipleship implied what we would call conversion, a radical break with the past that involved leaving family, previous work, possessions (e.g. Lk 14, 26; Mk 2, 14; Mk 10, 21) – indeed everything (Lk 5, 11) – for the sake of the gospel. The price of this radical change and transformation is sometimes characterized as taking up the cross or losing one's life in order to find it (e.g. Mt 10, 38–39). Finally, the call to discipleship implies sharing in the work of Jesus in bringing God's Kingdom into being. Thus, the great missionary discourse in the Gospel of Matthew, Chapter 10, lists the work of the disciple as proclaiming the good news, curing the sick, raising the dead, cleansing lepers, and casting out demons (Mt 10, 7–8). This sharing in Jesus' work and life is also bound up with the notion of "taking the lowest place" or of service (in Greek *diakonia*) as in the Gospel of Mark 9, 35, or even giving up one's life out of love (Jn 15, 12–13).

In the post-resurrection Christian communities, the understanding of discipleship moves even more strongly in two related directions. First, the disciple is not simply someone who knows and follows the *teachings* of Jesus or who models his life on the pattern of Jesus (imitation). The disciple is someone who is also profoundly *united* to Jesus as a person and who through that union shares in Jesus' own relationship with God as Father. Thus, in baptism the disciple enters into the same dynamism of Jesus' passage through death to new life. The letters of Paul, for example, express this as *participating* in the Cross of Jesus and in his resurrection – in other words, in the triumph of glory over suffering and life over sin and death (Rom 6, 3–5; Phil 3, 8–11). This baptismal dynamic is renewed and strengthened again and again by the celebration of the Eucharist in early Christian communities. The notion of union with and participation in Jesus Christ is further developed in Paul who also uses the language of adoption – that Christian disciples are now adopted as sons and daughters of God and thus co-heirs to God's promise in Jesus (Rom 8, 15; Gal 4, 6). Second, and closely related to this language of participation, is the emphasis on discipleship as membership of a family or community. Thus, "discipleship," and all that may be said about it, expands beyond a few close confidants to embrace all who follow Jesus within the community of believers, initiated in baptism and nurtured in the Eucharist. This community is described in the language of union and participation as a body, the living body of Christ (see, e.g., 1 Cor 12, 12–13).

Spirituality in the New Testament

Once we turn from general scriptural markers for Christian spirituality to the spirituality of the New Testament writers, the first and most important thing to bear in mind is that the New Testament is a first-century document. That is to say that however much the New Testament is given a privileged status in Christian spirituality, the actual spiritualities in the New Testament books are context-specific. The four gospels, for example, are creative re-workings of earlier oral or perhaps written traditions about Jesus that the gospel writers then allowed to interact with the contexts and needs of their specific audiences. This explains the considerable differences of emphasis alongside the sense of a common tradition about the person, teachings, and the ultimate significance of Jesus Christ. The New Testament, therefore, includes four gospels (and the Acts of the Apostles linked to the Gospel of Luke), a range of letters, and the apocalyptic Book of Revelation. In this very brief summary, I will concentrate on the material with the strongest influence on Christian spirituality, namely the gospels, Acts, and the letters ascribed to the apostle Paul.

Three of the gospels, Mark, Matthew, and Luke, are commonly grouped together as "the synoptic gospels" because of the amount of content they share and their similarities in wording and structure. It is generally accepted that these similarities arise not merely from a common oral background but also from direct literary connections. That said, the emphases and therefore the spiritualities of the three texts are quite particular to each.

For example, a dominant emphasis in the Gospel of Mark (the shortest and the earliest) is on Jesus' constant action rather than on his spoken teaching – in the sense that there is a large proportion of narrative but relatively few parables and only one major collection of sayings in discourse form (Chapter 13). In that sense, Jesus' own life is the primary parable and provides basic teaching about the nature of the Kingdom of God. So, discipleship, as it was for the first followers, is a question of "being with" Jesus in his mission. At the heart of Mark's presentation is the cross. Jesus is the suffering Messiah. Jesus' actions, healings, and teaching can only be understood in the light of the cross. It is therefore not surprising that the Gospel also emphasizes a secrecy surrounding Jesus' identity and the failure of the disciples to understand him. Just as the real meaning of Jesus' life, revealed in the passion and resurrection, is properly understood only in hindsight, so the power of God is revealed paradoxically in weakness. This also places the cross at the heart of the spirituality derived from this Gospel. Just as the Son of Man must suffer (e.g. Mk 8, 31), so too the disciple must deny self and take up the cross in imitation of Jesus (Mk 8, 34–35).

In the Gospel of Matthew, the emphasis is on Jesus as fulfillment of the promises of the Jewish scriptures. Jesus is the authoritative interpreter of the Law and of God's desires for the chosen people. Consequently, a related emphasis in the Gospel is on practicing a life of "righteousness" in response to the presence of "God with us" in Jesus (e.g. Mt 1, 23) and the permanently abiding presence of Jesus in the community of believers (e.g. Mt 28, 20). However, "righteousness" is not reducible to moral rectitude but means both repentance and acceptance of God's requirements, or obedience to God's way of seeing and being (Mt 5, 6). It is the option for the "righteous," single-minded, hard way (that also embraces service of God in serving the needy) that ultimately divides the people of the Kingdom from the others (e.g. Mt 25, 31–46). Not surprisingly, a related Matthean emphasis is on the totality of commitment, expressed in the double commandment to love God and neighbor (e.g. Matt 5, 38–42).

In the Luke–Acts tradition, the important themes are God's faithfulness and the all-embracing or inclusive nature of those who are heirs of God's promises. With the coming of the Messiah, universal salvation is possible in an age now filled with God's Spirit. The response is gratitude and joy. This is Jesus' own attitude. "Jesus rejoiced in the Holy Spirit and said, 'I thank you Father, Lord of heaven and earth, because you have hidden these things from the wise and intelligent and revealed them to infants'" (Lk 10, 21). The joyful reception of salvation is extended to "the poor" for whom Jesus and his teaching is "good news." Jesus himself is recorded as affirming this in his reading and commentary on the prophecy of Isaiah at Nazareth (Lk 4, 16–21). The classic New Testament themes of conversion and a life of following Jesus are also present in Luke but with the additional twist that those most likely to respond are "the poor" – that is, those who are in some way marginal, physically, socially, or spiritually (Lk 6, 20–26). Luke–Acts also spells out the universality of Jesus' message and God's salvation by highlighting in the Acts of the Apostles the role of the apostles, the Church, and most importantly the Holy Spirit who guides the community of Jesus and guarantees the spread of the gospel "to the ends of the earth" (Acts 1, 8). This includes the painful and difficult expansion of consciousness where the disciples are brought to recognize the presence and action of God's Spirit in "otherness," in situations and people who are outside their normal world of experience and religious assumptions (in this case the Jewish Law, see the story of Peter and the centurion Cornelius in Acts 10).[1]

The Gospel of John stands apart from the other three gospels. Its emphasis moves in more developed theological directions (which is not to say that the other gospels are not also theological). That is to say that the relationship of Jesus to God – especially the identification of Jesus with a pre-existent Son of God – is more to the foreground than the content of his preaching of the Kingdom. There is a much greater sense of top-down Christology – that is, Jesus is presented as the one sent from heaven by the Father as the definitive expression of God's love and desire for humanity and creation. He is the Word and wisdom of God made flesh. Discipleship is therefore focused more on coming to participate in Jesus' relationship to the Father (his divine life) by believing in the "signs" he does (both in words and in actions such as healings). Believers will be born anew in the Spirit (Jn 3, 5) into eternal life – that is, a life not subject to death-as-final-destiny. Discipleship is therefore a union with God in love and knowledge and union with all who are Jesus' "friends" (Jn 15, 12–15). Knowledge is expressed in terms of light or enlightenment and salvation is expressed more as the imparting of light and life than as sacrifice (see the "sign" expressed in the healing of the man born blind, Jn 9). This pattern of discipleship is also offered to those who come after the time of Jesus and believe in him through the Gospel rather than by directly witnessing the signs. What has attracted many people to this Gospel is this "mystical" dimension of New Testament spirituality that emphasizes God's presence, mutual indwelling, and a union of light and love rather than simply moral conversion.[2]

Apart from the four Gospels (and the related Acts of Apostles), the texts in the New Testament with the strongest influence on perceptions of the Christian life and discipleship are the collection of letters ascribed to the apostle Paul. I say "ascribed" because some of the most famous and important (e.g. 2 Thessalonians, Colossians, and Ephesians) belong to "the school of Paul" (reflecting Paul's insights) but were not written by Paul himself. It is helpful to begin by summarizing what differentiates the Pauline school from either the synoptic gospels or the Gospel of John. Distinctive features center on the person and role of Jesus Christ. While the synoptic gospels are dominated by the historical Jesus and his actions and teachings and while the Gospel of John is based on an understanding of the pre-existent Word of God, the spirituality of the Pauline letters focuses on the Jesus of the resurrection, the risen Christ who is also the crucified Jesus. Thus, the key to Pauline thinking is God's act of raising the crucified Jesus from the dead as the beginning of a new creation and as the hope of a transformed humanity (e.g. Rom 8.29; 1 Cor 15, 20; 2 Cor 5, 17). Thus, the status and future of humankind, as an act of divine creation, implies that "salvation" is God's act alone and that the Christian life is fundamentally a matter of receiving this gift. For Christians who live in the post-resurrection age, the medium for participating in salvation or in the new humanity is the Spirit present and active within us. This actually blends into the risen Christ. So, in 1 Cor 16, 45, it is the "second Adam" (Jesus Christ) who becomes a "life-giving spirit." So, it is the presence of the Spirit of the risen Christ who draws the Christian disciple into a pattern of death, resurrection, and transformed life (e.g. Rom 8, 12–17). The emphasis, therefore, is not so much on Christians "imitating" Christ but on *participation* in the new life given by God in and through Christ. So Christians are baptized into Christ's death but equally into new life (Rom 6, 3–4). Finally, this process of being made "other Christs" is not purely individual but in and through membership of Christ's "body," that is, the community of the Church. Equally, the Christian life is a bodily one rather than something conducted only on an elevated spiritual level – and embodiment remains the ultimate destiny of the new humanity, defined in terms of resurrection of the body (1 Cor 15).[3]

Spirituality and the Early Church

The development of spirituality in the early Church after New Testament times up to the fifth century was especially associated with four elements. First, from the very beginning Christian spirituality was expressed most strongly in the "way of life" of the community as a whole, not least its common prayer and liturgy. This is the feature of early Christian spirituality that is least often considered. Second, Christianity consistently had to respond to hostility and persecution in the public forum until it became itself a public religion in the fourth century and then had to change gear in important ways. Third, the expanding Christian community increasingly confronted internal controversies and was forced to address the need for greater doctrinal precision. Fourth, particularly in the aftermath of Christianity's adoption of a public role, the ascetical and countercultural tendency within Christianity found expression increasingly in the development of monastic ways of life. This last element will be held over until Chapter 3 which deals more generally with monastic spirituality.[4]

Liturgy

In very broad terms, the vast majority of evidence we have for early forms of spirituality is in written texts. This clearly does not and cannot express a rounded picture of the spiritual life of an average Christian community. For one thing, this kind of evidence often excludes women (who were rarely literate at this time) and their activity and contribution to early Christianity. Then, while early liturgical texts do survive, the writings on the whole do not really describe the actual experience of worship in the early communities or their day to day existence, let alone the inner or devotional life of individual Christians. We have already seen that the earliest spirituality of the Christian community centered on participation with Christ in the dynamism of baptism and Eucharist. Clearly, the earliest forms of worship were adopted and gradually adapted from a Jewish heritage. Slowly, too, distinctive hymns and prayers appeared as well as various art forms. However, we have to wait until Christianity emerges from persecution into an active public role in the fourth century before details of Christian worship are readily available. Before that date, there are merely some hints in a number of writings of which the Eastern *Didache* and the supposed writings of the Western Hippolytus are perhaps the best-known examples.

Contemporary authorities generally consider that the *Didache* ("teaching") derives from Syria and dates to the later part of the first century. It is not strictly a liturgical text but is concerned more broadly with Christian practice and morals including instructions on the Christian life (citing the Sermon on the Mount), on twice-weekly fasting, and on prayer three times daily based on the Lord's Prayer. However, it also has instructions on baptism and the Eucharist including forms that, from a contemporary viewpoint, suggest a more extended and extemporary blessing of the bread and wine than was usual in later times.

Hippolytus (c. 170–c. 236) is a confusing historical figure around whom gathered various traditions and legends. Most likely he was a priest and theologian in Rome during the early third century and, after conflicts with a succession of Bishops, was reconciled in his later years in the aftermath of a period of persecution. Apart from theological and biblical works, he is frequently but controversially credited with writing *The Apostolic Tradition*. This includes rites of baptism, Eucharist, and ordination. The Eucharistic prayer was used as the basis for the second prayer in the revised Roman liturgy after the Second Vatican Council. While it would be too crude to describe these texts as the actual Roman form of liturgy, they can be thought of as representative examples of early common worship. What stands out is both their simplicity and their spiritual depth. There is a strong emphasis on the Eucharist as symbol of unity and on the action of God's Spirit renewing the life and mission of the Christian community.

Spirituality and Martyrdom

Christianity continually confronted hostility and active persecution in the public arena until the edict of tolerance under the Emperor Constantine (313). Inevitably, this gave rise to a spirituality of martyrdom related very strongly to identification with the passion of Christ. The word "martyr," derived from the Greek *martus* or "witness," was originally applied to the first apostles as witnesses of Jesus Christ's life and, especially, of his resurrection (e.g. Acts 1, 8). Slowly it came to be associated with those Christians who had suffered hardship for their faith and eventually was limited to those who suffered death. The classic model for the latter referred back to the Book of Acts and the stoning of Stephen, the first Christian martyr (Acts 7), but the main reference was to the death of Jesus himself, whose death was deemed to be the pattern of all subsequent martyrdom. Thus, martyrdom became *the* ultimate symbol of faithful Christian discipleship and thus of Christian holiness. More than this, the tranquil acceptance of martyrdom was an affirmation of the believer's faith in Christ's promise of victory over death and of resurrection for all who accepted the good news of God's salvation. Martyrdom literature, whether the letters of Ignatius of Antioch (d. 107), or the stories of Polycarp of Smyrna (d. 155), or of Perpetua and Felicity of Carthage (complete with Perpetua's prison diary dated c. 203), infused the wider conceptions of a truly Christian life. This underlined the virtue of sacrifice, imitation of Christ, and the cost of allegiance to Christ, and resistance to an unquestioning acceptance of surrounding cultural norms.

Shrines, Devotion, and Pilgrimage

As any visitor to the surviving catacombs in Rome will quickly realize, the burial places of the Christian martyrs were an early example of sacred shrines which acted as focuses for popular devotion and for pilgrimage. In part, this reflected a characteristically Christian emphasis on the relationship between sacred place and sacred people. Despite its continued reverence for traditional Jewish sacred places, Christianity was based on a belief that God was revealed primarily not through a promised land or the Jerusalem Temple but in the person of Jesus of Nazareth. The itinerary of the earliest pilgrimages to the "Holy Places" was governed by the texts of the gospels. What mattered was that these places were the contexts where Jesus, the source of ultimate meaning and focus of Christian hope, lived, died, and was resurrected. Thus, sacred place materialized a life, a teaching, and an example. In some ways, as we shall see, such a perspective was projected onto the early Christian martyrs and then later saints. In other words, places were said to be sacred because of associations with human holiness.

The cult of martyrs was also the beginning of a more general devotion to saints in Christianity. Martyrs, because united with God, could now intercede for believers on earth. Festivals were instituted to mark their deaths (or "heavenly birthdays"), and this began a liturgical calendar of saints in the Christian Church. The burial places of martyrs became focuses of devotion where Christians could both pray for help, derive inspiration for their own lives, and, collectively, could continually reaffirm the flow of tradition within which each particular Christian community found its identity.[5]

Holy men and women were tangible links between heaven and earth. The earliest examples were the Apostles and the places, such as Rome, where they were believed to have worked, died, and been buried. These were followed by second- and third-century martyrs. Beyond them were successive generations of holy men and women across the centuries.[6] In acts of healing or intercession, as well as by their spiritual teachings, holy men and women from late antiquity through the Middle Ages and beyond personalized the presence and power of God for generations of ordinary believers.[7]

Spirituality and Doctrine

The forms of Christian spirituality express a certain understanding of God and of God's ways of dealing with the world. Yet, concrete spiritualities grow out of the actual practice of the Christian life rather than out of intellectual concepts conceived in isolation from experience and from reflection on experience. In other words, spiritualities arise from *human existence* and are not merely second order practices logically derived from pre-existing belief systems and doctrines. The characteristic Christian beliefs in God-as-Trinity and of Jesus Christ as the incarnation of God did not arise in the first instance from a change of intellectual horizons. They originated from the ways in which the first generation of Christians after Jesus' time sought to live their lives in relation to Jesus' life and teachings and how they experienced his abiding presence with them as Spirit. They then expressed this experience of the living Christ, and their new existence "in Christ," through prayer and through their attempts to live in obedience to God the Father in the pattern of Jesus. Doctrine and life certainly went together but a way of life came first. It is not that the early Christians were unconcerned with *truth*, it is just that the quest for truth was not a matter of detached speculation. Rather early Christians were concerned to preserve the fullness of a relationship with Christ and with God in Christ that they had come to understand to be the very heart of their identity as Christians.[8]

For all these reasons, it is not surprising that clarity concerning the nature of Jesus Christ, and his relationship to God, was one of the most critical theological issues of the early Christian period. The doctrine of Incarnation, that in the person of Jesus of Nazareth there was a true union of the divine and the human, not only governs all other Christian beliefs but is also the fundamental bedrock of Christian spirituality.[9] Our destiny is "deification" or, in the words of Irenaeus of Lyons (c. 130– c. 200), "The Word of God…did…become what we are, that He might bring us to be what He is Himself."[10] At an early stage, Christianity had to contend with what came to be called Gnosticism. This was a tendency that took a variety of forms rather than a coherent movement. The title itself reflects the Greek word *gnosis*, knowledge. The implication was that true knowledge of God was reserved to some special band of initiates. In addition, there were suggestions that material existence was a result of sin and that humans have a spiritual element that is trapped in the material body but really belongs to another world. Salvation is an escape from matter and a return to this divine world. In Christian terms, such beliefs undermined the notion of God as creator of matter and the doctrine of Incarnation. There were a variety of long-established dualist worldviews and "gnostic" mystery cults that were not of Christian origin but that had enough of an impact on Christianity to provoke strong response from orthodox theologians such as Irenaeus of Lyons.

It took some four hundred years for the classic boundaries of belief about Jesus Christ and his relationship to God to be determined. Thus, the Church Council of Nicea in 325 condemned the heresy of Arianism (named after an Egyptian priest Arius) that denied that the nature of God could be shared or communicated. Not only did Arianism hold that Jesus Christ was not divine but it also implied that there was no real relationship between God and humanity. The end and purpose of human life was not participation in the life of God. The only relationship humans have with God is as slaves to a distant, cold tyrant. So, against this, the Nicene Creed affirmed that Christ was God from God and "one in being with the Father." Later the Council of Chalcedon in 451 condemned the opposite (supposedly Monophysite) view that Christ was solely divine and not human. On the contrary, Chalcedon affirmed, Christ had two natures and was paradoxically both truly God and truly human without resolving precisely how this could be understood. In the end, the origin of all this debate was practical – the nature of human life – and its purpose was to affirm that God in Christ truly assumed human bodily nature and thus raised humanity into the divine life. As a corollary, an orthodox understanding of the Incarnation preserved a positive understanding of the world and of material, bodily existence.

A number of key personalities in Eastern and Western Christian thought stand out in the early centuries as having a particularly strong influence on Christian spirituality. It is to these that we will now turn our attention.[11]

Origen

Origen of Alexandria (c. 185–c. 254) was strongly influenced by Greek Neoplatonist philosophy with its emphasis on the spiritual path of the individual back to union with "the One" – in Christian terms, with God.[12] This was attained through ethical purification from everything that stands in the way of desire for union, through contemplation and through a mystical exegesis of the Christian scriptures. Basing himself on the classic Neoplatonist threefold hierarchy of existence and knowledge, Origen suggested both a threefold contemplative model of scripture interpretation (literal, moral, and spiritual) and a threefold ascending pattern for spiritual progress associated with beginners (*praxis*), proficients (*theōria*), and the perfect (*theologia*). The spiritual journey was conceived as a recovery of the likeness of God in the soul in a movement upwards from the material realm towards greater light.

Evagrius

In the late fourth century, a promising cleric and theologian in Constantinople, Evagrius Ponticus (d. 399), became a monk in Egypt. He adopted Origen's language of mystical scriptural exegesis and also of spiritual progress. His theology has been described as "apophatic," describing God primarily in terms of negations. He used Origen's three-fold model of the spiritual journey beginning with a stage of overcoming passion, moving on to the stage of contemplation of creation and ending in "theology" (*theologia*) – that is, mystical union with the Trinity itself. Evagrius combined speculative Neoplatonism with desert monastic practice to produce teachings on imageless contemplative prayer that had a long-standing influence, particularly on Eastern Christian spirituality.[13]

The Cappadocians

Evagrius had been a pupil of two great theologians, Basil the Great (330–379) and his friend Gregory Nazianzen (329–390). Together with another major figure, Gregory of Nyssa (c. 335–c. 395), Basil's brother, they were at the heart of a close-knit fourth-century group of ascetics and thinkers in Asia Minor known collectively as the Cappadocian Fathers (although one member, Macrina, Basil's sister, was a woman). Basil became bishop of Caesarea and is best known for his ascetic instructions for monks, or "rules," which will be discussed in Chapter 3. His ascetic works remain at the heart of Eastern monasticism. Together with his sermons, the emphasis of Basil's writings is a practical-ethical (ascetical) theology of the highest quality.

Gregory Nazianzen was also concerned with monastic asceticism (with less emphasis on leaving the city for the "desert" or on the hermit life) but is better known as one of the greatest theologians of the early

Church. For Gregory, strongly influenced by Origen's thought, the spiritual life was a journey away from materiality towards a kind of spiritual luminosity or refinement. He was a strong proponent of the orthodox party against Arianism and presided over the Council of Constantinople (381). One of his major contributions to the alliance of doctrine and spirituality was his highly developed theology of the Holy Spirit within his conception of the Trinity. He saw this theology of the Spirit as critical for an adequate understanding of Christian life, particularly the transfiguration of human existence in a process known as "deification." Deification describes the notion that human destiny is to share in God's life of immortal glory not by nature or by will but by the work of the Spirit within.

Gregory of Nyssa is perhaps best known as a spiritual theologian of the highest quality, not least through his text of mystical theology, *The Life of Moses*. Gregory represented the contemplative journey in terms of stages and ascent, but, in contrast to Origen, the journey was towards darkness rather than light. As his frame of reference, Gregory used the story of Moses' experiences in the Book of Exodus. Here, the metaphor is the ascent of Mount Sinai as Moses enters into ever deeper clouds of darkness in his encounter with God. Because of Gregory of Nyssa's "apophatic" understanding of the climax of the contemplative ascent as deep darkness in which God is experienced but never finally *known*, the spiritual journey is a never-ending progress *towards* perfection in which we strive ever more to be perfect but never conclusively arrive. Along with Origen, Gregory's exposition of the spiritual journey (allied with the writings of the sixth-century pseudonymous Dionysius) had a considerable influence on spirituality in both the East and the West.[14]

Augustine

Augustine of Hippo (354–430) was without doubt the greatest thinker of Western Christianity in the early period, and his writings have dominated Western theology and spirituality ever since. His spiritual autobiography, the *Confessions*, has had a particular impact. This work offers an account of Augustine's early life, his inner conflict as he struggled with a desire both for God and for personal pleasure, and his conversion. The most relevant fact about Augustine is that he wrote in the context of a Western Roman Empire in the process of terminal decay. This fact, combined with a sense of his own weaknesses, means that Augustine portrays a stark understanding of human weakness and guilt. He analyzed with great perception the depths and deviousness of the human heart and emphasized the gratuity of God's salvation. The strong emphases on sin, conversion, and forgiveness that have been prominent in Western spirituality may be attributed to Augustine's influence. On a more positive note, Augustine is also a theologian of desire. In his *Confessions*, Augustine refers to "my heart, where I am whatever I am."[15] For Augustine, God created humans with the divine image in their heart. In his *Tractates on the Gospel of John*, Augustine invites us to reconnect with this real self: "Return to thy heart; see there what, it may be, thou canst perceive of God, for in it is the image of God. In the inner man [sic] dwelleth Christ, in the inner man art thou renewed after the image of God."[16] However, the language of the heart does not imply a privatized spirituality. The heart is also where we are united, in God, with the whole human family. Indeed, in Augustine's *Commentary on Genesis*, Adam's sin was to live for himself. The most insidious sin was privacy or self-enclosure. So for Augustine, the Heavenly City was the community in which there would be the fullness of sharing.[17]

Pseudo-Dionysius

The Neoplatonist theology of an anonymous monk who wrote in Syria around the year 500 was perhaps the single greatest influence on the development of Christian mysticism, Eastern and Western. He wrote under the pseudonym of Dionysius, the convert of Paul in Acts 17. He is best known in the West for what is somewhat misleadingly called his "apophatic (or negative) spirituality" expounded in his shortest work, the *Mystical Theology*, translated into Latin in the ninth century by the Irish theologian John Scotus Eriugena. This stressed divine darkness – that God is ultimately incomprehensible and beyond all names or affirmations. Consequently, God is to be "known" paradoxically by denying or negating all the symbols or images for God that we conventionally use. However, merely to stress Dionysius' "negative" theology or spirituality in isolation would be entirely misleading. Not only did another treatise, *The Divine Names*, deal with God as revealed and known in the many names used of God in the scriptures, but the whole of Dionysius' spiritual theology is centered on the liturgy. In *The Ecclesiastical Hierarchy*, the liturgy is portrayed as drawing the believer into the pattern of divine outpouring and the reunion of created reality with God. Liturgy not only provides a rich symbolism of the divine but is also an earthly manifestation of the hierarchies that proceed in ordered fashion from God. It would be more accurate to say that Dionysius' spiritual theology emphasizes that, while God may be encountered in affirmation as well as negation, it must also be said that God is ultimately beyond *both* affirmation and negation.[18]

Christian Spirituality as Transformation and Mission

It is now possible to describe briefly the fundamental characteristics of all forms of Christian spirituality. As a beginning, we can return to the scriptures. According to the first chapter of the Gospel of Mark, the message of Jesus' initial preaching in Galilee is a call to "discipleship" – in other words, to follow his way. Thus, at its heart, Christian spirituality is founded on "discipleship," a dual process of conversion (a turning away from disorder and towards new life offered by God in Jesus Christ) and of learning how to follow in the way of Jesus and, like him, to proclaim God's Kingdom.

In the Gospel of John, Jesus is recorded as speaking of himself as "the way" for all disciples (John 14, 6), and in the Book of Acts Christianity is described as "the way" and Christians as "people of the way" (Acts 9, 2 and 18, 25) – "the way" being the way of Jesus which all disciples seek to follow. However, following the way of Jesus itself has two elements, one receptive and the other proactive. Discipleship is not simply a matter of responding to Jesus' proclamation of the Kingdom of God by sharing his way of life, but it is also a question of actively sharing in his work. This is expressed as the task of extending his proclamation of the Kingdom to the whole world (thus Mt 28, 18–20; Mk 16, 15; Lk 24, 46–49). Christian spirituality is inherently rather than accidentally connected to continuing Jesus' mission.

Having said this, it would be too narrow to understand the call to proclaim the Kingdom simply in terms of verbal communication of information about God or of moral teachings about human behavior. Proclaiming the way of Jesus was understood from the start as living life "after the manner of Jesus Christ." Thus, disciples are to extend the mission of Jesus by the kind of people they are. This means being a living message (see 2 Cor 3, 3). To proclaim the Kingdom of God is to *embody the gospel in a way of life*, both individually and collectively as the Church.

Any later explanations of the nature of Christian spirituality and all later forms of spirituality are based on these foundations. Because the spiritualities of the New Testament are unavoidably first-century documents, they are therefore context-specific. Consequently, when any subsequent spiritual movement or tradition refers to scriptural foundations, this is always an act of re-interpretation within a different and specific religious and cultural context.

With this caveat, it is nevertheless possible to say that, taken as a whole, the scriptural foundations of Christian spirituality suggest a *way of transformation* towards fullness of life in God and at the same time a *way of mission* through following the way of Jesus and by means of the power of God's indwelling Spirit. Transformation and mission are therefore key ideas for understanding Christian spirituality although, as we shall see, these dual elements are expressed differently in the various styles of spirituality. Every Christian spiritual tradition is an articulation in specific time–place contexts of the New Testament "model" of following Jesus faithfully. This implies a transformation of consciousness and conduct after the pattern of Jesus but not one based on mere *repetition* of Jesus' actions. The "event" of Jesus Christ is also set in a particular time and place. Christian discipleship necessarily implies a relationship to this inaugural "event" of Jesus Christ. Yet, in their teachings, the classic historical forms of Christian spirituality are both faithful to that event and also necessarily different from those beginnings. This is because they too are set within particular times and places. Faithful "following," discipleship, actually implies *going beyond* Jesus' actions but in a way that is opened up by them. To put it another way, the particularity of Jesus' life is the measure of all authentic forms of Christian spirituality, yet at the same time the particularity of the event of Jesus Christ permits, as it were, the equally particular nature of all subsequent discipleship.[19]

The history of Christian spirituality is a kind of rich and varied commentary on how transformation and mission are to be understood. In broad terms, all classic spiritual traditions address certain questions, sometimes implicitly rather than explicitly. First, what needs to be transformed or what are we to be transformed from and why? In other words, spiritual traditions offer some kind of perspective on the nature of, and remedies for, human disorder. Second, what factors stand in the way of transformation? These factors are described theologically, although nowadays we should also note the role of psychological or social factors. Third, where does transformation take place? In other words, is the context for transformation the normal processes of everyday life or is it only in some kind of special context set apart (e.g. the desert or the monastery)? Fourth, how does transformation take place? This will usually involve some theory of spiritual growth as well as wisdom about lifestyles or spiritual practices that assist transformation. Finally, what is the purpose of or end-point of transformation? In other words, what is the vision of holiness and human completeness?

Theories of Spiritual Transformation

At this point, it is worth summarizing some of the classic theories of spiritual growth. Different spiritual traditions have offered various theories of spiritual transformation and wisdom about the lifestyles or spiritual practices that assist transformation. One of the most widespread images is that of a pilgrimage or a journey with various stages or dimensions. This has been expressed in different times and places through themes such as *theosis* (or deification), ascent (up mountains or ladders), *conversatio* (in the Rule of St Benedict [subsequently RB] as we shall see in Chapter 3), the *triplex via* (or threefold path), or, more recently, in terms adapted from modern psychological theories of development. Equally, in broader terms the theme of the Christian life as a pilgrimage has been a rich one in spiritual literature ranging from Augustine's *City of God* in the fifth century to John Bunyan's *Pilgrim's Progress* in the seventeenth century and onwards to the anonymous nineteenth-century Russian work on the spirituality of the Jesus Prayer, *The Way of the Pilgrim*.

The metaphor of "journey" expresses the radically dynamic nature of the Christian spiritual life. Sometimes, two rather static concepts, "perfection" and "union," have been used to express the "where to?" of the journey, but ultimately the end in view is a more mysterious and dynamic fullness of life in God.

Beginning with the theologian Irenaeus in the second century, who developed a dynamic understanding of the Christian life in contrast to more static teachings on illumination (e.g. in the heresy of Gnosticism), the theology of the early Church gradually developed a theory of stages of the spiritual life. The Alexandrian theologian Origen (c. 185–c. 255) explained the contemplative life in Neoplatonic terms as three ascending stages away from material existence towards greater light associated with beginners (*praxis*), proficients (*theōria*), and the perfect (*theologia*).[20] The goal of the journey was a recovery of the original created likeness of God in the soul. In the following century, the Cappadocian theologian Gregory of Nyssa (c. 335–c. 395), notably in his *Life of Moses*, also described the contemplative journey in terms of the stages of ascent but in this case towards darkness rather than light. He used as his metaphor the story of Moses' on Mount Sinai entering into ever deeper clouds of darkness in his encounter with God.[21] Because of Gregory of Nyssa's "apophatic" (i.e. imageless) understanding of the climax of the contemplative journey as a deep darkness in which God is experienced but never finally *known*, there is a certain open-ended quality to his teachings about spiritual transformation.

Origen's and Gregory's expositions of the spiritual journey (allied with the writings of the sixth-century anonymous monk known by the pseudonym Dionysius or Denis) had a considerable influence in both the East and the West.[22] During the Western Middle Ages, the conception of the spiritual journey developed strongly in the direction of what became known as the "three ways" or *triplex via* (purgative, illuminative, and unitive "ways") which, while described in terms of consecutive stages, are more properly interweaving *dimensions* of transformation. Subsequent spiritual literature also employs metaphors for the spiritual journey – often the classic theme of "ascent" whether of mountains, for example, the sixteenth-century *Ascent of Mount Carmel* of John of the Cross, or of ladders, for example, the fourteenth-century Walter Hilton's *Ladder* – or *Scale* (from the Latin *scala* – stairs) *of Perfection*.

In terms of asceticism and the monastic life, John Climacus, the seventh-century Abbot of St Catherine's monastery in Sinai, employed the image of a ladder of ascending virtues in his *The Ladder of Divine Ascent*. The dominant Western monastic rule, the sixth-century *RB*, also described the spiritual journey in terms of a ladder – the twelve degrees of humility (Chapter 7), "a ladder of our ascending actions." This is developed further in monastic commentaries such as that by the twelfth-century Cistercian, Bernard of Clairvaux, *Steps of Humility and Pride*. Another influential monastic description of the spiritual journey was the twelfth-century *Ladder of Monks* by Guigo II, a Carthusian, but this referred to the ancient contemplative practice of reading scripture, *lectio divina*, but structured more systematically as four stages, *lectio*, *meditatio*, *oratio*, and *contemplatio*.[23]

Although the classic metaphor of "ascent" retains a certain value in emphasizing a continuous journey rather than a succession of disconnected experiences, it also suggests a separation of the material world from a truly spiritual existence. There are also some more general problems about the notion of successive stages. First, what is represented by the distinct stages (purgation/repentance, illumination/enlargement of vision, and union with God) are likely to be present in different proportions at *all* points of the spiritual journey. Second, in a more fundamental way, union with God should not be understood only as a stage beyond other stages and achieved through contemplative practice.

In another sense, Christianity understands the power of God (expressed in the language of "grace") as a prerequisite of all spiritual growth. Third, the notion of distinct stages can support a questionable hierarchy of spiritual and moral values and therefore of lifestyles in which the contemplative way is seen as distinct from and superior to the way of action. Thus, the twentieth-century German Jesuit theologian Karl Rahner questioned the concept of distinct stages as based on an outdated Neoplatonist anthropology in which the summit of human existence is total detachment from bodily passions. He also rejected an approach which seems, theologically, to involve an objective and inevitable increase of *grace* or, ethically, the limitation of higher moral acts to one stage rather than another.[24]

While the classic approaches to the spiritual journey in Christian spirituality continue to offer valuable wisdom for our own times, a contemporary perspective suggests that their sometimes individualistic tone must nowadays be complemented by a renewed biblical emphasis on the collective understanding of discipleship. The Second Vatican Council also clearly emphasized that it is the Christian community as a whole that is a pilgrim people "led by the Holy Spirit in their journey to the kingdom of their Father" (*Gaudium et Spes*, Chapter 1). This recovery of a more collective understanding of the spiritual journey also provided a pointer towards the solidarity with others expressed by Liberation Theology as it emerged in Latin America in the 1960s. This led to the use of the Old Testament image of the Exodus, a desert journey in which God leads the oppressed peoples from a state of slavery to the possession of a land of their own as in the work of Gustavo Gutiérrez.[25]

Conclusion

The brief exploration of scriptural foundations and their development in relation to doctrine and practice in the early Church underline a number of distinctive features in Christian spirituality overall. First, and in particular, Christian spirituality is intimately related to a specific understanding of God and of God's relationship to the world and to humanity. God is understood to be a dynamic interrelationship of "persons in Communion" (Trinity). Second, this understanding of God extends to a belief that God overflows into an outgoing dynamic of creativity. Christian spirituality is creation-centered in the sense that it understands all material reality as the gift and reflection of a loving God. Third, and closely related to this, is a belief that God's engagement with humanity is expressed particularly by God taking on human embodied existence in the person of Jesus Christ (the Incarnation). This makes all Christian spiritual traditions Christ-centered in differing ways. A fundamental framework for understanding Christian spirituality is "discipleship" which implies conversion and following a way of life in the pattern of Jesus Christ. Fourth, consequently, Christian spirituality, when it is true to its foundations, has a positive view of the material world and of the body. Such an approach to spirituality is said to be "sacramental" in the sense that material reality (including our embodied selves and everyday experience and action) is a medium for God's self-revelation and human encounters with the sacred. Fifth, despite this positive view of the material world as a revelation of the sacred, a Christian understanding of God's creativity and relationship to humanity is not naïvely optimistic. It recognizes disorder and sin in the world. Consequently, God's relationship to humanity is also seen as redemptive. That is, in Jesus Christ, God is said to confront human disorder with a call to repentance yet at the same time is portrayed as promising ultimate restoration. The Christian disciple is called both to conversion and to follow in the way of Jesus Christ. Sixth, such a following is not individualistic but is essentially communal, within the community of believers, sustained by a common life, shared rituals, and expressed ideally in mutual love and acceptance. In fact, the heart of Christian spirituality is precisely a way of life rather than an abstract code of a priori beliefs. Finally, at the center of the Christian understanding of spiritual transformation is both the notion of God's abiding presence in the Christian community and also God's indwelling in every person as Spirit, empowering, guiding, and inspiring the journey of the community and of each person towards an ultimate union with the divine in eternal life.

Notes

1 For a good summary of the spirituality of the synoptic gospels, see, for example, Stephen Barton, *The Spirituality of the Gospels*, London: SPCK, 1992.

2 For a good summary of Johannine spirituality, see Sandra Schneiders, *Written That You May Believe: Encountering Jesus in the Fourth Gospel*, New York: Crossroad Publishing, 1999.

3 See, for example, Tom Deidun, "Pauline spirituality" in *The New Dictionary of Christian Spirituality*, London: SCM Press and Louisville: Westminster-John Knox Press, 2005.

4   For a good essay on early Christian spirituality, see: Columba Stewart, "Christian spirituality during the Roman Empire 100–600" in Arthur Holder, ed., *The Blackwell Companion to Christian Spirituality*, Oxford/ Malden: Blackwell Publishing, 2005, pp. 73–89. See also Bernard McGinn, John Meyendorff, and Jean Leclercq, eds., *Christian Spirituality: Origins to the Twelfth Century*, New York: Crossroad Publishing, 1985, Chapters 2, 3, 4, and 6 and Bernard McGinn, *The Foundations of Mysticism: Origins to the Fifth Century*, New York: Crossroad Publishing and London: SCM Press, 1991, Chapters 4, 5, 6, and 7.

5   For a technical study of early martyrdom stories, see Alison Goddard Elliott, *Roads to Paradise: Reading the Lives of the Early Saints*, Hanover: University Press of New England, 1987, Chapter 2. Rowan Williams has insightful things to say about martyrdom in his section on Ignatius of Antioch in *The Wound of Knowledge: Christian Spirituality from the New Testament to St John of the Cross*, 2nd revised edition, London: Darton Longman & Todd, 1990, pp. 14–23. For a concise general summary of the early tradition of martyrdom in relation to Christian spirituality, see John McGuckin, "The early Christian Fathers" in Gordon Mursell, ed., *The Story of Christian Spirituality*, Oxford: Lion Publishing, 2001, pp. 50–54.

6   Peter Brown, *"A debate on the Holy" in The Making of Late Antiquity*, new edition, Cambridge MA: Harvard University Press, 1993.

7   See Peter Brown, *Authority and the Sacred: Aspects of the Christianisation of the Roman World*, Cambridge: Cambridge University Press, p. 74.

8   For a concise account of the intimate relationship between spirituality and doctrine in the early Church, see Williams, *Wound of Knowledge*, Chapters 2 and 3.

9   See for example, Rowan Williams, "Beginning with the incarnation" in *On Christian Theology*, Oxford/Malden: Blackwell Publishing, 2000, pp. 79–92.

10 Irenaeus, "Preface" in *Against Heresies*, Book 5, *The Ante-Nicene Fathers*, vol. 1, Edinburgh: T & T Clark, 1996.

11 For a classic study of the personalities and theologies that follow, see Andrew Louth, *The Origins of the Christian Mystical Tradition*, Oxford: Clarendon Press, 1992.

12 For a selection of texts, see Rowan Greer, ed., *Origen: An Exhortation to Martyrdom, Prayer and Selected Works*, Classics of Western Spirituality, New York: Paulist Press, 1979.

13 See, for example, John E. Bamberger, ed., *Evagrius Ponticus: The Praktikos. Chapters on Prayer*, Kalamazoo: Cistercian Publications, 1970.

14 See, for example, Abraham J. Malherbe and E. Ferguson, eds., *Gregory of Nyssa: The Life of Moses*, Classics of Western Spirituality, New York: Paulist Press, 1978.

15 Augustine, Chapter 3, in Mary T. Clark, ed., *Confessions*, Book 10, *Augustine of Hippo: Selected Writings*, Classics of Western Spirituality, Ramsey: Paulist Press, 1984. See also Thomas Martin, *Our Restless Heart: The Augustinian Tradition*, London: Darton Longman & Todd and Maryknoll: Orbis Books, 2003.

16 Tractates on the Gospel according to St John, Tractate XVIII, 10, in Philip Schaff, ed., *A Select Library of the Nicene and Post-Nicene Fathers of the Christian Church*, vol. VII, Edinburgh: T & T Clark, reprint, 1991.

17 On this point, see R.A. Markus, *The End of Ancient Christianity*, Cambridge: Cambridge University Press, 1998, p. 78.

18 C. Luibheid and P. Rorem, eds., *Pseudo-Dionysius: The Complete Works*, Classics of Western Spirituality, New York: Paulist Press, 1987.

19 For a more developed treatment of this idea, see the essay by the great French Jesuit scholar of spirituality Michel de Certeau, "How is Christianity thinkable today?" in Graham Ward, ed., *The Postmodern God*, Oxford: Blackwell Publishing, 1997.

20 See "The Prologue to the Commentary on the Song of Songs" in R. Greer, trans. and ed., *Origen*, Classics of Western Spirituality, New York: Paulist Press, 1979.

21 See E. Ferguson and A.J. Malherbe, trans. and eds., *Gregory of Nyssa: The Life of Moses*, Classics of Western Spirituality, New York: Paulist Press, 1978.

22 See C. Luibheid and O. Rorem, trans. and eds., *Pseudo-Dionysius: The Complete Works*, Classics of Western Spirituality, New York: Paulist Press, 1987.

23 See E, Colledge and J. Walsh, eds., *Guigo II: The Ladder of Monks & Twelve Meditations*, New York: Doubleday Image Books, 1978.

24 See Karl Rahner, "Reflection on the problem of the gradual ascent to perfection" in *Theological Investigations*, vol. 3, London: Burns & Oates, 1967.

25 For example, Gustavo Gutiérrez, *We Drink from Our Own Wells: The Spiritual Journey of a People*, Maryknoll: Orbis Books, 1984. For discussions of the different approaches to the spiritual journey in Christian spirituality, see, for example, Lawrence S. Cunningham and Keith J. Egan, *Christian Spirituality: Themes from the Tradition*, New York: Paulist Press, 1996; Andrew Louth, *The Origins of the Christian Mystical Tradition: From Plato to Denys*, Oxford: Clarendon Press, 1981; and Margaret R. Miles, *Practicing Christianity: Critical Perspectives for an Embodied Spirituality*, New York: Crossroad, 1988.

Chapter 3

Monastic Spiritualities:
300–1150

c. 250	Beginnings of Egyptian monasticism
c. 269	Antony of Egypt withdraws to desert
c. 290	Apostolic Church Order written
c. 296–373	Athanasius of Alexandria lives
c. 306–373	Ephrem of Syria lives: theologian and spiritual writer
c. 320	Pachomius founds monastery of Tabennisis
c. 356	Death of Antony of Egypt
c. 360–435	John Cassian lives: monastic writer. Settles near Marseilles c. 420
371	Martin of Tours becomes bishop
c. 451–525	Brigid of Kildare lives
c. 480–547	Benedict of Nursia lives: author of the Rule of St Benedict
c. 500–c. 583	Brendan the Voyager lives
c. 550	Latin edition of the Apophthegmata Patrum (Sayings of the Desert Fathers)
540–604	Gregory the Great lives: pope and theologian
c. 543–615	Columbanus lives: monastic founder and missionary
563	Columba founds Iona
c. 580–662	Maximus the Confessor lives: Eastern theologian
597	Augustine of Canterbury lands in Kent
c. 634–687	Cuthbert of Lindisfarne lives: monastic founder
730–787	Iconoclastic controversy
c. 747–821	Benedict of Aniane lives: monastic reformer
768–814	Charlemagne, Emperor and Church reformer
909	Foundation of monastery of Cluny

Spirituality: A Brief History, Second Edition. Philip Sheldrake.
© 2013 John Wiley & Sons, Ltd. Published 2013 by John Wiley & Sons, Ltd.

927–942	Odo is Abbot of Cluny
949–1022	Symeon the New Theologian lives: Eastern theologian
c. 970	Regularis Concordia
1007–1072	Peter Damian lives: monastic founder
1023	Romuald founds Camaldoli
1033–1109	Anselm of Canterbury lives: monk, philosopher, theologian, Archbishop of Canterbury
1075–1148	William of St Thierry lives: monastic theologian
1080–1157	Guerric of Igny lives: Cistercian writer
1084	Bruno founds Grande Chartreuse
1098–1179	Hildegard of Bingen lives: abbess, poet, and musician
1098	Foundation of Citeaux
1109–1167	Aelred of Rievaulx lives: English Cistercian spiritual writer
1133	Consuetudines Cartusiae (Carthusian Rule) approved
1152	Carta Caritatis (Cistercian constitutions) approved
1153	Death of Bernard of Clairvaux
1169	Death of Isaac of Stella, Cistercian writer
c. 1207–c. 1294	Mechtild of Magdeburg lives: Cistercian mystical writer
1221	Death of Adam of Perseigne
1240–1298	Mechtild of Hackeborn lives: Cistercian spiritual writer
1256–1307	Gertrude of Helfta lives: Cistercian spiritual writer
1296–1359	Gregory Palamas lives: hesychast theologian

The period from the fourth to the twelfth centuries was a time of major social and political change in the parts of Europe and the Mediterranean world that had made up the Roman Empire. First, and most significantly, at the beginning of the period the Empire itself began to break apart as a result of both internal and external factors. Internally, during the reign of Diocletian in the late third century, the administration of the Empire was first divided into eastern and western parts. Under the Emperor Constantine, the eastern capital was fixed at Constantinople, nowadays Istanbul, on the site of ancient Byzantium. By the end of the fourth century, the division was complete. While the Eastern Byzantine Empire survived politically, the Western Empire collapsed during the fifth century under pressure from a mixture of internal instability and invasions by tribes from beyond the Rhine and the Danube. New kingdoms emerged and further settlement from Scandinavia took place leading eventually to the birth of nation states in Western Europe with their own vernacular languages as well as to a new Holy Roman Empire under Charlemagne. A second major factor for change was the emergence of Islam as a major religion in Arabia and its political and military expansion into the Middle Eastern, North African, and Iberian parts of the Roman world from the seventh century onwards. The subsequent encounter between Islam and historic Jewish and Christian cultures in the Mediterranean world was always complex – at times antagonistic and violent but sometimes creative and surprisingly harmonious.

The period from the fourth century onwards was also one of major consolidation in the history of Christianity. First of all, Christianity emerged from its persecuted position into the public mainstream as a result of the Emperor Constantine's edict of toleration (313) and, within a relatively short time, became the official religion of the Empire. Inevitably, the shift from being a persecuted minority to becoming the public and cultural establishment led to readjustments in the self-understanding and spiritual values of Christianity.

One consequence was the expansion of what was initially a counter-cultural ascetical movement that gave birth to monasticism. For the next seven centuries, the history of Christian spirituality both East and West was in many different ways dominated by the ascetical-monastic "type" of spirituality.

After the fifth century, monastic communities in Western Europe played a significant role as a kind of "survival capsule" for Greco-Roman culture in the turbulent world of a collapsing Empire, barbarian invasions, and the eventual emergence of the new kingdoms. In other words, monasteries became important centers for transmitting classical civilization to a post-imperial world. The Rule of St Benedict (subsequently RB), which came to dominate Western monasticism, presupposed that most monks were literate (and that meant able to read and write in Latin), and it has been conjectured that the Rule also presupposes some kind of monastic library which would have contained the scriptures, works of early theology (patristics), and some classical authors. One of Benedict's monastic contemporaries, Cassiodorus, wrote a programme of studies for monks and mentions Virgil and Aristotle. The famous Anglo-Saxon monk, the Venerable Bede (673–735), quotes Pliny and other classical authors such as Virgil and Ovid.

Monastic communities were also centers for missionary work during Europe's conversion to Christianity. An important element of this process was a certain fusion with pre-Christian practices as well as a growing cultural localism within Christian spirituality. Irish Christianity will be briefly explored as an example of a local spiritual culture.

Finally, the period was an important one in the development of Eastern Christianity, associated with the Byzantine Empire centered in Constantinople, and saw the gradual divergence of Eastern and Western forms of Christian spirituality.

The Emergence of Monasticism

Christianity has no monopoly on monasticism. Monastic life has existed in some form in most major world religions, usually associated with an austere non-materialistic lifestyle and contemplative practices. Christian monasticism is essentially a movement to the margins. The wilderness (desert, mountain, forest, or sea) has exercised a peculiar fascination throughout Christian history. One of the fundamental features of Christian monasticism is that it demands withdrawal. Why were physical deserts chosen for monastic communities? The theme of the "desert" is common to many monastic texts. It is both a paradise, where people may live in harmony with wild animals, and at the same time a place of trial where ascetics encounter inner and outer demons. The desert is frontier territory. Living on a physical boundary symbolizes a state of liminality – existing between the material and spiritual worlds.

The reasons why monastic life emerged by the early fourth century continue to preoccupy scholars.[1] Some people suggest that there were continuities with Jewish ascetical movements (e.g. Qumran) or with early Christian ascetical groups within Syriac Christianity. Others have even suggested contacts with pre-existing Buddhist or Hindu forms through trading links with India. More conventionally, the origins of monasticism have often been attributed to a combination of factors associated with the move of Christianity from persecuted minority to the dominant religion of the Empire. First, the rapid expansion in numbers of Christians, often for social reasons, led to a growing sense of laxity. Second, the ideals of martyrdom transferred from physical death to a spiritualized replacement (sometimes called white martyrdom). The pinnacle of holiness moved from victory over physical death to victory over "the world."

Widows and Virgins

There are also questions about *where* monasticism began. The conventional assumption is that it was in the Egyptian desert at the end of the third century. However, two realities existed before this. First of all, at an early date committed women emerged within the Christian Church. These were the widows and the virgins. New Testament evidence (e.g. Acts 6, 1–6; I Tim 5, 3–16) suggests that widows appeared very early on. Younger virgins possibly developed as a separate category within groups of widows. Certainly before the end of the third century, both groups were described in the "Apostolic Church Order." Some of these seem to have formed communities from which they undertook pastoral and spiritual tasks. Communities existed in the main cities of the Empire as well as in Palestine and Egypt. Their spiritual motivation was partly pastoral but the choice of virginity is significant. Scriptural teaching is not a sufficient explanation as the texts do not portray celibacy as an indispensable means of following Jesus Christ. It is possible that there was some inspiration from temple virgins in Greco-Roman religion. Socially, celibacy freed women from conventional social roles and enabled them to share with men in the quest for spiritual perfection. There may also have been a remaining sense that the "final days" were approaching when the current world order would end. Thus, virginity anticipated the perfect society of the Kingdom of God when the physical continuity of the human race would cease to have meaning and when all would live in harmonious, voluntary relationships ("like the angels").[2]

Syrian Ascetics

A second group that predates Egypt was in Syria-Palestine. However, as the prestige of Egyptian monasticism became dominant, this earlier Syriac tradition was largely forgotten. From what we can work out, the dating of the Syriac ascetical tradition may have been very early. Indeed it may have derived from the understanding in Luke's Gospel that Christian discipleship was to be a literal imitation of Jesus portrayed as poor, homeless, and single. So, radical asceticism was closely related to costly discipleship – total abandonment of homes and possessions in imitation of the one who had nowhere to lay his head. The Syrian word for such ascetics was *ihidaya* (the single one) of which the Greek *monachos* was a translation (from which the English "monk" derives). The ascetic "single one" certainly left family life behind but was also single-hearted and bound to Christ, "The One," in an exclusive relationship. Interestingly, no doubt partly because of physical environment (there was no deep desert in the Syrian wilderness) Syriac ascetics remained close to villages as visible challenges to ordinary life yet often with significant roles as guides and arbitrators. Their "otherness" tended to be expressed by eccentricity or ascetical extremes. Early Syriac asceticism remained largely expressed in the lives of single hermits.[3]

Egyptian Monasticism

Egypt was where monasticism emerged in an organized sense. Yet even here, the movement remained essentially a lay one. The reasons for the emergence of monastic life in Egypt include local factors. There was a major economic crisis in third- and fourth-century Egypt, and this may have driven numbers of people to seek alternative lifestyles away from the cities. However, in the case of St Antony (died c. 356), who came to be known as the "father of monasticism," the famous *Life* by Athanasius of Alexandria suggests that the inspiration was purely spiritual. Thus, Antony, a relatively wealthy young farmer with a religious disposition, received a final impetus from hearing the story of the rich young man read in church.[4] Athanasius' account also stresses the ideal of dispossession and the desert as the place where the full gospel may be practiced. These emphases may have owed something to the influence of neo-Platonic philosophy in Egypt, particularly through the teachings of the theologian Origen in Alexandria. This emphasized the soul's alienation from God but also stressed human potential for ascent back to God through scriptural contemplation, repentance, purification, and celibacy.

Egyptian monasticism developed broadly in three forms associated with geographical locations and by 400 numbered many thousands of ascetics, both men and women. The first, and earliest, form was the hermit life of which St Antony was the archetype. This flourished especially in what was called Lower Egypt to the south of the Nile Delta. Antony withdrew into solitude c. 269 and gradually went further into the desert wilderness. Yet he attracted many disciples. The notion of total solitude needs some modification as two hermits sometimes lived together and disciples stayed in close proximity to their "spiritual father" or "mother" from whom they received guidance. The second form consisted of small groups of ascetics to the West of the Nile Delta. Several monks lived together as disciples with their spiritual father (*abba*) or mother (*amma*) in monastic "villages," known as a *lavra* or *skete*. The most famous settlements were at Nitria and Scetis near Alexandria which became important meeting places of desert and city worlds. At Nitria, visitors like John Cassian (who became a key figure in the foundation of monasticism in Europe) first made contact with the desert tradition.

A more educated, Greek-influenced monasticism evolved around theologically sophisticated figures such as Evagrius (345–399). The third form
of monasticism was in Upper (or southern) Egypt, in a region close to the
ancient city of Thebes. This form consisted of relatively ordered and large
communities of men or women. The leading figure was Pachomius
(290–347) who founded the monastic settlement of Tabennisis which is
conventionally described as the origin of organized monasticism.

Wisdom of the Desert

The earliest sources for the spiritual wisdom of Christian monasticism
were either lives of the great founders (e.g. Athanasius' *Life of St Antony*)
or collections of sayings and anecdotes about monks. The sayings and
stories were gathered mainly from the hermits of Lower Egypt or from
the groups at Nitria and Scetis. These were passed on in oral fashion and
later written down (the *Apophthegmata Patrum*) during the fifth century.
There were two major collections organized by subject matter (the
Systematic Series) or under the names of well-known teachers
(the Alphabetical Collection).[5] These writings record a period of
informality. Once institutionalization took place with the foundation of
large communities, normative texts such as the Rule of Pachomius began
to appear.[6]

The early desert ascetics were motivated by a desire to live the life
demanded of all Christians – but they did so with particular intensity.
What they sought was simply the way to salvation.

> A brother asked a hermit, "What must I do to be saved?" He took off
> his clothes, and put a girdle about his loins and stretched out his hands
> and said, "Thus ought the monk to be: stripped naked of everything,
> and crucified by temptation and combat with the world."[7]

This story also graphically illustrates two other key elements of desert
spirituality that passed into the monastic traditions. The first is the theme
of spiritual combat. Here the image is a boxer preparing to fight. In other
stories, the image is one of warfare – battling with temptation or even
literally with demons. So, for example,

> They said of Sarah that for thirteen years she was fiercely attacked by
> the demon of lust. She never prayed that the battle would leave her,
> but she used to say only, "Lord, give me strength."[8]

Mature desert ascetics, such as Sarah, did not pray to be relieved from temptations – indeed, sometimes they even asked their spiritual guide to pray that temptation continue because they believed that struggle had a spiritual value in itself. A second, related theme is asceticism. The word itself comes from the Greek *askēsis*, training – hence the athletic images in the story. Asceticism in its proper sense does not imply an anti-body attitude. On the contrary, asceticism takes the body with great seriousness, understanding it to be a vital element of spiritual progress in need of proper ordering. The goal of ascetical discipline was a properly directed rather than a fragmented life. The training was fundamentally for the Kingdom of God, which monastic life anticipated.[9]

The greatest teachers of wisdom in the desert were the monk's cell and the spiritual father or mother. The action of staying in the cell, even when bored, frustrated, and tempted, was both a practical discipline and a spiritual symbol. Practically, the cell provided the necessary silence, solitude, and absence of external distraction for prolonged prayer. Symbolically, the simplicity of the cell represented a shedding of worldly possessions and staying put represented the value of stability and endurance as the foundations for the inward journey.

> A hermit said, "The monk's cell is the furnace in Babylon in which the three children found the Son of God. It is the pillar of cloud out of which God spoke to Moses." (Ward 2003, p. 72, number 74)

> In Scetis a brother went to Moses to ask for advice. He said to him, "Go and sit in your cell, and your cell will teach you everything." (Ward 2003, p. 10, number 9)

The second quotation also expresses the strength of the relationship between the ascetics and their spiritual mentors.[10] In the hermit or *skete* ways of life, reliance on the spiritual father or mother was vital for practical advice on how to survive the rigors of desert life, on how to avoid illusion, and on how to become wise in the ways of the heart. This is not really "spiritual direction" in the modern sense. The spiritual guides were chosen because of their wisdom and experience – hence they are often called "an old man (or woman)." The purpose of guidance was simply to open the pupil's heart to be taught by God. On the whole there was no lengthy discussion or instruction but a preference for few words and pithy sayings. At the heart of the relationship was obedience. This was both a discipline – a correction of any tendency to rely on one's own powers – and an expression of receptivity to God.

A hermit said, "Someone who hands over his soul in obedience to a spiritual guide has a greater reward than one who retires alone to a hermitage." (Ward 2003, p. 147, number 19)

The theme of obedience also highlights two further central values of the desert tradition: humility and discernment. The cultivation of honesty and self-awareness – the real meaning of humility – was thought to be a critical means of spiritual progress. It was the greatest defense against spiritual pride which was seen as the classic temptation of the hermit. Humility was often linked to a capacity to forgive others their faults.

A hermit was asked, "What is humility?" He answered, "Humility is a great work and a work of God. The way of humility is to undertake bodily labour, and believe yourself a sinner, and make yourself the servant of all." A brother said, "What does that mean, to be the servant of all?" He answered, "To be the servant of all is not to look at the sins of others, always to look at your own sins, and to pray to God without ceasing." (Ward 2003, p. 167, number 82)

In a sense, discernment or spiritual wisdom – the capacity to judge well and to choose properly – was a corollary of humility. Discernment, *diakrisis*, was the most prized of the ascetic virtues. In the mind of desert ascetics, discernment was often associated with an ability to recognize the difference between the inspiration of God and the illusory promptings of the demons. Discernment (or "discretion") was a gift of God received through deep prayer and ascetic practice. It marked out the true ascetic from the spiritual gymnast who could carry out prodigious acts of endurance but in an unbalanced way.

A hermit was asked by a brother, "How do I find God? With fasts, or labour, or vigils, or works of mercy?" He replied, "You will find Him in all those, and also in discretion. I tell you, many have been very stern with their bodies, but have gained nothing by it because they did it without discretion. Even if our mouths stink from fasting, and we have learnt all the Scriptures, and memorized the whole Psalter, we may still lack what God wants, humility and love." (Ward 2003, p. 111, number 94)

If humility is what God seeks, so is charity. A lack of self-centeredness should also overflow into care for others. The desert fathers and mothers were very clear that their ascetic way was not one of spiritual self-preoccupation but rather of ever greater sensitivity to those in need, and a greater freedom to respond. The scriptural injunction to love God and neighbor was always before their eyes.

> A brother asked a hermit, "Suppose there are two monks: one stays quietly in his cell, fasting for six days at a time, laying many hardships on himself: and the other ministers to the sick. Which of them is more pleasing to God?" He replied, "Even if the brother who fasts six days hung himself up by his nose, he wouldn't be the equal of him who ministers to the sick." (Ward 2003, p. 180, number 18)

In terms of spiritual practices, what was done should serve the fundamental values of the ascetical life – discipline, spiritual struggle, endurance, charity, and, above all discernment. When we read the sayings and lives of the desert fathers and mothers, it is clear that silence and solitude (especially staying in one's cell) played a central role. The notion of "unceasing prayer" sometimes implied extended recitation of the psalms or meditation or long vigils, especially throughout the night, or it might mean praying "in the heart" while doing other tasks such as manual labor or making mats to sell. Indeed, apart from its practical necessity, physical labor was also a form of spiritual discipline that countered any temptation to sink into idleness. Fasting or a broader frugality with food underlined the value of bodily self-control as opposed to dissipation. However, it is also notable in the sayings and stories that the virtues of charity or hospitality had a high priority. An ascetic might put aside more overtly spiritual activities such as prayer to serve the needs of others. This too was an important form of "spiritual practice."

Monastic Rules

Pachomius (c. 290–346) founded the first known communitarian monastery at Tabennisis c. 320. He is credited with writing the first monastic Rule, with a significant influence on the later Rules of St Basil in the East and St Benedict in the West. This move codified the monastic way of life and the hierarchy to which the individual should give obedience. It provided a vehicle of continuity, but, equally, it moved away from the spontaneity of obedience to a spiritual father or mother. Obedience was now to a Rule of which the superior was the spiritual interpreter and legal monitor. In general terms, Rules are normative texts which set out the spiritual principles guiding communities. A Rule is not essentially a *legislative* document but a medium for the communication of a spiritual ethos. Across its broad history, monasticism has been dominated by three Rules, St Basil in Eastern Christianity and St Augustine and St Benedict in the West.

The Rule of St Basil derives from Basil the Great (c. 330–379), one of the theologians known as the Cappadocian Fathers. He bequeathed to Eastern monasticism the ethos on which it is still based.[11] The title "Rule" (the *Asceticon*) is perhaps a misnomer as the material is fundamentally an anthology of advice. Even during Basil's lifetime, a number of versions of the *Asceticon* were in circulation and questions of authenticity are complex. The Small *Asceticon* is the earliest and is probably the version that influenced the RB. The most widespread form, the Great *Asceticon*, has influenced most modern translations. The tone of Basil's "Rule" is strict, yet it is also relatively moderate when compared to the extremes of early desert asceticism. The emphasis is on community life and a balance of liturgy, manual work, and other tasks. Basil's vision of monasticism is also pastoral, and provision is made for the education of children and the care of the poor.

The so-called Rule of St Augustine is the earliest Western Rule. There is a dispute about whether it was written by Augustine himself. Whatever the case, this rule in turn influenced the RB and inspired hundreds of religious communities of varying forms up to the present day. After his conversion to Christianity in 387 and eventual return to North Africa when he was made Bishop of Hippo, Augustine seems to have written a rule. The "Rule" actually refers to two texts, the longer *Praeceptum* and the shorter *Ordo Monasterii*, supplemented by a letter of Augustine (letter 211) that seems to be a version of the *Praeceptum* addressed to women. Although the influence of the Rule was overtaken by that of St Benedict from the mid-sixth century onwards, it had a major resurgence in the late eleventh century. St Augustine's Rule does not promote rigid separation from the world and leaves space for active work outside the monastery. Its fundamental spiritual emphasis is on community, the model for which is the life of the earliest Christian community in the Acts of the Apostles.[12]

> Do not call anything your own; possess everything in common....For you read in the Acts of the Apostles: "They possessed everything in common," and "Distribution was made to each in proportion to each one's need." (*Praeceptum*, Chapter 1. 3)

The Rule does not offer detailed or complex structures, and the language stresses love more than obedience. There is also a strong emphasis on a community of equals (whatever their social background) held together by bonds of mutual friendship – something that presumably reflected Augustine's own experiences at Hippo.[13]

The RB draws on the Rules of St Basil and St Augustine and, even more, on the *Rule of the Master* (although there are still some authorities who maintain a reverse influence or that both Rules rely on a common source now lost). Another major influence was the writings of John Cassian who became familiar with monastic life in Egypt. Beyond that, Cassian is an obscure figure who seems at one point to have been a monk in Palestine. By c. 420 he had settled near Marseilles where he became part of the emerging monastic network and where he composed his two famous works on monastic life, the *Institutes* and the *Conferences*.[14] It has often been asserted that Cassian brought the wisdom of Egyptian monasticism to the West. The reality is more complicated. Certainly elements of his writings show the intellectual influence of Origen and Evagrius, but scholars raise serious questions about the extent of his practical knowledge.[15]

The RB, written in sixth-century Italy, became the most influential monastic guide in the Western Church. In the period from the sixth to the tenth centuries, it gradually replaced other traditions. Given his iconic status in Western monasticism, remarkably little is known about Benedict of Nursia apart from the fact that he lived in the mid-sixth century, reputedly founded the abbey of Monte Cassino, and compiled a monastic rule.[16] While the RB is characterized by relative moderation, urbanity, and balance, it nevertheless presupposes a life of withdrawal from the outside world. The outward looking ethos of the Augustinian tradition is largely absent although hospitality to strangers (who are to be received as Christ) is a major injunction (RB 53). The Prologue of the Rule opens with the word *Obsculta*, listen!

> Listen, O my son, to the teachings of your master, and turn to them with the ear of your heart. Willingly accept the advice of a devoted father and put it into action. Thus you will return by the labour of obedience to the one from whom you drifted through the inertia of disobedience. (RB Prologue 1 & 2)

Listening and obedience (both to God and to the spiritual master, the abbot) are intertwined. In many respects, the RB contrasts with the Rule of St Augustine in its hierarchical stance (although fraternal charity is mentioned later in the Rule, RB 72). The God of the Rule is an awesome figure, and the abbot, who stands "in the place of Christ," is a ruler rather than "first among equals" (RB 2). The Rule is also detailed and programmatic rather than a collection of spiritual wisdom. Its popularity is partly explained by a well-organized structure and the priority given to good order. However, its spiritual success also relates to a healthy balance of work, prayer, and rest and the creative tension between the values of the individual spiritual journey and of common life under the authority of an abbot. The central task of the monk is common prayer or the *opus Dei* ("nothing is to be preferred to the Work of God," RB 43) supplemented by personal meditation, spiritual reading (*lectio*), and manual work. Other spiritual practices mentioned in the Rule include silence (and generally refraining from idle gossip), fasting, and sleeping less during Lent. Apart from its emphasis on obedience and on humility as the primary image of spiritual progress (RB 7), the Rule also teaches the complementary spiritual values of stability (faithfulness expressed by staying in the monastery until death) and the virtually untranslatable concept of *conversatio morum* (literally "conversion of manners"). This stands for an overall commitment to a monastic lifestyle including deep conversion and spiritual development throughout life.

Benedictine Expansion

The history of Western monasticism after the sixth century is rich and complex. However, at the risk of simplification, the Benedictine style gradually gained ascendancy until by the tenth century it was the dominant monastic ethos. An initial impetus came from Pope Gregory the Great in the late sixth century who not only wrote the life of Benedict and promoted his Rule but sent a community of Roman monks under Augustine (later of Canterbury) as missionaries to England. However, in the period up to the ninth century, the RB co-existed with other monastic rules and ways of life, for example, the rules of Martin of Tours and Columbanus. Martin, a former Roman soldier, settled as an ascetic near Poitiers and moved as bishop to Tours in 371. To some degree, Martinian monasticism reflected the East, especially the asceticism of Asia Minor. Another major monastic personality was Columbanus (c. 543–615), an Irishman who arrived with his followers in Gaul. Eventually he traveled widely across Gaul, Switzerland, and settled finally in Bobbio, Italy, where he died. While his monastic rules are fairly conventional, Columbanus frequently employed "the journey" as a favored metaphor for the Christian life. The Christian is a guest of the world. "Therefore let this principle abide with us, that on the road we...live as travellers, as pilgrims, as guests of the world...."[17]

In England, Irish monastic ideals were also present through the influence of Iona (founded from Ireland by Columba in 563) on Northumbria. However, from the mid-seventh century, it seems that the RB increasingly dominated. On the continent, a critical moment was the reign of Charlemagne (768–814) who used monasticism, and particularly the promotion of the RB, as part of his quest for uniformity, both secular and ecclesial, throughout his empire. A key figure was Benedict of Aniane. Supported by Charlemagne, Benedict effectively imposed the RB (subtly mixed with other ancient monastic customs) in many monasteries. By the time of Charlemagne's successor, the RB was imposed by Church council on all the monasteries of the empire.

A further critical moment was during the tenth century in England. Mainly as a result of the Danish invasions, monastic life had virtually ceased. However, by the middle of the tenth century, a reform process, inspired by continental models, had been started by Dunstan, Archbishop of Canterbury, and two other bishops, Ethelwold of Winchester and Oswald of Worcester. Eventually men's and women's houses agreed to a form of Benedictine observance in a document called the *Regularis Concordia*. On the continent earlier expansion gave way to decline largely because of excessive interference by powerful families. However, a spirit of reformism emerged, centered on a new monastery at Cluny in Burgundy, founded in 909. This adopted the reforms of Benedict of Aniane and was freed from secular interference by being placed directly under papal protection. Cluny adopted a high standard of observance during the long abbacy of Odo (927–942) and his talented and saintly successors. By the end of the eleventh century, the Cluniac reform numbered around a thousand monasteries and had spread across France, to Italy (including Monte Cassino), and to England. The strength of Cluniac monasticism lay partly in its independence and centralized organization. However, it also cultivated a strong spiritual ethos both in the personal life of the monks and in its stress on the solemnity of liturgy. However, it was precisely the increasingly complex liturgy and virtual absence of manual labor that provoked more austere reform movements in the twelfth century.

A range of important spiritual teachers and personalities existed during these monastic centuries. Three people may be taken as indicative examples: Gregory the Great, Anselm, and Hildegard of Bingen. Gregory the Great (540–604), a diplomat and monk who eventually became pope, is famous not only for sending Augustine (eventually of Canterbury) and other monks as missionaries to Anglo-Saxon England but also for his important spiritual writings. His *Dialogues* contain all the biographical detail we know of St Benedict, his *Letters* stress especially the contemplative nature of monastic life, his *Pastoral Care* is an early example of pastoral theology, and there were commentaries on Job, Ezekiel, the gospels, and the Song of Songs. From these writings emerge an important but not systematically structured spiritual theology which had a major impact on medieval spirituality. Among his important themes are contemplation, discernment, the role of suffering, stages of spiritual growth, compunction, and joyful desire.[18]

Anselm of Canterbury (1033–1109) was a monk, later abbot, of Bec in Normandy who became Archbishop of Canterbury in 1093. Apart from being a significant philosopher, his important ascetical-spiritual theology, present especially in his *Prayers and Meditations* and in his *Proslogion*, bridged the worlds of patristic thought and Western medieval devotion. His approach to prayer is intellectual (meditation as a form of theology), scripturally reflective (providing teaching on and material for *lectio divina*), devotional (not least in reference to the Virgin Mary), intensely fervent, experiential, and personal.[19]

Hildegard of Bingen (1098–1179) has achieved cult-like status in recent decades. A German aristocrat and Benedictine abbess, Hildegard was not only a visionary mystic (e.g. her *Scivias*) but also a prophetic figure of reform in Church and society and a public preacher – an activity approved by the pope but unusual for a woman at that time. Part of her present-day attraction is that she was a prolific writer on a broad range of topics including theology, biblical commentary, the natural sciences, herbal medicine, spiritual teachings, and poetry. She was also a talented musician who composed over seventy spiritual songs with highly distinctive music. Finally, Hildegard was an artist, able to illustrate her visionary works with striking images and designs.[20]

The New Hermits

The expansion and reform of western monasticism continued in the eleventh and early twelfth centuries in two notable but contrasting directions. First, a number of monastic reforms sought to return to earlier hermit traditions. Two major examples, the Camaldolese and the Carthusians, survive to the present day. These combined the eremitical ideal with community structures. The new hermit monasteries also emphasized a simple "apostolic" life expressed by poverty, a simplified liturgy, solitude, and manual labor.[21]

The "Camaldolese" trace their origins to two people and two locations. Romuald (c. 950–1027) became a monk of the Abbey of Classe in northern Italy but retired as a hermit near Venice. After a further period as a solitary in Catalonia, Romuald returned to Classe as abbot in 998. However, the community were not receptive to his viewpoint and he once again retired as a solitary. Eventually, towards the end of his life around 1023 he founded the hermitage of Camaldoli, close to Florence, and an associated cenobitic community which continue to this day. There are no surviving writings from Romuald. The other figure, Peter Damian (1007–1072), was strongly influenced by the memory of Romuald and reformed his monastery of Fonte Avellana and its founda-tions on a similar pattern to Camaldoli. Although the family of Camaldoli, both men and women, drew upon earlier hermit traditions, it eventually adopted the RB.[22]

In 1084, Bruno (1032–1101) with six companions founded a monas-tery at Grande Chartreuse near Grenoble. He had previously been canon and chancellor of the diocese of Cologne and then spent some time under the guidance of Robert of Molesme who later founded the monas-tery of Citeaux. At the beginning, the monks of the Grande Chartreuse (later the center of the Carthusian Order) had no special rule but the lifestyle was semi-eremitical. Eventually Guigo I, the fifth prior wrote the *Consuetudines Cartusiae* which were approved in 1133 and, with some later additions, remain the rule of the Order. This combines Benedictine inspiration, particularly the monastic Offices, with ancient monastic and eremitical literature. The Carthusians espouse a mixture of hermit and community life characterized by great austerity, contemplation, and hid-denness. The Order has always remained small with houses of both monks and nuns. Carthusians inhabit hermitages linked together by a main cloister. Apart from the long night Office, community Mass, and Vespers, the average day is spent in the cell, praying, studying, or gardening – with meals together only on Sundays and feast-days and common recreation (a long walk) generally once a week. Despite the strong emphasis on solitude and anonymity (a motto is *O beata solitudo*, Oh blessed solitude), the Carthusians paradoxically have a strong community sense (conceived as "shared solitude") and a significant tra-dition of writing. Guigo II (c. 1188) in his treatise *Ladder of the Monks* systematized the monastic style of meditative scripture reading known as *lectio divina* which influenced the later development of systematic meditation.[23]

The Cistercians

The final great monastic movement – and perhaps one of the most important medieval traditions of spirituality – was the emergence of the Cistercian Order in the twelfth century. This reform exists on a kind of cultural and religious cusp. On the one hand, it was intended as a purification of the Benedictine tradition by returning to a literal observance of the Rule. On the other hand, the Cistercian ethos was clearly the product of new cultural currents in the twelfth century. This is particularly so with the emphasis on love in a period that became known as the century of love, both secular and religious. The period was one of great intellectual and artistic flourishing such that the term "Twelfth-Century Renaissance" is frequently used. One element of this was the emergence of a kind of "humanism" with its emphasis on the value of human nature, on human dignity, and on virtue. Medieval scholars speak of the discovery of "the individual" or the discovery of "the self."[24] The birth of a romantic emphasis on love, not least courtly love, is one aspect of this shift of sensibilities.

The word "Cistercian" derives from the Latin name for Cîteaux, the reformed Benedictine monastery in Burgundy founded by Robert of Molesme in 1098 and subsequently consolidated by Alberic and the Englishman Stephen Harding. The process of developing a distinct Order is complex. However, the major texts (apart, of course, from the Rule itself), especially the *Exordium* (texts of foundation) and the *Carta Caritatis* (or Charter of Love), were initially endorsed by the pope in 1119 and finally approved with the formal statutes or customaries by 1152. After initial problems, the Cistercians expanded rapidly after the arrival of Bernard (later abbot of Clairvaux) as a monk in 1112. The fervor and idealism expressed in an emphasis on austere simplicity, community and fraternal love, and manual labor, as well as the recovery of a deeply biblical and patristic spirituality, caught the imagination of a whole generation, and by the death of Bernard of Clairvaux in 1153 the Order numbered some 339 monasteries.

The Cistercians produced a substantial body of spiritual writing, such as the eight large volumes of treatises, homilies, and letters by Bernard himself. His work is a classic expression of patristic-monastic theology (notably mystical-contemplative responses to scripture) in contrast to the emerging "new theology" of the cathedral schools and the universities. In tune with the spirit of his age, Bernard espoused an optimistic view of human nature and especially the innate human capacity for God, expressed not least in his attraction to Augustine's theme of human desire and its fulfillment in union with the divine. One of Bernard's most famous expressions of mystical theology is his *Sermons on the Song of Songs*.[25] Other Cistercians such as Bernard's friend William of St Thierry (c. 1075–1148) and the later English monks Gilbert of Hoyland and John of Ford continued the tradition of spiritual commentaries on the Song of Songs, and this became a hallmark of Cistercian monastic spirituality. William was, like Bernard, much indebted to Augustine's theology of desire at the heart of the human quest for God. The list of medieval Cistercian writers is long, numbering among others Guerric of Igny (c. 1080–1157), Isaac of Stella (d. 1169), and Adam of Perseigne (d. 1221). Their spiritual teachings are expressed especially in biblical or liturgical sermons, scriptural commentary, and letters.[26] One of the most strikingly attractive figures was Aelred of Rievaulx (1109–1167), "the Bernard of the North," born in what is now Northumberland and the son of a priest. After an early life in the Scottish court, Aelred entered the monastery of Rievaulx in Yorkshire and became novice-master and eventually abbot. During his time, the abbey flourished numerically and spiritually. His best-known writings are *The Mirror of Charity*, a classic theology of Cistercian monasticism exploring the notion of spiritual progress as a deepening capacity for love, and *Spiritual Friendship* on human relationships as a reflection of God's intimacy – "God is friendship." Influenced both by Cicero and Augustine, it takes the form of a Socratic dialogue between Aelred and several other monks.[27]

A striking aspect of the Cistercian spiritual school was the unofficial as well as official expansion of women's monasteries. By the late thirteenth century, Cistercian women had developed a notable tradition of spiritual and mystical writings – for example, the outstanding group of nuns at Helfta in Germany who produced such spiritual giants as Mechtild of Magdeburg (whose visionary work *The Flowing Light of the Godhead* was written in the vernacular while she was still a Beguine), Mechtild of Hackeborn (*The Book of Special Grace*), and Gertrude of Helfta (*Exercises* and *The Herald of Divine Love*).[28]

Cistercian spirituality is characterized by two fundamental values, simplicity and love. The first was expressed in a preference for minimalism. This involved stripping away accretions of all kinds, liturgical, material, social, and architectural-aesthetic. At the heart of simplicity was a desire to follow the poor Christ, and the lifestyle involved an emphasis on manual work. A corollary was the inclusion of a new class of monk, the lay brothers (*conversi*). This was not merely a structural innovation for it also opened up the spiritual life to people from the uneducated majority of the population who were normally excluded from access to the sources of spiritual wisdom. Parallel to simplicity was the emphasis on affectivity. On the one hand, this led to the development of devotion to Jesus Christ and the Virgin Mary as well as conceiving the spiritual journey as a movement of the human heart into the heart of God. On the other hand, it led to a stress on the power of community life.[29]

The Spiritual Values of Monasticism

"Monasticism" is not a single, simple reality. However, as a "style" of Christian spirituality, it is possible to summarize some of the overall spiritual values. The foundation of monastic spirituality may be summarized as "asceticism." While this implies *a disciplined life*, asceticism is not reducible to physical exercises or bodily deprivations. At its heart lies the notion of living in readiness for the Kingdom of God, valued above all else. In turn this implies communion with God expressed in prayer. Trust in God as the ultimate destination of the human journey demands singleness of heart as opposed to a divided heart. Everything that is extraneous to the search for God is stripped away in a life of simplicity, temperance, and frugality.

Contemplation is also a central value for monasticism – although an early monastic founder such as Columbanus taught that all humans are called to contemplation *by nature*. The same might be said about simplicity as a basic Christian virtue. This implies that monastic life is an *exemplary* form of Christian life rather than a substitute for ordinary human-Christian existence. Contemplation, in turn, demands attentiveness to God and, indeed, to the way God "speaks" through events and people. This attentiveness lies at the heart of the monastic practice of silence in which one can learn the language of the heart and also cultivate the virtue of discerning wisdom. To live the pattern of contemplation-attentiveness-silence demands stillness rather than multiple distractions, and this is expressed in monastic teachings about the importance of stability. Stability is not simply staying in one place but, more importantly, is a matter of remaining focused rather than dispersed and of remaining faithful to, rather than distracted from, the demands of the spiritual journey.

While Christian monasticism embraces a variety of styles from the solitary life to formally structured communities, the notion that monastic life overall anticipates paradise has been a frequent theme. So, as we have seen, a monastic rule such as St Augustine's may promote the breaking down of barriers between different groups of people, while the stories of early desert ascetics sometimes explicitly speak of their life as a restoration of the harmony of paradise.[30]

The spiritual values of particular traditions within monasticism are graphically expressed in the layout and architecture of monastic settlements – a kind of spirituality in stone. Early forms of Egyptian cenobitic community as well as Irish monastic settlement had no grand architecture but were clusters of buildings essentially on the village model. Here, the solitary tradition blends with moderate forms of shared life. In contrast, the classic monastic ground plan of the Benedictine tradition gave prominence to a common way of life. Thus, the largest buildings were the church (expressing the centrality of the common liturgy), the chapter house where the community met daily for the reading of the rule and for business, and the refectory where the community ate together with a degree of ceremonial. At the center of the complex was a space open to the sky (and to the infinite) surrounded by the passageways of a square cloister which offered a route for ritual processions and for meditation but also offered an easy pathway to link the common buildings. The Cistercian variant followed basically the same pattern but in accordance with the values of austerity and simplicity – expressed especially in the starkness of a flat-sided and square-ended church building. By contrast the Camaldolese and the Carthusians, with their semi-hermit lifestyles, limited the size and prominence of common buildings. For example, Carthusian churches, chapter houses, and refectories were relatively small, and the largest and most obvious feature of a Charterhouse (or Carthusian monastery) was the great cloister linking together a series of two-storey houses which were the hermitages of the monks.

At the heart of the spiritual practices of monasticism lay the practice of scriptural meditation known as *lectio divina*. The remote origins lie in early desert monasticism where the famous collections of sayings often mention meditating and ruminating upon scripture. *Lectio* is also mentioned as a spiritual practice in the RB but without any further development. The process was classically described in terms of four dimensions or stages although, as we have seen, this was only given a systematic framework in the twelfth century by the Carthusian monk Guigo. The first stage, *lectio*, originally implied not simply reading a scripture text with the eyes but pronouncing it quietly with the lips. The second stage, *meditatio*, embraced a range of elements such as memorization, repetition of words or phrases, reflection on the meaning of the words, and "rumination" or chewing and digesting the words so that they are inscribed in the heart. Thus, meditation was a free exercise with no fixed timespan or precisely prescribed method. Overall it was an extension of reading and led the monk towards *oratio*. This third dimension literally means "prayer" but fundamentally implied a heart-felt and spontaneous offering of oneself to God. *Contemplatio* was the fourth dimension. Originally this did not designate, as it later did, being finally drawn into an elevated spiritual state or immediacy of presence to God. Rather it summarized the deepened spiritual attitudes that arose from the overall practice of *lectio divina*.[31]

Spirituality and the Conversion of Europe

Christianity has regularly been identified as one of the great missionary religions. It is certainly true that, from the beginning, the instinct actively to proclaim the message of God's salvation to the whole world has often been a powerful one. The early medieval period up to the eleventh century witnessed the gradual conversion of European, post-imperial, largely tribal peoples and the general expansion of Christianity especially in the West. Conversion was as much cultural as religious because it involved a degree of "civilizing" by reference to a Roman imperial past. Hagiographies of the saints of the conversion period often portray a missionary model of Christian holiness associated with wonder-working and visions and sometimes the renewal of the older martyrdom tradition.[32] The spread of Christianity led to the development of local "spiritualities." As a general remark, Christian missionaries were often monks (e.g. Augustine in England or the Englishman Boniface the "apostle of Germany" in the mid-eighth century). They worked by collaborating with local chiefs or kings often assisted by special relationships with the queen or other senior women.

The question about when, or indeed whether, Europe was fully "Christianized" is a contested one but is not especially relevant to the story of spirituality – except in one respect. Despite references to destroying pagan temples, for example, in the legends of St Boniface, Christianity succeeded partly because its spirituality regularly fused with older practices and beliefs. Thus, it absorbed elements of ancient magic, it took over sacred days (e.g. *Samain*, the greatest festival of the Celtic year, corresponded to the Feasts of All Saints and All Souls at the beginning of November), its holy men and women often reproduced the healing and teaching roles of pre-Christian shamans, and it regularly offered continuity by occupying pre-Christian sacred sites. In England, this was sometimes indicated by the dedication of churches to, for example, St Helen (absorbing Ellen, a Celtic goddess) or to St Michael and All Angels (absorbing pre-Christian pantheons).[33]

Local Spiritualities: Ireland

Although Western Christianity formally supported the value of religious unity, the emergence of relative uniformity only began with the neo-imperialism of Charlemagne in the ninth century and took a long time to develop. In practice, spiritual cultures in the early medieval period were fundamentally local.

One tradition that has received a great deal of attention in recent years is so-called Celtic spirituality. However, any notion that "Celtic" spirituality was totally distinct from other local forms (e.g. the neighboring early English tradition) and was also opposed to "Roman Christianity" is a recent invention. "Celtic" Christianity was a variant of the Western "Catholic" Church, owing allegiance to the Bishop of Rome, at a time when considerable divergence in local customs was the norm. The label "Celtic" is also misleading. This suggests that prior to the arrival of the Normans, there was a common spiritual culture across all six lands in the Celtic language group, Ireland, Scotland, Wales, Cornwall, Brittany, and the Isle of Man. In fact, these were not a single unit culturally or religiously. Most of what is popularly known as "Celtic spirituality" actually refers to Ireland and to Irish foundations in Scotland and Northumbria.

If we think of early medieval Irish spirituality, there are obvious connections between a spiritual culture and its natural and social environment. Ireland was never part of the Roman Empire and consequently had no city tradition or road system. Social life was predominantly tribal with local kingship. Centers of habitation were small with no monumental architecture. The landscape had not been partly tamed by estates or country villas but remained largely wilderness. On a relatively small island, the sea was a dominant feature – not least because it provided transport routes for a country with an inhospitable interior. It does not take a vast leap of imagination to make connections between these realities and a particular spiritual "temperament." An indigenous form of Church organization and spirituality flourished in Ireland (and is well documented), at least from the time of St Patrick's mission sometime in the mid-fifth century to the twelfth century when the Norman invasion exposed Ireland to the practices of the continental European Church and its reform movements.

The Irish Church had a particularly strong monastic flavor, often based on the traditional tribal centers and overlapping with tribal organization. Monastic colonies spread to Scotland (most notably Colm Cille or Columba on Iona in the mid-sixth century), Northumbria (Aidan then Cuthbert on Lindisfarne in the seventh century), and across much of Western Europe (e.g. Columbanus). Irish asceticism also valued solitude, often accompanied by a vigorous penance, pursued on lonely headlands and islands. A characteristic feature was the social as well as religious importance of monastic asceticism, possibly influenced by Eastern models mediated through the traditions of John Cassian and Martin of Tours in Gaul. Monastic "towns" were sometimes mixed settlements of men, women, celibates, and married people, that fulfilled political, social, economic, educational, as well as religious functions.

The closeness of religion to the life of the people was also reflected in a profound sense of the presence of a Trinitarian God and the saints and angels all around them. Even after the coming of Christianity, the wealth of prayers and poetry is marked by powerful natural imagery. Yet, the so-called nature spirituality of Irish Christianity, often written by monastic hermits, portrays nature as of only relative value. What matters are the classic monastic themes of solitude and simplicity and closeness to God.

> I wish, O son of the Living God,
> O ancient, eternal King
> For a hidden little hut in the wilderness
> That it may be my dwelling.
>
> An all-grey lithe little lark
> To be by its side,
> A clear pool to wash away sins
> Through the grace of the Holy Spirit.[34]

Equally, the legends of someone like St Kevin of Glendalough befriending birds and wild animals is not uniquely Irish but echoes the myth of paradise recreated in early desert monastic literature.

There was also a practice of voluntary exile far from home and familiar landscapes. This wandering of individual ascetics and groups led many of them, sometimes reluctantly, to evangelize the people among whom they settled. Throughout the history of Christian spirituality, religious explorers have often sought refuge in some form of "desert." The distinctive geography of Ireland produced a particular kind of "desert" ascetic – the seafarer. The ultimate point of such wandering was to "seek the place of resurrection." This involved living in the world as a stranger for Christ's sake. The "place of resurrection" was the place appointed by God for the particular wanderer to settle, waiting for death. It is significant that this place was not determined by tribe or culture but by God alone. A famous story is the Voyage of St Brendan or *Navigatio Brendani* probably dating from the late ninth century even though the saint lived from c. 500 to c. 583. Its simple plot blends pre-Christian Irish journey traditions, folklore, a strong narrative, poetry, and monastic imagery. Interesting attempts have been made to prove that there really was such a voyage by St Brendan (in which he may even have reached North America). However, it is more likely that this particular tale is a parable of the monastic inner journey.

Irish spirituality, especially because of its strong monastic ethos, paid close attention to the spiritual needs of the individual. From this developed the widespread practice of spiritual guidance among both monastics and laypeople known literally as "soul friendship" exercised by a "soul-friend" (*anamchara*). Its centrality is illustrated by a saying associated with St Brigid, one of the great female monastic leaders, "A person without a soul-friend is a body without a head." Out of this tradition grew the practice of private confession and penance (associated with the *Penitentials* or books of guidance for confessors) that eventually spread from the Irish Church to the remainder of the Western Catholic tradition.[35]

Spirituality in the East

As we have already seen, many of the key movements, personalities, and themes of the spirituality of early Christianity have their origin in what might be called the Eastern Church. The point at which it is meaningful to speak of a separation of Western and Eastern Christian spiritualities is difficult to pin down and was, in any case, never absolute. There was no single moment but an extended process, deepened by key institutional or political changes. Among these was the decline in the number of Easterners working in Rome, particularly after the death of the Emperor Constans II in Sicily (668) ended the last serious attempt to keep Italy within the Byzantine Empire, and also the death of the last Greek pope in 752. After this, the papacy became virtually identified with the West and increasingly involved with the new "Holy Roman Empire" deriving from Charlemagne and his successors.

The dominant strain of Eastern Christian spirituality at least until the end of the Middle Ages is often called "Byzantine spirituality" because of its association with the Byzantine Empire, based in Constantinople. Until the expansion of Islam in the eighth century, the Empire covered the Balkans, Turkey, Syria-Palestine, and North Africa and saw itself as the direct successor of the Roman Empire. Byzantine spirituality remained associated with the Eastern Empire until the fall of Constantinople in 1453 and continues through the medium of the Orthodox family of Churches.

It is risky to try to summarize such a culturally varied tradition in a short space. However, there are a number of characteristics that define Eastern Christian spirituality even if they are not exclusive to the Eastern tradition. First, it is characteristically theological-mystical. Unlike later Western theology, the Eastern tradition retained a more unified approach in which doctrine, ethics, pastoral practice, and spiritual theory form an interconnecting whole. Theology engages doctrine with the inner life of Christians and also with outward behavior. In particular, Eastern spirituality is explicitly Trinitarian. The Christian life engages with a God who is mysteriously Other, yet become human in Jesus Christ and also indwelling as Spirit. One of the most characteristic features of Eastern spirituality is the concept of *theōsis* or deification, coined by Gregory Nazianzus, one of the Cappadocian theologians in the fourth century, and further developed by such figures as Maximus the Confessor in the seventh century and Gregory Palamas in the fourteenth century. *Theōsis* teaches that the destiny of humanity and of the created order as a whole is ultimate communion with God-as-Trinity – indeed to share in the divine life itself not by nature but through God's grace.

Second, Eastern spirituality is ascetic. Since the fourth century, the spiritual traditions of the East have been formed especially under monastic influence. The basic liturgical practice of the East is deeply monastic as is the emphasis on fasting and repentance. Monastic life continues to play a central role in Orthodox (Eastern) Christianity as the context par excellence for transmitting spiritual wisdom and the traditions of prayer. As we shall see in later chapters, the widespread spiritual influence of the monasteries of Mount Athos in Greece (not least through the compilation of monastic-ascetic and contemplative texts known as *The Philokalia*) and the role of the Russian monastic spiritual guide (*staretz*) in the lives of many laypeople are cases in point.

Third, Eastern spirituality is sacramental-liturgical. While private prayer is strongly encouraged, many of the private devotions actually reflect the service books of public liturgy. The latter is based both on scripture and on patristic texts. The repetitive nature of Eastern liturgy, in the sense both of repetitive prayers and hymns and the repetition of particular images, tended to deflect any tendency to develop formal meditative techniques, detached from liturgy, as happened in the West. For a figure like Symeon the New Theologian (eleventh century), our ultimate destiny of communion with God is anticipated by every Christian in baptism, reinforced in the Eucharist. Thus, mysticism and the everyday sacramental life of the Church are bound together rather than separated. The sacramental-liturgical dimension of Eastern spirituality overflows into a "high" view of the Church and the position of the individual believer within it. The Eastern concept of Christian community extends to include all those who have gone before us and also the whole court of heaven. Hence the strong emphasis on what is called the "communion of saints," our connections with it, and the role of saints.

Fourth, balancing the ascetic element, there is also what might be called an aesthetic dimension at the heart of Eastern spirituality. While this is expressed in the visually and musically rich Divine Liturgy and also in the great body of religious poetry, the aesthetic element is best known through the tradition of icons. Although there were violent battles during the eighth and ninth centuries concerning the validity of venerating icons (the so-called Iconoclastic Controversy), a highly theological and spiritually rich understanding of religious art was and remains characteristic of Eastern spirituality. The role of such art is not fundamentally didactic but spiritual – that is, icons are understood as channels of God's power. There is also a quasi-mystical sense that through interaction with the icon the Christian may somehow become united with what the icon represents – whether this is Christ or the Virgin Mary and the other saints.

Finally, Eastern spirituality may be thought of as mystical – that is, concerned with apprehension of and communion with the divine. While this mystical element is intimately related to all the preceding elements, not least the theological, it has often been associated in people's minds with the tradition of "hesychasm" (from the Greek for quietness or stillness, *hesychia*). From the time of the desert fathers and mothers to the Middle Ages, the concept was virtually synonymous with the life of monastic withdrawal and contemplation. Gradually, however, the term took on a more technical sense as the "state" of stillness achieved through spiritual practice whereby we can be freed from mental image and from desire as a prelude to communion with God.

By the late thirteenth century, under the influence of monastic settlements at Mount Athos or Sinai and of such figures as Gregory Palamas (1296–1359), "hesychasm" became a more distinct tradition. In it, the early Syriac emphasis on the inner presence of the Spirit plus the Macarian tradition (e.g. the *Fifty Spiritual Homilies* by pseudo-Macarius) with its emphasis on ceaseless prayer fused with the broader Eastern Byzantine tradition of stillness of heart. The result, in part, was a growing emphasis on what is known as the Jesus Prayer (or the Prayer of the Name).[36]

Eastern Christianity, unlike Western teachings on prayer, has been reluctant to emphasize methods or techniques. Nevertheless, the Jesus Prayer has been deemed particularly helpful in pursuit of inner silence and in deepening the Christian's personal relationship with the incarnate Son of God. In broad terms, this involves the frequent repetition of an invocation "Lord Jesus Christ, Son of God, have mercy on me a sinner." This may be shortened to "Lord Jesus, have mercy." It is not usual practice to invoke the name "Jesus" on its own. The Jesus Prayer may be recited as a formal exercise of prayer or it may more informally accompany ordinary daily work. This form of prayer was not understood in a purely mechanistic way but involved complex inner transformation and demanded careful guidance. This is clear from the nineteenth-century Russian narrative of an anonymous spiritual seeker, commonly known as *The Way of the Pilgrim*, through which this tradition became familiar in the West.[37]

Syriac Spirituality

Until relatively recently, it has been regularly assumed that Eastern Christian spirituality merely refers to the Greek-Byzantine tradition. However, there was another spiritual culture in the early Church of the East and that is the Syriac tradition. It is only within the last hundred years that the vast literature of this tradition has been studied and appreciated as a distinctive spirituality.[38]

The Syriac tradition covered a large area, centered in Antioch and Edessa in modern Syria but also covering much of eastern Turkey, northern Iraq, and Iran. The origins of the tradition are unclear, but from an early date it seems to have had a starkly ascetical streak that was touched upon earlier in the chapter. In early works such as the *Acts of Judas Thomas* and the *Odes of Solomon* (probably second century), baptism and sexual abstinence were closely linked. The emphasis was on the superiority of virginity and even on abstinence in marriage. In the fourth-century *Book of Steps* or *Book of Degrees*, this was brought together with another important Syriac theme, the central position of the Holy Spirit. The "just" are those who lead normal human lives (including marriage) and receive only a pledge of the fullness of the Spirit. However, the "perfect" do not marry and lead lives of total renunciation. These receive the fullness of the Spirit.

The best-known and greatest spiritual teacher and writer of the Syriac tradition is St Ephrem (c. 306–373) who was born in Nisibis in Mesopotamia but eventually moved to Edessa. Ephrem's theologically rich work is expressed especially in poetry. His collections of hymns, which had an extensive influence on both Greek and Western spirituality, are characterized stylistically by the use of metaphor and intellectually by the notion of paradox. God is immanent yet transcendent, unapproachable yet accessible through natural symbols as well as in the life of Christ. Again, there is a strong emphasis on the role of the Spirit and the movement towards final absorption into the Spirit of God as the climax of the Christian life.[39]

Conclusion

The period from the fourth to the twelfth centuries was crucial both for the consolidation of the Christian spirituality in general and for the development of the specifically monastic paradigm in particular. By the end of the period, it is fair to say that for a range of reasons the Western Church had developed a life of its own that was significantly different from Eastern Christianity. It is also important to note that Christianity in its Eastern Syrian form moved at an early date into parts of Asia such as India and China. Legend has it that the apostle Thomas reached India in the first century, and certainly by the fourth century there was an organized Christian community in what is now Kerala. By the seventh century, Christianity had also reached China, and several monasteries were founded. The beginnings of distinctive approaches to spirituality beyond Europe, North Africa, and the Middle East will be discussed in Chapter 5.

To return to Western Europe, by the twelfth century, major cultural and social shifts were taking place, especially the so-called Twelfth-Century Renaissance and the rebirth of cities. These inevitably had a considerable impact on the further development of spirituality during the Middle Ages, and it is to this that Chapter 4 turns its attention.

Notes

1   For an up to date study of the origins and early history of monasticism
    see Marilyn Dunn, *The Emergence of Monasticism: From the Desert Fathers to
    the Early Middle Ages*, Oxford: Blackwell Publishing, 2003.

2   On early widows and virgins, see Rosemary Rader, "Early Christian forms
    of communal spirituality: Women's communities" in W. Skudlarek, ed.,
    The Continuing Quest for God, Collegeville: Liturgical Press, 1982, pp. 88–99
    and Jo Ann McNamara, "Muffled voices: The lives of consecrated women
    in the Fourth Century" in J. Nichols and L. Shank, eds., *Distant Echoes:
    Medieval Religious Women*, Kalamazoo: Cistercian Publications, 1984,
    pp. 11–30.

3   On the Syriac ascetical tradition see, for example, Gabriele Winkler "The
    origins and idiosyncracies of the earliest form of asceticism" in Skudlarek,
    The Continuing Quest for God, pp. 9–43; Peter Brown "The rise and function
    of the holy man in Late Antiquity" in his *Society and the Holy in Late
    Antiquity*, London: Faber, 1982; and Robert Murray "The features of the
    earliest Christian asceticism" in Peter Brooks, ed., *Christian Spirituality:
    Essays in Honour of Gordon Rupp*, London: SCM Press, 1975.

4   There is a relatively recent translation of this life in Robert C. Gregg, ed.,
    Athanasius: The Life of Antony & The Letter to Marcellinus, Classics of Western
    Spirituality, New York: Paulist Press, 1980.

5   An excellent selection translated and introduced by the scholar of early
    monasticism, Sister Benedicta Ward contains examples from both
    collections. See Benedicta Ward, trans., *The Desert Fathers: Sayings of the
    Early Christian Monks*, London/New York: Penguin Books, 2003.

6   The most comprehensive recent study of desert monasticism is William
    Harmless, *Desert Christians: An Introduction to the Literature of Early
    Monasticism*, Oxford/New York: Oxford University Press, 2004. One of the
    best studies of early desert spirituality is Douglas Burton-Christie, *The Word
    in the Desert*, Oxford/New York: Oxford University Press, 1993. There is
    an excellent short summary of desert spirituality in Andrew Louth,
    The Wilderness of God, London: Darton Longman & Todd, 1991, Chapter 3.

7   Benedicta Ward, trans., *The Desert Fathers: Sayings of the Early Christian
    Monks*, London/New York: Penguin Classics, 2003, p. 57, number 16.

8   Ward, *The Desert Fathers*, p. 36, number 10.

9   For a brief but first-rate summary of asceticism and the role of the body
    in the desert tradition, see Peter Brown, *The Body and Society: Men, Women
    and Sexual Renunciation in Early Christianity*, London: Faber & Faber,
    1991, Chapter 11.

10 On spiritual guidance in the desert, see the classic study by Irénée
    Hausherr, *Spiritual Direction in the Early Christian East*, Kalamazoo:
    Cistercian Publications, 1990. This edition includes an excellent

summary of the tradition in the Foreword by Kallistos Ware. See also, Benedicta Ward, "Spiritual direction in the desert fathers" *The Way*, 24/1, January 1984, pp. 61–70.

11 For a translation of and commentary on key passages of St Basil's Rules, see Augustine Holmes OSB, *A Life Pleasing to God: The Spirituality of the Rules of St Basil*. London: Darton Longman & Todd, 2000. For general background, see Dunn, *Emergence of Monasticism*, pp. 34–41.

12 See R.A. Markus, *The End of Ancient Christianity*, Cambridge: Cambridge University Press, 1998, p. 78.

13 For the text of the Rule and its associated documents, see George Lawless, *Augustine of Hippo and His Monastic Rule*. Oxford: Clarendon Press, 1987.

14 See the translations by Colm Luibheid, *John Cassian: Conferences*, Classics of Western Spirituality, New York: Paulist Press, 1985.

15 See Dunn, *Emergence of Monasticism*, pp. 73–81.

16 Most of the details of Benedict's life come from the *Dialogues* of the pope Gregory the Great in the late sixth century. Gregory greatly promoted the "Benedictine way" without perhaps being technically himself a Benedictine monk. There are several good editions of the RB with translations and scholarly commentaries and one of the best is Terrence C. Kardong OSB, ed., *Benedict's Rule: A Translation and Commentary*, Collegeville: The Liturgical Press, 1996. For reliable and accessible introductions to Benedictine spirituality and the Rule, see Columba Stewart OSB, *Prayer and Community: The Benedictine Tradition*, Traditions of Christian Spirituality Series, London: Darton Longman & Todd and Maryknoll: Orbis Books, 1998; also Esther de Waal, *Seeking God: The Way of St Benedict*, Collegeville: The Liturgical Press, 1984. A classic study of monastic theology and culture remains Jean Leclercq OSB, *The Love of Learning and the Desire for God: A Study of Monastic Culture*, new edition, New York: Fordham University Press, 2003.

17 Sermon VIII, 2 in G.S.M. Walker, ed., *Sancti Columbani Opera*, Dublin: The Dublin Institute for Advanced Studies, 1970, p. 97, lines 11–13. This volume also contains three monastic rules associated with Columbanus.

18 See Jean Leclercq, *The Love of Learning and the Desire for God: A Study of Monastic Culture*, third edition, New York: Fordham University Press, 1982, Chapter 2, "St Gregory, Doctor of Desire."

19 See Benedicta Ward, ed., *The Prayers and Meditations of St Anselm with the "Proslogion."* London/New York: Penguin Books, 1984.

20 See C. Hart and J. Bishop, eds., *Hildegard of Bingen: Scivias*, New York: Paulist Press, 1990. Also, Barbara Newman, *Sister of Wisdom: St Hildegard's Theology of the Feminine*, Berkeley: University of California Press, 1989.

21 The classic study is Henrietta Leyser, *Hermits and the New Monasticism*, London: Macmillan, 1984.

22   Apart from material on the Camaldolese reform in Leyser 1984, see Peter-Damian Belisle, ed., *The Privilege of Love: Camaldolese Benedictine Spirituality*, Collegeville: The Liturgical Press, 2002 and Peter-Damian Belisle, *The Language of Silence: The Changing Face of Monastic Solitude*, London: Darton Longman & Todd and Maryknoll: Orbis Books, 2003, especially Chapter 8.

23   On Carthusian spirituality see, E. Colledge and J Walsh, eds., *Guigo II, The Ladder of Monks & Twelve Meditations*, New York: Doubleday, 1978 and Dennis Martin, ed., *Carthusian Spirituality: The Writings of Hugh of Balma & Guigo de Ponte*, Classics of Western Spirituality, New York: Paulist Press, 1997; Belisle, *Language of Silence*, Chapter 9.

24   For a critical discussion of this theme, see Caroline Walker Bynum, "Did the twelfth century discover the individual?" in *Jesus as Mother: Studies in the Spirituality of the High Middle Ages*, Berkeley: University of California Press, 1984, pp. 82–109.

25   For translations of and an introduction to Bernard's writings, see G.R. Evans, ed., *Bernard of Clairvaux: Selected Works*, Classics of Western Spirituality, New York: Paulist Press, 1987.

26   There is a useful one-volume selection in English of early Cistercian spiritual writings in Pauline Matarasso, ed., *The Cistercian World: Monastic Writings of the Twelfth Century*, London/New York: Penguin Books, 1993. The most complete collection of critical modern translations of these and other Cistercian writers are produced by Cistercian Publications in the USA in its *Cistercian Fathers Series*. There is a parallel series of studies of monastic history and spirituality in its *Cistercian Studies Series*.

27   For modern translations see E. Connor, trans., *Aelred of Rievaulx: The Mirror of Charity*, Kalamazoo: Cistercian Publications, 1990 and M.E. Laker, trans., *Aelred of Rievaulx: Spiritual Friendship*, Kalamazoo: Cistercian Publications, 1977.

28   For a good study of these Cistercian women, see Bynum, "Women mystics of the thirteenth century: The case of the nuns of Helfta"in *Jesus as Mother*. Two modern translations are Frank Tobin, ed., *Mechtild of Magdeburg: The Flowing Light of the Godhead*, Classics of Western Spirituality, New York: Paulist Press, 1998 and Margaret Winkworth, ed., *Gertrude of Helfta: The Herald of Divine Love*, Classics of Western Spirituality, New York: Paulist Press, 1993.

29   For broad summaries of Cistercian spirituality, see Louis Lekai, *The Cistercians: Ideals and Realities*, Kent: Kent State University Press, 1977; André Louf, *The Cistercian Way*, Kalamazoo: Cistercian Publications, 1989; and Esther de Waal, *The Way of Simplicity: The Cistercian Tradition*, London: Darton Longman & Todd and New York: Orbis Books, 1998.

30   See, for example, the notion of monastic life as paradise regained in "Life of Onnophrius" in T. Vivian, *Journeying into God: Seven Early Monastic Lives*, Minneapolis: Fortress Press, 1996, Chapter 7.

31   For a modern study of *lectio divina* see Michael Casey, *Sacred Reading: The Ancient Art of Lectio Divina*, Ligouri: Trijmph Books, 1996.

32   See Ian Wood, *The Missionary Life: Saints and the Evangelisation of Europe 400–1050*, London: Longman, 2001.

33   On fusion with pre-Christian forms see, Valerie Flint, *The Rise of Magic in Early Medieval Europe*, Oxford: Clarendon Press, 1991; Philip Sheldrake, *Living Between Worlds: Place and Journey in Celtic Spirituality*, 2nd edition, London: Darton Longman & Todd and Cambridge MA: Cowley, 1997; and Anton Wessels, *Europe: Was it ever really Christian?* London: SCM Press, 1994.

34   The Hermit's Song in Patrick Murray, ed., *The Deer's Cry: A Treasury of Irish Religious Verse*, Dublin: Four Courts Press, 1986, pp. 36–37.

35   For some reliable works on Celtic or Irish spirituality in general, see Thomas O'Loughlin, *Celtic Theology*, London/New York: Continuum, 2000 and his *Journeys on the Edge: The Celtic Tradition*, London: Darton Longman & Todd and New York: Orbis Books, 2000; Ian Bradley, *Celtic Christianity: Making Myths and Chasing Dreams*, New York: St Martin's Press, 1999; Oliver Davies, ed., *Celtic Spirituality, Classics of Western Spirituality*, New York: Paulist Press, 1999; and Philip Sheldrake, *Living between Worlds: Place and Journey in Celtic Spirituality*, 2nd edition, London: Darton Longman & Todd and Cambridge MA: Cowley, 1997.

36   On the Eastern spiritual tradition, see, for example, John McGuckin, *Standing in God's Holy Fire: The Byzantine Tradition*, London: Darton Longman & Todd and New York: Orbis Books, 2001; John Chryssavgis, *Light Through Darkness: The Orthodox Tradition*, London: Darton Longman & Todd and New York: Orbis Books, 2004; C. Luibheid and N. Russell, eds., *John Climacus: The Ladder of Divine Ascent*, Classics of Western Spirituality, New York: Paulist Press, 1982; and John Meyendorff, ed., *Gregory Palamas – The Triads*, Classics of Western Spirituality, New York: Paulist Press, 1983.

37   For a recent edition, see Aleksei Pentkovsky, ed., *The Pilgrim's Tale*, New York: Paulist Press, 1999.

38   See R. Murray, *Symbols of Church and Kingdom: A Study of Early Syriac Tradition*, Cambridge: Cambridge University Press, 1975 and also Roberta Bondi, "The spirituality of Syriac-speaking Christians" in Bernard McGinn, John Meyendorff, and Jean Leclercq, eds., *Christian Spirituality: Origins to the Twelfth Century*, New York: Crossroad Publishing, 1985, pp. 152–161.

39   Ephrem's hymns are available in the Classics of Western Spirituality series: Kathleen McVey, ed., *Ephrem the Syrian: Hymns*, New York: Paulist Press, 1989.

Chapter 4

Spirituality in the City:
1150–1450

c. 1050–c. 1250	Rebirth of Western European cities
1073–1085	Gregory VII as pope initiates "Gregorian Reform"
c. 1080–1134	Norbert of Xanten lives: leader in the vita evangelica movement
c. 1081–1151	Suger lives: Abbot of St Denis, reputed originator of Gothic style
c. 1096–1164	Peter Lombard lives: theologian
Twelfth century	Twelfth-Century Renaissance
c. 1135–1202	Joachim of Fiore lives: Cistercian abbot and apocalyptic prophet
1141	Death of Hugh of St Victor: mystical theologian
c. 1160–1240	Jacques de Vitry lives: bishop, reformer, Beguine chronicler
1170–1221	Dominic de Guzman lives: founder of Dominicans
1173	Death of Richard of St Victor
1177–1213	Mary of Oignes lives: Beguine writer
1182–1226	Francis of Assisi lives: founder of Friars Minor (Rule 1223)
1194–1253	Clare of Assisi lives: collaborator of St Francis and founder of Poor Clares (Rule approved 1253)
Thirteenth century	Hadewijch lives: Beguine poet and mystic
1204	Sack of Constantinople during Fourth Crusade
1217–1274	Bonaventure lives: Franciscan mystical theologian
c. 1232–c. 1315	Ramon Llull lives: religious philosopher in dialogue with Islam
1247	Carmelite Rule approved

Spirituality: A Brief History, Second Edition. Philip Sheldrake.
© 2013 John Wiley & Sons, Ltd. Published 2013 by John Wiley & Sons, Ltd.

c. 1260–c. 1328	Meister Eckhart lives: Dominican mystical theologian
c. 1293–1381	John Ruusbroec lives: Flemish priest and mystical theologian
1295–1366	Henry Suso lives: Dominican mystical theologian
c. 1300–1361	Johannes Tauler lives: Dominican mystical theologian
1304–1374	Petrarch (Francesco Petrarca) lives: Renaissance thinker
1310	Marguerite Porete, the Beguine, burned at the stake
1311–1312	Council of Vienne condemns Beguine movement
c. 1342–c. 1417	Julian of Norwich lives: English mystic and writer
1347–1380	Catherine of Siena lives: mystic
c. 1350–1450	Italian Renaissance
1433–1499	Marsiglio Ficino lives: Renaissance philosopher
1439	Council of Florence seeks to reunite Western and Eastern Churches
1453	Fall of Constantinople to the Turks. End of Byzantine Empire

An overview of medieval spirituality from the twelfth to the fifteenth centuries must begin with five critical religious and cultural factors. These are the Gregorian reform, apocalyptic movements, the *vita evangelica* movement, the so-called Twelfth-Century Renaissance, and the rebirth of cities. In a range of ways, these had an immense impact on Church life and spirituality over the next three centuries. This was also the period that not only witnessed the foundation of new religious orders better suited to the cities but also the particular growth of what I call the second, "mystical type" of Christian spirituality, particularly in Western Europe.

The Gregorian Reform

The Gregorian reform was an important movement of renewal between the mid-eleventh and mid-twelfth centuries and took its name from Pope Gregory VII (1073–1085). The core of the reform was the purification of the Church from secular and political domination. However, Gregory's programme was fundamentally structural-institutional – particularly in a growing separation of the clergy from the laity expressed by universal celibacy and in securing the unity of the Church through a centralized papacy. One effect of the reforms was to focus supernatural power increasingly in a clerically controlled sacramental system.

While the reform had a spiritual and moral content, especially a concern for the quality of clerical life and pastoral care, it unlocked a radical evangelical fervor which the hierarchy of the Church found difficult to contain. In the end, it could be argued that the Gregorian reform failed to satisfy laypeople and the outstanding religious spirits of the age. Two things resulted from this. First, a new spiritual climate developed which favored evangelical simplicity and piety. Second, there was a movement outwards from the world of the cloister and a growing resistance to forcing the spiritual life into organized systems. At its most extreme, this dissatis-faction contributed to the birth of dissident movements such as the Waldensians (who re-emerged as a reformed church in Italy during the Reformation) and the Humiliati. There also emerged various radical-popular apocalyptic groups, even some within established religious orders, who predicted the imminent second coming of Christ or the establishment of a new world order.[1]

Apocalyptic Movements

Apocalyptic movements, based on the Book of Revelation in the New Testament, involved intense eschatological fervor concerning the immi-nent second coming of Christ. From the time of St Augustine, such movements persistently reappeared throughout Christian history. In times of religious or social upheaval and change, apocalypticism offered an alternative hope in response to fear or insecurity. Its symbolic power also responded more broadly to the overall uncertainty and instability of the human condition.

The twelfth century witnessed an overtly apocalyptic spiritual movement in the writings of the Italian Cistercian abbot, Joachim of Fiore, who by his death in 1202 had become one of the most noted figures of his day. Like all apocalyptic prophets, Joachim saw himself as the secret bearer of a new age.[2] He believed in the imminent coming of a "third age" of the Holy Spirit. First, during an imminent crisis, two new religious orders would arise to confront the Antichrist and his forces – an order of preachers and an order of hermits. Finally, there would be a process of monasticization throughout the whole Church which would bring about the gradual triumph of spirit over flesh and contemplation over worldly thought. This teaching is found in *The Book of Figures*. In Joachim's Twelfth Table, "The Arrangement of the New People of God," the Church is divided into seven "Oratories" of which the seventh is the Oratory of St Abraham the Patriarch and of All the Holy Patriarchs.

Joachim commented that "under the name of this oratory will be gathered the married with their sons and daughters living a common life." While living in separate dwellings they will share food and clothing and be obedient to the Spiritual Father (who governs the whole community). The biblical allusions make it clear that the model for this is the early Jerusalem community of *The Books of Acts*.[3]

The Vita Evangelica

The birth of the so-called *vita evangelica* was not an organized movement but a way of describing a widespread spiritual fervor. It centered on a return to gospel values expressed in simplicity, the literal imitation of the poor and homeless Jesus (mendicancy and wandering), and in preaching. It is noticeable that women played an active role at the start although eventually this was curtailed in significant ways. This can be seen with the eventual enclosure of some women's groups (e.g. the Poor Clares) and a general suspicion of others (e.g. the Beguines).

In the case of the various elements that went to make up the *vita evangelica*, some were absorbed into the spiritual mainstream. Thus, the mendicant groups found an accepted place through formal recognition of new religious orders such as the Franciscans in the thirteenth century. Some people who began as radical wandering preachers, such as Norbert of Xanten, eventually settled down to a fairly orthodox monastic life (Norbert founded the Canons Regular of Premontré). Even the mendicants, while retaining their relative simplicity, mobility, and emphasis on popular preaching, took on a structured lifestyle as religious orders. However, they continued close connections with lay Christians by founding associated groups, known as Tertiaries (or "Third Orders"), for men and women who were unable to take on the full lifestyle of the parent order. Some Tertiaries lived in community, but the majority continued to live at home in normal married and working environments while undertaking a life of prayer and charitable work compatible with everyday commitments.

One category that bridged the gap between the Gregorian reforms and the *vita evangelica* was the so-called canonical life. The defining style was one of clergy or groups of women who lived in community as Canons (or Canonesses) Regular yet exercised a pastoral ministry. The most notable expression was a revival of the fifth-century Rule of St Augustine. This canonical revival also integrated clerical reform with elements of the new evangelical fervor – not least its encouragement of a more active spirituality of service. Many of the new communities of men and women ministered to the poor, nursed the sick, or cared for pilgrims. Some male communities took on the pastoral care of geographical areas. Some communities of Canons Regular or of Canonesses integrated pastoral care with contemplative-monastic observance. The Canons Regular of Premontré (Premonstratensians) in particular were influenced by elements of Cistercian austerity, and the Canons of St Victor in Paris (or Victorines) became notable for the foundation of a contemplative-mystical tradition that combined the Augustinian theological tradition with the mystical theology of pseudo-Dionysius and with the new "scientific" theology of the schools. The two most notable exponents were Hugh of St Victor (d. 1141) and Richard of St Victor (d. 1173) who exercised a major influence on the development of a distinct spiritual theology. Richard's doctrine was condensed into two important works, *Benjamin minor* and *Benjamin major*, which describe the contemplative journey. Richard and his disciples increasingly made a certain reading of the teachings of pseudo-Dionysius the yardstick to judge a mystical way of life. Richard had considerable influence, for example, on St Bonaventure's *Journey of the Mind into God* and on *The Cloud of Unknowing*, the fourteenth-century English mystical text.[4]

Twelfth-Century Renaissance

The expression "Twelfth-Century Renaissance" is now commonly accepted as a way of describing an extraordinary flourishing of creative intellectual, spiritual, and aesthetic currents. Intellectually the so-called father of Scholasticism, Peter Lombard, completed his *Sentences*, Gratian's codification of canon (i.e. church) law was completed, leading spiritual figures such as Dominic and Francis were born, and the cathedral of Notre Dame in Paris was begun and, with the Abbey church of St Denis under Abbot Suger, inaugurated the great age of Gothic architecture. Theology was in transition from rural monasteries to urban cathedral schools and eventually to the new city universities, and an abundant literature, both courtly poetic and spiritual, came into being.

From the point of view of spirituality, a number of features stand out. First, there was a shift in sensibility as well as in theological emphasis towards the development of a religiously based humanism. For example, there was a growing emphasis on the humanity of Jesus rather than on the ascended, glorified Christ. This had an impact of religious iconography as representations of the suffering Jesus on the cross gradually replaced images of Christ the King. At the same time, this growing emphasis on the humanity of Christ enhanced devotion to the Virgin Mary as mother of Jesus. As we shall see later, this change in sensibilities also gave rise to an increased role for devotional practices. Second, the twelfth century also witnessed a notable cultivation of the theme of love in both religious and secular culture. This parallel discovery of divine and human love was expressed in subjective mysticism and in courtly love. The degree to which the latter influenced the former is a matter of discussion. However, it is notable that the imagery of romantic, erotic love as found in the Old Testament book, the Song of Songs, offered a ready expression for a contemplative spirituality of intimacy. As we shall see later in the writings of the Beguines, this tendency became known as "love mysticism" or "bridal mysticism." Finally, the Christian humanism of the twelfth century led to an increase of interest in the concept of the human individual and in the realm of subjectivity (though not in a modern, autonomous, psychological sense).[5] This undoubtedly fed into the development of affective mysticism which in turn encouraged greater interest in the development of spiritual guidance.

The Rebirth of Cities

From the eleventh to the thirteenth centuries, Western Europe underwent a major urban revival for the first time since the days of the Roman Empire. This had a serious impact on religious perspectives. The new urbanization, while still relatively modest in relation to a large rural population, created a growing literate merchant class. It is precisely the needs of this group, and the new complexity of European society, that partly explains the proliferation of new forms of Christian life and diverse spiritual practices outside the traditional (largely rural) monastic cloister.

The new spirituality can be summarized as a search for an evangelical life in imitation of Jesus and the early disciples. This sometimes led to the reform of the older orders (such as the growth of the Cistercians from the Benedictines) or the foundation of new ones (the mendicant, preaching, and pastoral groups such as Franciscans and Dominicans) or lay groups such as the Beguines. The new orders, the lay movements, the proliferation of cathedrals, and the new Gothic architecture and the birth of new theological and intellectual centers in the universities were all associated with cities and reflect urban sensibilities. Urban growth also led to the development of the notion that "the city" itself could be understood as a holy place.

Cathedrals and Urban Vision

Among the most evident consequences of the new urbanism were the great "Gothic" cathedrals. Cathedrals represented a theological-spiritual as well as geographical shift. Previously "the sacred" was located primarily in rural monastic communities where, not surprisingly, the dominant image of paradise was a recreation of a Garden of Eden. Now, images of "the sacred" shifted from Genesis to the Book of Revelation, from the Garden of Eden to the New Jerusalem.[6]

In the urban cathedral, heaven was not only invoked symbolically but also, as it were, brought down from heaven in the spirit of the Book of Revelation, Chapter 21. To enter the cathedral was to be transported into heaven on earth by the vastness of the space, by the progressive demate-rialization of walls with a sea of glass and a flood of light, and by the increasingly elaborate liturgies in which, sacramentally, the living Church was united with the whole court of heaven. For Abbot Suger of St Denis in Paris, one of the greatest patrons of early Gothic, the church building had to be more impressive than other city buildings. The trea-sures should evoke the splendor of heaven, and the priests, like the blessed in heaven, would dress in silks and gold.

The art of the cathedrals acted as a microcosm of the cosmos and sought to evoke and invoke a peaceable oneness between Creator and creation. This was a utopian space in which an idealized harmony, to be realized only in heaven, was anticipated in the here and now. But it was *idealized*. As Georges Duby, the distinguished French medievalist, reminds us, "Yet it would be a mistake to assume that the thirteenth century wore the beaming face of the crowned Virgin or the smiling angels. The times were hard, tense, and very wild, and it is important that we recognise all that was tumultuous and rending about them."[7] The social symbolism of cathedrals was thus also ambiguous. While cathedrals symbolized a Christian vision of human-divine unity, they also solidified the divisions of the social order. The gothic cathedrals of the Middle Ages sanctioned the new urban wealth from which they derived. They also proclaimed in their design and layout the realities of episcopal power and religious orthodoxy.

Yet, at best, the cathedral promoted more than a two-dimensional, static, urban "map." It portrayed a third and a fourth dimension – movement through space on both vertical and horizontal planes and human transformation *through time*. Cathedrals were repositories for the cumulative memory and constantly renewed aspirations of the community. Even today, to enter such a building is to engage with centuries of human pain, achievements, hopes, and ideals. The American philosopher Arnold Berleant suggests that the cathedral acted as a guide to an "urban ecology" that contrasts with the monotony of the modern city "thus helping transform it from a place where one's humanity is constantly threatened into a place where it is continually achieved and enlarged."[8] Such an urban "center" offered communion with something deeper than the need for ordered public life. Cathedrals deliberately spoke of "the condition of the world."

The City as Sacred

Notions of "the sacred" in the city were not restricted to ritual sites such as cathedrals. There was a clear sense that the city as built environment embraced a wider "sacred landscape of the streets." What seems clear is that medieval people often sought to take the heavenly Jerusalem as a model applicable to the material city. There were various attempts to make the concept of the divine city visible not merely in the structure of cathedrals and churches but even in the layout of cities. For example, the Statutes of Florence of 1339 spoke of the sacred number of twelve gates even though by that stage the city had extended to fifteen gates.[9]

Italy also gave birth to the notion that civic life itself, an organized community of people living in concord, could be just as much a way to God as monasticism.[10] The city was often seen as an ideal form of social life that was in effect an image in this world of the heavenly Jerusalem. There is a literary genre, *laudes civitatis*, or poems that articulated a utopian ideal of civic life. Like the glories of the heavenly city, the human city is depicted in the *laudes* as a place where diverse people are able to live together in peace. Cities were renowned for the quality of communal life in which every citizen or group found a particular place that contributed to building up the whole. Finally, medieval cities were regularly praised as places of hard work. The point was that the city itself was idealized as a kind of metaphor for the City of God.[11]

Streets in predominantly Catholic countries even today retain medieval examples of religious plaques and statues. For example, the rich collection of street shrines in the *città vecchia* of the Italian city of Bari, ranging in age from the twelfth century to the present, has been the subject of scholarly writing.[12]

The sense that the city as a whole was a sacred landscape was reinforced by processions and blessings. In medieval cities, the Eucharist was a *public drama*, not only in the many churches but also the feast-day pageants, mystery plays, and street processions, for example, on the feast of Corpus Christi. Processions, before Lent and on Rogation Days, and ceremonies to mark out the boundaries of each parish (known as "beating the bounds") together symbolized a purification of the city from the spirit of evil.[13]

Universities as Sacred Space

Interestingly, the *laudes civitatis* sometimes mention teachers among the people who lend a sacred quality to the city. The centers of intellectual and theological enquiry increasingly moved during the twelfth century to new cathedral "schools" that eventually gave birth to the great European universities. This involved a geographical shift of learning from countryside to new cities. However, the move involved more than geography. The theological enterprise was no longer focused in centers explicitly dedicated to a religious way of life. The new universities existed primarily to foster teaching and learning. The new theology gradually gave birth to a belief that the discipline of the mind could be separated from the discipline of an ordered lifestyle, *ascesis*, or what we call "spirituality."

The new mendicant religious orders were essentially an urban phenomenon. Their foundation in so many ways parallels the birth of the universities, and it was not long before the new orders became deeply involved in teaching – indeed often taking a leading role in university development. Inevitably, this link gave birth to an intellectualist shift in spirituality. So, for example, the Dominicans entered the universities initially to educate their own members to be effective preachers. Gradually, however, they developed an intellectual ministry – indeed were the originators of the idea that the intellectual life was a spiritual path. The Dominicans led the way in exploring how to cope theologically and spiritually with the rediscovery of Greek philosophy, especially Aristotle (as in the works of Thomas Aquinas).

Although by the sixteenth century, the Protestant reformers decried to a large extent the curriculum and focus of late medieval universities – because it seemed to prepare students in a form of theology devoid of spirituality – it should be remembered that throughout the greater part of the Middle Ages, the university in the city was an institution that acted as a bearer of religious life and spirituality for the Western world.

Vita Evangelica *and Urban Sensibilities*

The new urban spiritual movements, gathered around an ideal of the evangelical life, expressed the sensibilities and the complexities of the merchant class. It has been said that St Francis of Assisi's choice of radical poverty as *the* gospel value was not solely the result (as it was in St Bonaventure's biography of Francis) of a sudden inspiration while listening to the reading of scripture in church. It was in part a spiritual reaction to the growing wealth and power of urban society and to the characteristic sins of Francis' own social class. Yet, at the same time, close ties grew up between the new mendicant orders and the new city political class in ways that gave birth to a kind of civic religion in which local city saints (not least members of the new orders themselves) were venerated and their love of the local commune was emphasized.

The gradual development of the great city piazzas of late medieval Italy owes much to communities of friars and their large preaching churches built for mass communication and opening out onto relatively large open spaces that could accommodate even bigger audiences. These provided a suitable urban setting for crowds to gather, drawn initially by the reputation of preachers. Florence has many examples such as San Marco, Santa Maria Novella, Santa Croce, and Ssma Annunziata. As the colonnades of ancient Rome gave birth to the monastic cloister, so in the new laicized city spirituality of the later Middle Ages the monastic cloister moved out into the city to give birth to the colonnaded piazza. What began as a functional space for preaching gradually gave birth to a concept of public space where people could gather and intermingle for a variety of purposes, and particularly during the Renaissance they also offered a means of enhancing and safeguarding the panorama of cities.

The new cities gave birth to lay spiritual movements in the same period, such as the groups of women known as Beguines who came largely from the new city merchant class and flourished in northern Germany, the Netherlands, Belgium, and northern France (although some scholars extend the term to Italy and also to England). These groups were thoroughly assimilated into the life and surroundings of the city. This is clear from their unenclosed existence and engagement with city life in running schools for girls, working with the poor and sick, and engaging in trade, for example, of lace. Some continued to live with their families; others (e.g. in Cologne) lived in small groups in tenements. Where Beguines did occupy or build discrete buildings, these were distinctively urban as we shall see.[14]

The Mendicant Movement

The notion of mendicancy or begging alms was a particular characteristic of many of the new religious groups of the thirteenth century. Eventually, this way of life solidified into a number of new religious orders whose male members were popularly known as "friars" (from the Latin *fratres*, brothers). The most important groups were the Friars Minor or Franciscans founded by Francis of Assisi in 1208/1209, the Friars Preacher or Dominicans founded in France (1215) by a Spaniard Dominic de Guzman, the Carmelites whose origins are obscure but can be traced back to groups of hermits in the Holy Land and whose rule was approved in 1247, the Augustinian Hermits (Austin Friars) founded c. 1244, and, later in the fourteenth century, the Servants of Mary (Servite Friars) founded in Florence.

These communities of "evangelical life" gave special emphasis to poverty and itinerancy, following in the footsteps of Christ and living like the early disciples and preaching a gospel of repentance. While there were commonalities between the new mendicant orders, there were also differences of emphasis. The Dominicans, for example, retained elements of the life of Canons Regular which had been St Dominic's original calling and, combining this with Cistercian influences, had a more communitarian and liturgical lifestyle than other groups. As an order explicitly dedicated to preaching, they placed a high value on study and the intellectual life. The Carmelites, on the other hand, in memory of their hermit origins retained a strongly contemplative and even quasi-monastic dimension to their lifestyle with some houses in remote locations. With the exception of the Dominicans who had more clerical origins, the mendicant communities began as groups of laypeople. The mendicant movements, including the Dominicans, involved women. In the case of the Franciscan family, this was expressed by the special place in the formation of the tradition of Clare of Assisi and the significance of the Second Order (popularly known as Poor Clares).

In general, the mendicants had their strongest influence on laypeople in the towns with which they developed strong spiritual as well as pastoral bonds. As already noted, this was expressed by the foundation of lay groups related to the mendicant orders, known as Tertiaries or Third Orders. The mendicant movement responded to two contemporary spiritual needs. First, it attempted to free spirituality from an older monastic dominance. Second, there was a realization that the Church in new city and traditional countryside needed preachers who were not tied down by owning estates and maintaining large building complexes like the older monastic communities. Mendicants were free to move around the streets and to be absorbed into the flow, a transgression of fixed boundaries which, even at such an early stage, was characteristic of city life.

As exponents of a mixed, contemplative-active life, the mendicants made contemplative values accessible to their urban contemporaries. They not only engaged with the general population in ways that traditional monasticism had not done by preaching, teaching, and spiritual guidance but their religious houses were more accessible architecturally to the outside and their churches were built with the spiritual needs of the city populations in mind with large, open preaching naves and relatively small and unpretentious areas for the chanting of the liturgical offices.[15]

Dominic, Francis, Clare, and Bonaventure

It is not unfair to suggest that the character of the two largest mendicant orders, the Dominicans and the Franciscans, reflected the personalities and backgrounds of their founders.

St Dominic (1170–1221) was originally a Canon Regular of St Augustine at Osma in Castille. In 1203, he and his bishop were in southern France on diplomatic business when they came across the papal preaching mission confronting the dualist heretics known as Cathars or Albigensians. Bishop Diego and Dominic bolstered the mission by gathering together a band of dedicated preachers who, in line with the spiritual fervor of the time, also espoused a life of gospel poverty. As early as 1206, an associated community of women was founded at Prouille. On the bishop's death in 1207, Dominic remained in France and developed his group of preachers into a religious order. Basically Dominic followed his background experience as a Canon Regular. Thus, he sought to combine liturgy, contemplation, and pastoral ministry. The Order of Preachers was formally approved in 1216 and from the start embraced women and lay associates, although their full incorporation only happened years after Dominic's death. Dominican spirituality does not originate in high theory or in a particular spiritual wisdom embodied in clearly defined techniques. Effectively, Dominic's vision was to respond to concrete pastoral needs. This, and a reliance on structures that he already knew, suggests a fundamental pragmatism and functionalism in his approach to the spiritual life. The Dominican structures were relatively simple and democratic rather than hierarchical. Clearly, preaching as a medium for spreading the gospel lies at the heart of Dominican spirituality. In that sense, Dominican spirituality is evangelical and missionary. As a foundation for preaching, Dominic placed a strong emphasis on study which really replaced the traditional monastic emphasis on manual labor as a critical spiritual discipline. *Veritas* (truth) became a kind of motto of the Order expressing its deepest ideals of intellectual integrity at the service of the gospel. Behind the ability to minister effectively also lay a contemplative spirit focused especially on liturgy. This connection between contemplation and action was expressed in a traditional phrase *contemplata aliis tradere* – it is what is contemplated that leads to everything else.[16]

St Francis of Assisi (1182–1226) was very much the child both of the new urban renaissance and of the spiritual ferment of his times. He was the son of a wealthy merchant in a central Italian hill town. It is not far-fetched to see his spiritual emphasis on poverty as partly a response to a concern for material success that characterized his class. Equally his spiritual temperament reflected the spiritual currents around him – a sense of being called to renew the Church through simplicity and evangelical piety; a sensitivity to the humanity of Christ, inspired partly by the "humanism" of figures like St Bernard and partly by an awareness of the holy places of Jesus' own life fostered by the contemporary crusading spirit; an emphasis on flight from the world interpreted not in classic monastic terms but in terms of the life of contemporary wandering preachers. Thus, his *Later Rule* says: "As pilgrims and strangers in this world who serve the Lord in poverty and humility, let them [the friars] go begging for alms in full trust." Overall, the development of the Franciscan Order from its initial form submitted to the pope in 1209 to the final confirmation of the Rule in 1223 reflects above all a desire to live a gospel existence inspired by Jesus and the early disciples. The key theme was imitation of Christ the brother of all, and especially the poor and crucified Christ, by serving him in poor and marginalized people. This spirituality of imitation is expressed symbolically in the intensity of Francis' mystical experiences, not least the appearance of the marks of the crucifixion on Francis' body (known as stigmata) in 1224.

In the opening verses of his *Testament* written in 1226 shortly before his death, he also recalls the motivation for his original conversion:

1. The Lord granted me, Brother Francis, to begin to do penance in this way: While I was in sin, it seemed very bitter to me to see lepers. 2. And the Lord Himself led me among them and I had mercy upon them.

3. And when I left them that which seemed bitter to me was changed into sweetness of soul and body; and afterwards I lingered a little and left the world.

Francis' famous embrace of the leper he met on the road was not merely a response to human suffering but, in medieval terms, an encounter with the excluded "other." Lepers were not simply infected with a fearful disease. They symbolized the dark side of existence onto which medieval people projected a variety of fears, suspicions, and guilty sinfulness that must be excluded from the community of the spiritually pure. Lepers were outcasts banished from society. As his *Earlier Rule* enjoins, the brothers that Francis gathered around him "must rejoice when they live among people of little worth and who are looked down upon, among the poor and the powerless, the sick and the lepers, and the beggars by the wayside." Even the famous Canticle of Creation expresses more than a rather romantic love of the natural world. The underlying meaning is more complex. The key notion is that all our fellow creatures as brothers and sisters reflect to us the face of Christ. The first nine verses speak of the cosmic fraternity of all elements of creation. For example:

> Let everything you have made
> Be a song of praise to you,
> Above all, His Excellency the Sun (our brother);
> Through him you flood our days with light.
> He is so beautiful, so radiant, so splendid,
> O Most High, he reminds us of you.

This notion of cosmic fraternity conceals a prophetic edge. Verses 10–11 celebrate the peace that comes from mutual pardon or reconciliation.

> Be praised, my Lord,
> Through those who forgive for your love,
> Through those who are weak,
> In pain, in struggle,
> Who endure with peace,
> For you will make them Kings and Queens,
> O Lord Most High.[17]

The created world is to be a "reconciled space" because of the fraternity of all things in Christ. There is no room for violence, contention, or rejection of the "other."

Although Francis' life and writings are a primary source for Franciscan spirituality, it is now widely recognized that Clare of Assisi (1194–1253) was not merely a dependent figure but a significant personality in her own right in the origins of the Franciscan tradition. Inspired by Francis' preaching, Clare dedicated herself to a gospel life in 1212 and became the first woman member of the Order. She held to the same vision of poverty and gospel living in the face of considerable opposition from Church officials. Some historians have suggested that Clare originally wished her sisters to have an unenclosed lifestyle of service rather along the lines of the lay movement of Beguines. Whatever the case, Clare was forced to accept the Rule of St Benedict for her sisters, but this was mitigated in 1216 by papal permission to observe the same "privilege" of poverty as the friars – that is, freedom from normal monastic possessions, buildings, estates, and complex finances. However, her moderate Rule for the Poor Sisters (the Poor Clares) was only finally approved on her deathbed in 1253. Although the sisters were dedicated to a life of contemplation, this should not be contrasted with the men's dedication to preaching in poverty. Enclosure was not the end purpose of Poor Clare life. This was the bond between poverty and contemplation – contemplation in poverty and poverty as itself a form of gospel-centered contemplation. In her famous *Letters to Agnes of Prague*, Clare writes of Christ the Mirror into which the contemplative gazes and there discover the poverty of Christ and his intense love of the world expressed in the Cross. In turn, Clare suggests that the sisters are to be mirrors to those living in the world – mirrors in which people can see the gospel life.[18]

A key figure in the consolidation of Franciscan spirituality was Bonaventure (1217–1274), theologian, mystic, and superior of the Franciscan Order. Two years after his election as Minister General in 1257, Bonaventure (later called the Seraphic Doctor) spent some time at the hermitage of Mt Alverna where Francis had had his own mystical experiences. Here, Bonaventure came to understand that the spiritual journey of Francis was a model for others. This conviction, allied to his use of the mystical theology of pseudo-Dionysius mediated through the Victorines, resulted in his greatest work of mystical theology: *The Soul's Journey into God*.[19] Here, the contemplative way is open to all men and women. The spiritual journey to union with God is expressed in the classic metaphor of ascent, with Christ as the ladder, and combines the two Franciscan themes of contemplation of God indwelling in creation and intense love of Christ crucified.

The Beguines

A further striking expression of the new urban spirituality and the classic values of the *vita evangelica* was a lay movement of women known as the Beguines. The Beguines emerged towards the end of the twelfth century in northern Europe. It is not clear that we should really call the Beguines a "movement" as there was no single founder, no original rule of life, and the Beguines are sometimes difficult to distinguish from a range of individuals or groups who sought a radical Christian life outside the monastic cloister. Many of these were similarly based on the classic values of the *vita evangelica* – imitation of the early Christian communities, service of the poor, gospel simplicity, and chastity.

The Beguines were essentially a city phenomenon. Their emergence reflects the appeal of the spiritual reform movement to laypeople, especially to educated and relatively affluent ones, and coincides with a more lively participation in matters of faith by townspeople who were often dissatisfied by the ministrations of poorly educated priests and who had relatively little access to the spirituality of traditional monastic life. As a result, numbers of literate laypeople became involved in spiritual teaching and even informal preaching. They also created associations for prayer and charitable works and began to read the Bible in the vernacular. In the specific case of women, there was a move towards associations for mutual spiritual support as an alternative to traditional convent life. The Beguine life offered women the possibility of shaping their own spiritual experience and a degree of freedom from clerical control. While some continued to live with their families, others banded together in houses they bought by pooling resources. Eventually during the thirteenth century, two dominant forms emerged. In Germany, there were very few large units but small houses or tenements of between three and twenty individuals. In Flanders, the Beguines tended to create fairly sizeable building complexes known as "beguinages" that often became independent parishes. These might resemble a walled city within a city with a large church at its hub as at Bruges or a tree-covered square hardly distinguishable from others in the city as in Ghent. In either case, the architecture was domestic or urban rather than classically religious and monastic. The life of Beguines, even in structured communities, was far less ordered than a convent. For example, personal possessions were often permitted, there was no strict enclosure, and formal vows were not taken although Beguines were expected to obey the statutes of the beguinage and the elected Mistress during residence.

Beguines expressed two particular religious motivations – a cult of chastity and a desire for voluntary poverty. The latter led not simply to a simple style of life but also to the virtue of self-sufficiency achieved by the labor of their own hands. Eventually, the Beguines became famous for the quality of their weaving and lace-making. To this may be added a lively interest in serving the poor and devotion to the Eucharist that expressed both a desire for greater affectivity in spirituality and an emphasis on the humanity of Christ. Indeed, even when some Beguines practiced a fierce asceticism, this was motivated less by a rejection of the body than by a desire to imitate the human life of Christ and his sufferings on behalf of humanity. The emphasis on the passion of Christ and on the Eucharist showed itself in a strongly affective mysticism. In this they were often inspired by Franciscan and Cistercian sources – two religious Orders with whom Beguines had close connections. These features were present in someone like Mary of Oignies (b. 1176) who made the area around Liège a center of the new lay spirituality and inspired a reformist priest Jacques de Vitry (later a bishop and papal advisor) to become a supporter and one of the most noted chroniclers of Beguine life. Mary became noted for her visions of Christ while she contemplated the Eucharist. Because of their relative freedom from clerical control, some of their independent spiritual practices, and their production of a vernacular spiritual literature, it was inevitable that the Beguines would attract the suspicion of Church authorities. By the fourteenth century, they were being accused of heresy – especially that people could become one with God and as a consequence may ignore the moral law. A notable figure, Marguerite Porete, was burned as a heretic in Paris in 1310, and the Beguines were condemned by the Council of Vienne (1311–1312). Despite this, Marguerite's book (in English *The Mirror of Simple Souls*) survived to the present day and is now widely accepted as a spiritual classic. Despite an understandable decline after Vienne, and the gradual conversion of larger communities into conventional convents, a few small groups of Beguines survive to the present day in Belgium and the Netherlands.[20]

The mysterious figure of Hadewijch may be taken as a classic example of the mystical strand of Beguine spirituality. We really know very little about Hadewijch. She was Flemish, perhaps from Antwerp, and was probably writing in the first half of the thirteenth century. She was clearly highly educated and familiar with the conventions of courtly love lyrics which may indicate either an aristocratic or a musical background. She also appears to be influenced by Augustine, the Cistercians, and the Victorines. Her undoubted writings are forty-five poems in stanzas, sixteen poems in couplets, thirty-one letters (both of spiritual guidance and spiritual mini-treatises), and fourteen visions. Hadewijch is one of the clearest examples of the Western tradition of love mysticism. Her writing is not systematic but pursues three basic themes: love (both as God's own nature and as the response of the human soul); our relationship with God culminates by entering into an abyss (she even risks speaking of somehow *becoming* God); and participation in the sufferings of Christ. Love is the term that appears most prominently in her poetry. We can only lay hold of God by love, and this is expressed in the language of courtly lover relating to a highborn mistress (God).[21]

Fourteenth-Century Mysticism

It is commonly suggested that the period from 1150 to 1450 saw a great flourishing of mysticism. This needs some qualification. First, according to the researches of the French Jesuit Michel de Certeau, the word "mysticism" (and therefore the idea of a distinct area of spiritual experience or knowledge) only appeared in France during the seventeenth century.[22] Second, while "experience" appears in medieval mystics, for example, as the basis for teaching or authority, a preoccupation with subjective experience in itself was most noticeably reinforced by modern psychology in the late nineteenth century and its application to religious experience in such influential works as William James' *Varieties of Religious Experience* (1902). This later emphasis on "experience" in isolation served to separate mysticism from systems of belief and religious practice. This would have been completely alien to medieval people.[23] It is with these qualifications in mind that it is possible to suggest that the period was an age of mystical flourishing and to talk about the emergence of a "mystical type" of spirituality.

Broadly speaking, two factors favored the increased attention to individual spiritual journeys. The first was the development of an intellectualist approach to theology. In the construction of the "new" theology, philosophical categories (especially those of Aristotle) and a dialectical method came to dominate. Gradually, the new theology with its more "scientific" method led to an inevitable separation of spirituality from theology. The second factor was, as we have seen, the recovery of interest in, and reinterpretation of, the mystical theology of the anonymous sixth-century figure, pseudo-Dionysius.

Within this period, the fourteenth century is particularly rich in major mystical writers. A number of key figures or writings may be taken as significant examples: Eckhart and his disciples Henry Suso and John Tauler, Jan Ruusbroec, Catherine of Siena, and Julian of Norwich.

Eckhart (c. 1260–1328), the German Dominican theologian and preacher, is known only by his academic title of "Meister" or Master. He studied at Cologne and Paris and may have been taught by Albert the Great from whom he gained a taste for the Neoplatonic mysticism of pseudo-Dionysius, tempered by the Aristotelianism of Aquinas. Eckhart is the subject of a great deal of contemporary fascination even outside Christianity because of his paradoxical religious language. On the one hand, there is an absolute abyss separating us from the transcendent God. This leads Eckhart to speak of a necessary negation of our understandings and concepts of "God" in order to touch the divine "ground" itself, what may be called "God beyond God." Yet, at the same time, Eckhart made daring assertions of mystical identity between us and God. He is at his most radically paradoxical in his vernacular German sermons where metaphor is used in contradictory ways to reveal deeper meanings. His obscure language led to suspicions of heresy and the condemnation of some of his teaching – although this is now generally thought to be based on misunderstandings.[24]

Henry Suso (1295–1366) trained as a Dominican at Cologne and then worked largely at Constance and Ulm. He is the most literary of the Dominican trio and left many treatises, letters, and sermons as well as an autobiography. Suso was also a theological mystic, directly influenced by Eckhart's ideas on negativity and on union with God in his *Little Book of Truth* but offering a very different spirituality in his *Little Book of Eternal Wisdom*. This became a devotional classic and has strong elements of love mysticism and Christocentric devotion.[25] Johannes Tauler (c. 1300–1361) was born near Strasburg and as a Dominican was known especially for his preaching, available in a surviving collection of some eighty sermons which later influenced Martin Luther. Tauler "translated" the negative mysticism of Eckhart in terms of a more practical and active spirituality. He spoke of the eruption of the eternal into human life to which the only adequate response was a continual process of conversion and a firm emphasis on our necessary humility before the otherness of God.[26] Eckhart, Suso, and Tauler developed a widespread network of relationships in the Rhineland and beyond with lay men and women, communities of nuns, and above all with groups of Beguines where exchanges of spiritual insight were clearly mutual.

John Ruusbroec (1293–1381) was the most influential and substantial of the Flemish mystics, influenced by the Beguines and especially the works of Hadewijch. Evelyn Underhill describes him as one of the greatest of Christian mystics. Originally a parochial priest in Brussels, at the age of fifty Ruusbroec went with two colleagues to live a secluded life at Groenendaal where they founded a community of Augustinian Canons. Ruusbroec wrote in the same dialect as Hadewijch, and one of his major works, *The Spiritual Espousals*, was written while working in Brussels. At Groenendaal, he built upon this work in a number of other treatises such as *The Sparkling Stone*. Like Hadewijch, Ruusbroec wrote of the contemplative union with God without difference – not as a fusion but as a communion of love. His love mysticism is more theological than devotional and is notable for a strong emphasis on the image of the Trinity in the human soul. Ruusbroec also strongly criticized any tendency to separate contemplation from Christian action, from ethical behavior, or from the sacramental life of the Church.[27]

Catherine of Siena (1347–1380) was a mystical activist and visionary who battled with her family to avoid early marriage and at eighteen became a lay member of the Dominican Third Order living at home. Her precocious spiritual life (apparently visions at six, private vows at seven) and extreme fasting (with anorexic overtones) has attracted unfavorable psychological interpretations. However, Catherine is equally notable for the richness of her spiritual teachings (expressed in many letters and in her *Dialogue*), for her hard work with the sick, poor, and marginalized, and for the impact of her public interventions to bring peace between Italian city states and to persuade Pope Gregory XI to return to Rome from Avignon. In the *Dialogue*, based on her experiences of contemplative union with God, Catherine taught the positive power of human desire which, she wrote, is one of the few ways of touching God.[28]

Julian of Norwich

Julian of Norwich (c. 1342–1417/1420) is a particularly rich example of late medieval mysticism. In the judgment of many, Julian was one of the greatest English theologians and is the most original of the fourteenth-century so-called English mystics who flourished during a period of immense social and religious upheaval (the Black Death, the Hundred Years' War, the Peasants' Revolt, Lollard heresy, and the Great Schism when the Western Church was divided in loyalty to competing Popes). The other major figures are Walter Hilton, Richard Rolle, Margery Kempe, and the anonymous author of *The Cloud of Unknowing*.

We know little about Julian – even her name is taken from the dedication of the Norwich church where she became a solitary (or anchoress).

This happened sometime after an almost mortal illness in 1373 when, over a twenty-four-hour period, she had sixteen visions provoked by the sight of a crucifix in her sick room. Her *Showings* (or *Revelations of Divine Love*) are available in a Short Text and the more famous Long Text (cited as LT), a highly sophisticated but not structurally systematic work of mystical-pastoral theology written after twenty years of contemplative reflection.

The overall teaching of the *Showings* is addressed to all Julian's fellow Christians. "In all this I was greatly moved in love towards my fellow Christians, that they might all see and know the same as I saw, for I wished it to be a comfort to them, for all this vision was shown for all men" (LT, Chapter 8). For Julian, love rather than judgment or anger is God's reality. She begins with her visions of the Passion. The point of these was to find in the broken figure of Jesus the reality of God. Thus in Jesus Christ, all humanity, creation, life, and eternal future are caught up into the very life of God-as-Trinity. "And in the same revelation, suddenly the Trinity filled my heart full of the greatest joy, and I understood that it will be so in heaven without end to all who will come there. For the Trinity is God, God is the Trinity. The Trinity is our maker, the Trinity is our protector, the Trinity is our everlasting lover, the Trinity is our endless joy and our bliss, by our Lord Jesus Christ and in our Lord Jesus Christ" (LT4).

From the vision of Christ on the cross, Julian learned that everything is filled with God and enclosed by God. There is also longing in God, and this quality is part of God's everlasting goodness. "For as truly as there is in God a quality of pity and compassion, so truly there is in God a quality of thirst and longing....And this quality of longing and thirst comes from God's everlasting goodness" (LT31). Because of God's painful longing for us, the longing we feel is our unsatisfied desire for God and God's own desiring acting within us.

In her teaching on God as Mother Julian is fully Trinitarian. Jesus as Mother is not distinguished from the Father as Ruler or Judge – ultimately, the Trinity is our Mother. "And so in our making, God almighty is our loving Father, and God all wisdom is our loving Mother, with the love and the goodness of the Holy Spirit, which is all one God, one Lord" (LT58).

Julian also seeks to articulate something of how God *sees*. Because of this, she offers a radically alternative vision of created reality, including human existence. This results in two striking assertions. First, there is neither blame nor wrath in God (LT45–49). Second, and related to it, sin is "no deed" (LT11). In seeing God in everything (LT11), Julian also sees all things in God and therefore "in all this sin was not shown to me." Later, as she considers how sin hinders her longing for God (LT27), she is taught that she could not see sin as she contemplated the Passion because "it has no kind of substance, no share in being, nor can it be recognized except by the pain caused by it." Sin is the cause both of human pain and of the Passion, and yet "sin is necessary." In the end, God does not "see" sin but only the bliss that will be ours. In God's vision, this is the ultimate truth of human existence, and so Julian, in her God's eye view, cannot see sin even though she knows its effects within human life and experience.

The famous parable of the lord and the servant makes clear (LT51) that everything depends on how we see. In the parable, the servant rushes to do his lord's will but falls into a ditch. There he sees neither his loving lord "nor does he truly see what he himself is in the sight of his loving lord." Indeed, as Julian suggests in the next chapter (LT52), "God sees one way and man sees another way." Essentially, God can only see humanity in the light of his Son. "When Adam fell, God's son fell [into Mary's womb]; because of the true union which was made in heaven, God's Son could not be separated from Adam, for by Adam I understand all mankind" (LT51).

From this standpoint, the story of Adam (the Fall) and of Jesus Christ (the Incarnation) are to be seen as a single reality. The moment of Adam's fall becomes the moment of salvation as well. God looks upon us as we are "in Christ" and therefore sees us in our final integrity: healed, sinless, and glorified. In the light of eternity, we are always in union with God. In summary, this is a theology of the irrevocable love of God in whom there is no blame. The sinfulness and suffering of humankind is transformed by the re-creative work of Jesus our Mother into ultimate endless bliss. In Julian's words, despite the present pain of human existence, "all shall be well and all manner of thing shall be well."[29]

Crossing Spiritual Boundaries: The Influence of Islam

As a corollary to these explorations of late-medieval mysticism, it is fascinating to note the possible impact of Islamic mysticism on Christian spiritual writers, particularly in Spain. It used to be widely assumed by historians that the thirteenth-century Catalan thinker Ramon Llull (c. 1232–1315) learned Arabic merely to try to convert Muslims. It is now accepted that matters were more complicated. There seems to have been a dialogue between Islamic thought and his writings. This is especially true of the influence on Llull of the great Muslim thinker Al-Ghazzali. In his mystical work *The Book of the Lover and Beloved*, Llull explicitly admits that he was inspired by the Sufis. The recent work of Luce López-Baralt also suggests that the Al-Andalus school of Sufism, with its emphasis on spiritual illumination and spiritual drunkenness, influenced the fifteenth-century *alumbrados* and the Franciscan mystics Francisco de Osuna (1497–1541) and Bernardino de Laredo (1482–1540), both of whom in turn influenced Teresa of Avila. Baralt also outlines in some detail a controversial assessment of the impact of Sufism on the language and symbolism of John of the Cross.[30] Another even more speculative possibility is a credible but unproven Sufi influence on the third kind of prayer (prayer of the breath) in the appendix to Ignatius Loyola's *Spiritual Exercises*.

Devotional Spirituality

Devotion is generally associated with feelings rather than ideas, and, in spiritual cultures that value the mind above the body or emotions, religious devotions are often underestimated. Particular spiritual practices that engaged the affective side of religion were characteristically referred to as "popular devotions." There is a sense in which this was, and sometimes still is, thought of as "popular piety" rather than "spirituality." However, studies that give no attention to these practices and sentiments offer a very one-sided approach to the history of spirituality. Equally, a rigid distinction between "high" mystical spirituality and popular devotional spirituality is unhelpful. As the Franciscans and the Beguines both clearly show, devotional themes and practices were often an important backdrop to mystical writings.

One of the most striking elements of Western spirituality in the period from 1150 to 1450 was the rise of devotions and a devotional mentality. Once again, this was the product of the intense religious fervor provoked by reform movements in the Church, the growing laicization of spirituality outside the monasteries, and the spiritual climate in the cities. As literacy increased among lay urban Christians, a notable development was the growing production of devotional manuals. These included collections of saints' lives (such as the classic *Golden Legend* of Jacopo de Voragine), handbooks of prayers (often created to enable a personal appropriation of public liturgy), books of spiritual guidance and instruction, and collections of structured meditations, particularly on the life of Christ. A notable example is the thirteenth-century *Meditationes Vitae Christi* once thought to be written by St Bonaventure and still considered to be from a Franciscan writer. As we shall see in Chapter 5, manuals of meditation and instructions on meditative practice played an even more central role in the influential spiritual reform movement from the mid-fourteenth century onwards, the *Devotio Moderna*.

Apart from written sources, devotional spirituality was expressed through activities such as pilgrimage journeys (primarily to the Holy Land but also places such as Rome, Compostella, or Canterbury), processions (e.g. of the Blessed Sacrament), the production of religious art and the veneration of religious statues or icons in churches or on city streets, visits to shrines containing the relics of saints, and outdoor religious dramas such as the famous English Mystery plays. Apart from Eucharistic processions, for example, associated with the feast-day of Corpus Christi, three other devotional focuses or practices emerged in this period and survive to the present day: the Christmas crib, the rosary, and the Stations of the Cross. The crib (apparently derived from Francis of Assisi) expresses a devotion to the doctrine of the Incarnation – that is, God become human in the person of Jesus. The rosary is associated both with the development of devotion to Mary and also with meditations on the life of Christ and salvation history. The Stations reflects both a devotion to the passion of Christ and also a focus on the holy places associated with the life of Christ provoked by pilgrimage to the Holy Land and by the Crusades.

Thematically, apart from devotion to saints which had a long pedigree, devotional spirituality in this period derived especially from a growing emphasis on the humanity of Christ. This expanded into an emphasis on the suffering and Passion, on devotion to Mary, the source of Christ's humanity, and on liturgical and mystical devotion to the Eucharist.[31]

Spirituality and Eastern Christianity

As we saw in Chapter 3, an important element of Eastern Christian spirituality is the tradition of icons. Such images, whether painted on wooden panels or frescoes and mosaics on the walls of churches, are deemed to be a medium of direct engagement or communion with God and the saints (expressed powerfully in the fact that the figure depicted faces the viewer and gazes upon the believer directly), a source of sanctification or grace, and a privileged window onto a sacred realm. Iconographers do not see their role as being artistically innovative but seek to pass on a quasi-sacramental tradition whose way of production is in the context of prayer and whose purpose is communion with the divine.

Alongside what might be called "the way of images" (which embraces liturgical ritual and music as well as icons), there is also an important strand of Eastern spirituality that seeks to transcend thought and image. From its origins in the desert monastic quest for *hēsychia* or stillness, there gradually arose a way of prayer to aid inner calm. In broad terms, this developed at the monastery of St Catherine at Mount Sinai and was further promoted by John Climacus in the seventh century, who specifically taught the link between breathing and the name of Jesus. As we have already noted, the classic form of the "Jesus Prayer" or Prayer of the Name in time became a phrase based on Matthew 9, 27, "Lord Jesus Christ, Son of God, have mercy on me a sinner." The hesychast tradition of spirituality was still further refined by Symeon the New Theologian (949–1022). While a government official in Constantinople, Symeon undertook lengthy periods of quiet prayer, influenced by early monastic teachings. At one point, he had an experience of being suffused by light which he took to be a participation in divine light. Symeon and other writers linked this physical phenomenon to the transfiguration of Jesus on Mount Tabor. Symeon became a monk and his writings had a particular influence on the communities of monks which grew up on the Greek peninsula of Mount Athos.[32]

The hesychast tradition had its opponents, provoked in part by the exaggerated language used of experiences of union with God by some Athonite monks. However, an important defender of the tradition, and mystical theologian in his own right, was Gregory Palamas (1296–1359). Gregory entered one of the monasteries on Mount Athos aged twenty and was thoroughly steeped in the hesychast tradition. After a period away because of Turkish raids, he returned to Athos in 1331 when he began to publish his teachings. His most famous work was the *Triads for the Defence of the Holy Hesychasts* – both an explanation and theological defense of the whole tradition.[33] The critical issue in the debate between Gregory and the opponents of hesychasm was whether it was possible to experience the immediate presence of God. Gregory justified his affirmative answer by a famous theological distinction in reference to God between the divine essence (necessarily beyond human experience or knowledge) and God's "energies" (or action) which involve a direct and immediate presence of God in the world. Additionally, Gregory believed, like Symeon, that the mystical experience of God somehow transformed the body of the contemplative so that mystical illumination actually became a physical participation in the divine light itself.

Gregory's views were vindicated by a number of Church councils, and he ended as the Archbishop of Thessalonika.

Sadly, spirituality was one expression of the growing separation of Eastern and Western Christianity which, in so many other respects, was cultural and political. The theological speculations of Gregory Palamas did not fit easily with the mainstream of Western theology and were viewed with suspicion. Equally, the positive view of the body in hesychast spirituality did not correspond with a tendency in Western mysticism to suggest that the body had to be transcended. The so-called Great Schism of 1054 (involving mutual excommunications by Rome and Constantinople) can be seen as a relatively minor event that grew in symbolic importance only with hindsight. It was the growing tensions during the crusade period and especially the inexcusable sack of Constantinople in 1204 during the Fourth Crusade (and subsequent attempts to Westernize the Byzantine Church) that caused far more long-lasting damage. Various attempts to heal the wounds in the late thirteenth century and again at the Council of Florence in 1439 did not last, and the fall of Constantinople to the Turks in 1453 saw not only the end of the Byzantine Empire but the cementing of deep suspicions of the West by Orthodox Christians that are only slowly being overcome in the present day.

The Renaissance

In the century from about 1350 to 1450 and beyond, late medieval Western spirituality was touched in particular by the Renaissance. The Renaissance and its intellectual and artistic humanism are rarely considered in histories of Christian spirituality. This is unfortunate as it misunderstands both the Renaissance and the nature of spirituality. Broadly speaking, the Renaissance was the monumental intellectual and aesthetic movement that swept the Italian cities of the fourteenth century and eventually spread across the Alps. The apparent lack of interest in traditional theological sources, a re-engagement with the classical, especially ancient Roman, world, and the notion that the human was a proper object of study (hence, "humanism") misled some people into believing that the Renaissance was a kind of neo-pagan retreat from Christian religion. This is a caricature.

Francesco Petrarca (Petrarch 1304–1374) was one of the greatest figures of the Renaissance and one of the earliest agents in the recovery of classical culture. He was also deeply interested in theology but attacked the arid rationalism of the late-scholasticism of his time. As with other humanists, Petrarch was repelled by the sterility of much contemporary religion and sought to redirect attention away from abstractions towards a proper attention to the human and the aesthetic. This was a spiritual principle because for Petrarch, an emphasis on logic and intellectual order actually distracted people from God's action in the world, from the glory of human nature in the image of God, and fostered a religious climate that was irrelevant to everyday human experience. Petrarch was strongly influenced by Augustine, especially his *Confessions* which showed Augustine as a master of the classical rhetoric of his times. Petrarch and other humanists also emphasized the importance of rhetoric – not purely as a literary device but because of its persuasive power. Unlike late-scholastic theology, rhetoric penetrated the heart, transformed the will, aroused an emotional response, and so inspired action. The Renaissance emphasis on a return to ancient texts also inspired a concern for the authenticity of biblical texts. Petrarch, for example, compiled copious notes on the New Testament and emphasized the importance of dealing with biblical texts in their original languages.

In many respects, the city of Florence under the patronage of the Medici family was a kind of center of the Renaissance. Here, Marsilio Ficino (1433–1499) was commissioned to translate the whole of Plato's works into Latin. In this enterprise, the deeply spiritual Ficino revived the concept that the philosopher was a kind of spiritual guide. For Ficino, humanism was not in any way opposed to Christianity but, on the contrary, was to be a medium for the renewal of true religion.

The study of humanity or of the created order directed attention to what we would call both the sciences and the arts. As humans, we share in the creative activity of God. Thus, artists, architects, and engineers such as Michelangelo or Leonardo da Vinci were no mere craftspeople but were elevated to the rank of active co-creators with God. For humanists, the human personality was not to be reduced to the intellect ruled by higher mental powers. In religious terms, the search for God was also affective and could validly find expression in art and poetry. A remarkably positive view of the human body contrasted with an excessive emphasis on ascetic mortification as the measure of true spirituality. In terms of religious art, the emphasis was ever more strongly on the humanity of Christ, and artists dramatized the most humanly poignant episodes of his life. In such a richly incarnational framework, aesthetics itself became a form of spiritual discourse.[34]

Conclusion

Overall, the period from the late fourteenth century to the eruption of the Reformation in the early sixteenth century can best be described as one of slow fragmentation in Western Christianity. Above all, the period witnessed the slow death of what has been called "the medieval synthesis" – with its coherent worldview, its sense of a single "Christendom," its architectonic philosophical-theological system, its relatively stable social hierarchy, and carefully structured sense of authority based on a balance between Church and political Empire. Arguably the synthesis was never as coherent in reality as it has sometimes been portrayed, but the experience of late medieval fragmentation seems real enough. From 1350 to 1500, we only have to think of the devastating list: the Black Death, the Hundred Years' War, the gradual breakdown of the feudal system and the growing dominance of wealthy and educated urban classes, the decline of the Holy Roman Empire and the emergence of new nationalisms, the sapping of morale provoked by the Great Schism, the intellectual aridity of much late medieval theology, and the wider sense of a religious system that had run out of steam and was in need of major reform.

In this climate, it is not surprising that spirituality not only became increasingly laicized but also increasingly favored personal interior experience over ecclesiastical authority systems. The energy now lay with movements of evangelical and biblical piety often linked to calls for reform in the Church. It was the inability of the Church institution to respond speedily or adequately enough on either a spiritual or a structural level to both the criticisms and the fervor that made the final breakdown of medieval Christianity irreversible.

Notes

1   On the impact of the Gregorian Reform on spirituality, see, Karl Morrison, "The Gregorian reform" in Bernard McGinn, John Meyendorff, and Jean Leclercq, eds., *Christian Spirituality: Origins to the Twelfth Century*, New York: Crossroad Publishing, 1985, pp. 177–193. On the Twelfth-Century Renaissance, see Robert Benson, Giles Constable, and Carol Lanham, eds., *Renaissance and Renewal in the Twelfth Century*, Toronto: University of Toronto Press, 1991; and R.W. Southern, *Medieval Humanism and Other Studies*, Oxford: Basil Blackwell, 1970; and Caroline

Walker Bynum, *Jesus as Mother: Studies in the Spirituality of the High Middle Ages*, Berkeley: University of California Press, 1984, Introduction and Chapter 3.

2   See Marjorie Reeves, *Joachim of Fiore and the Prophetic Future*, London: SPCK, 1976.

3   English translation in Bernard McGinn, ed., *Apocalyptic Spirituality – Treatises and Letters of Lactantius, Adso of Montier-en-Der, Joachim of Fiore, The Spiritual Franciscans, Savanarola*, New York: Paulist Press, 1979, pp. 142–148.

4   On canonical spirituality, see Bynum, *Jesus as Mother*, Chapter 1. On the Victorines see Stephen Chase, *Contemplation and Compassion: The Victorine Tradition*, London: Darton Longman & Todd and New York: Orbis Books, 2003.

5   See Bynum, *Jesus as Mother*, pp. 82–109.

6   See Colleen McDannell and Bernhard Lang, *Heaven, A History*, New Haven: Yale University Press, 1988, pp. 70–80.

7   Georges Duby, *The Age of the Cathedrals: Art and Society 980–1420*, Chicago: University of Chicago Press, 1981, p. 95.

8   See Arnold Berleant, *The Aesthetics of Environment*, Philadelphia: Temple University Press, 1992, p. 62.

9   C. Frugoni, *A Distant City: Images of Urban Experience in the Medieval World*, Princeton: Princeton University Press, 1991, p. 27.

10   On the development of medieval cities see Jacques Le Goff, *Medieval Civilisation*, Oxford: Blackwell, 1988, pp. 70–78.

11   See Peter Raedts, "The medieval city as a holy place" in Charles Caspers and Marc Schneiders, eds., *Omnes Circumadstantes: Contributions Towards a History of the Role of the People in the Liturgy*, Kampen: Uitgeversmaatschappij J.H. Kok, 1990, pp. 144–154.

12   See Nicola Cortone and Nino Lavermicocca, *Santi di strada: Le edicole religiose della città vecchia di Bari*, 5 vols., Bari: Edizione BA Graphis, 2001–2003.

13   See Peter Ackroyd, *The Life of Thomas More*, London: Random House, 1999, p. 111.

14   For recent studies of the Beguines see, Walter Simons, *Cities of Ladies: Beguine Communities in the Medieval Low Countries 1200–1565*, Philadelphia: University of Pennsylvania Press, 2001; Saskia Murk-Jansen, *Brides in the Desert: The Spirituality of the Beguines*. Traditions of Christian Spirituality, London: Darton Longman & Todd and New York: Orbis Books, 1998; and Philip Sheldrake, "Context and conflicts: the Beguines" in *Spirituality and History*, New York: Crossroad, 1992.

15   On the mendicant orders and their spiritualities, see Jill Raitt, ed., "The mendicants" in *Christian Spirituality II: High Middle Ages*

and Reformation, New York: Crossroad Publishing, 1987 and C.H. Lawrence, *The Friars: The Impact of the Early Mendicant Movement on Western Society*, London: Longman, 1994.

16   On Dominican spirituality, see Richard Woods, *Mysticism and Prophecy: The Dominican Tradition*, London: Darton Longman & Todd and New York: Orbis Books, 1998 and Simon Tugwell, ed., *Early Dominicans: Selected Writings*, Classics of Western Spirituality, New York: Paulist Press, 1982.

17   Translated from the medieval Italian by Frances Teresa OSC in *Living the Incarnation: Praying with Francis and Clare of Assisi*, London: Darton Longman & Todd, 1993, p. 129.

18   For early Franciscan texts (including the texts cited in this chapter), see Regis Armstrong and Ignatius Brady, eds., *Francis and Clare: The Complete Works*, New York: Paulist Press, 1982. On general Franciscan spirituality, see W. Short, *Poverty and Joy: The Franciscan Tradition*, London: Darton Longman & Todd and New York: Orbis Books, 1999; Jacques Le Goff, *Saint Francis of Assisi*, English translation, London: Routledge, 2004 [1999]; and Marco Bartoli, *Clare of Assisi*, English translation London: Darton Longman & Todd, 1993 [1989].

19   See Ewert Cousins, ed., *Bonaventure – The Soul's Journey into God, The Tree of Life, The Life of St Francis*, New York: Paulist Press, 1978.

20   On the Beguines and their spirituality, see C. Hart, ed., *Hadewijch: The Complete works*, Classics of Western Spirituality, New York: Paulist Press, 1980; E. Babinsky, ed., *Marguerite Porete: The Mirror of Simple Souls*, Classics of Western Spirituality, New York: Paulist Press, 1993; Murk-Jansen, *Brides in the Desert*; and Sheldrake, *Spirituality and History*, Chapter 6.

21   Columba Hart, ed., *Hadewijch – The Complete Works*, New York: Paulist Press, 1980.

22   Michel de Certeau, *The Mystic Fable: The Sixteenth and Seventeenth Centuries*, Chicago: University of Chicago Press, 1992.

23   For critical commentaries on the experientialist turn in understandings of mysticism see Denys Turner, *The Darkness of God: Negativity in Christian Mysticism*, Cambridge: Cambridge University Press, 1995 and Bernard McGinn, *The Foundations of Mysticism: Origins to the Fifth Century*, New York: Crossroad Publishing, 1991, especially General Introduction and Appendix.

24   B. McGinn and E. Colledge, eds., *Meister Eckhart: The Essential Sermons, Commentaries, Treatises and Defense*, New York: Paulist Press, 1985 and B. McGinn and F. Tobin, eds., *Meister Eckhart: Teacher and Preacher*, New York: Paulist Press, 1987. See also, B. McGinn, *The Mystical Thought of Meister Eckhart*, New York: Crossroad Publishing, 2001.

25   F. Tobin, ed., *Henry Suso: The Exemplar, with Two German Sermons*, New York: Paulist Press, 1989.

26   M. Shrady, ed., *Johannes Tauler: Sermons*, New York: Paulist Press, 1985.

27   J. Wiseman, ed., *John Ruusbroec: The Spiritual Espousals and Other Works*, New York: Paulist Press, 1985.

28   S. Noffke, ed., *Catherine of Siena: The Dialogue*, New York: Paulist Press, 1980.

29   E. Colledge and J. Walsh, eds., *Julian of Norwich: Showings*, New York: Paulist Press, 1978. For a wider study of the English mystics, see Joan Nuth, *God's Loves in an Age of Anxiety: The Medieval English Mystics*, London: Darton Longman & Todd and Maryknoll: Orbis Books, 2001.

30   See, L. López-Baralt, *San Juan de la Cruz y el Islam: Estudios sobre las filiaciones semíticas de su literatura mística*, Madrid: Hiperion, 1990 and *The Sufi "trobar clus" and Spanish Mysticism: A Shared Symbolism*, Lahore: Iqbal Academy, 2000. Some John of the Cross scholars suspect that Baralt reads too much into the material but nevertheless believe there may be some Islamic influences.

31   See Richard Kieckhefer, "Major currents in late medieval devotion," Ewert Cousins "The humanity and the Passion of Christ," and Elizabeth Johnson "Marian devotion in the Western Church" in Jill Raitt, ed., *Christian Spirituality: High Middle Ages & Reformation*, New York: Crossroad Publishing, 1987.

32   C.J. de Catanzaro, ed., *Symeon the New Theologian: The Discourses*, New York: Paulist Press, 1980.

33   N. Gendle, ed., *Gregory Palamas: The Triads*, New York: Paulist Press, 1983.

34   There are few writings that deal directly with the spirituality of the Renaissance or Christian humanism. One useful survey essay (but limited to Italy) is William J. Bouwsma, "The spirituality of Renaissance humanism" in Jill Raitt, ed., *Christian Spirituality II: High Middle Ages and Reformation*, New York: Crossroad Publishing, 1987.

Chapter 5

Spiritualities in the Age of Reformations: 1450–1700

1300–1378	Ludolph of Saxony lives: Carthusian author of *Life of Christ*
1340–1384	Gerard Groote lives: a leader of the devotio moderna movement
1433–1503	Nilus Sorsky lives: Russian monastic founder
1440–1515	Joseph Volotsky lives: Russian monastic founder
1469–1536	Desiderius Erasmus lives: Christian humanist and reformer
1483–1546	Martin Luther lives: originator of German Reformation
c. 1484–1566	Bartolomé de las Casas lives: Spanish Dominican, Bishop of Chiapas, Mexico, and social reformer
1484–1531	Ulrich Zwingli lives: Swiss reformer
c. 1488–1524	Thomas Müntzer lives: leading figure in the Radical Reformation
c. 1490–1527	Hans Hut lives: leading figure in the Radical Reformation
1491–1556	Ignatius Loyola lives: author of the Spiritual Exercises, founder of Jesuit Order
1492	Christopher Columbus reaches the Americas. Fall of Granada and end of Muslim Al-Andalus
1497–1560	Philip Melanchthon lives: collaborator of Martin Luther
1509–1564	John Calvin lives: leading French reformer. *Institutes of the Christian Religion* written 1536
1515–1582	Teresa of Avila lives: Carmelite reformer, mystic, and writer
1521	Prague Manifesto
1524	Peasants' War in Germany
c. 1525	Anabaptist movement begins

Spirituality: A Brief History, Second Edition. Philip Sheldrake.
© 2013 John Wiley & Sons, Ltd. Published 2013 by John Wiley & Sons, Ltd.

1529	Luther's Small Catechism
1530	Augsburg Confession
1542–1591	John of the Cross lives: Carmelite mystic and major Spanish poet
1545–1563	Council of Trent – to counter Protestantism and to reform Western Church
1552	Thomas Cranmer's Book of Common Prayer
1552–1610	Matteo Ricci lives: Jesuit explorer in China
1556–1621	Johann Arndt lives: leading Lutheran Pietist
1560–1609	Jacob Arminius lives: Dutch Reformed theologian
1567–1622	Francis de Sales lives: Bishop of Geneva and influential spiritual writer
1572–1641	Jeanne de Chantal lives: collaborator of St Francis de Sales and founder of the Order of the Visitation
1572–1631	John Donne lives: leading poet, preacher, and Dean of St Paul's Cathedral
1572–1656	Roberto de Nobili lives: Jesuit missionary to India
1574–1629	Pierre de Bérulle lives: founder of the French Oratory, Cardinal, reformer
1580	Book of Concord: statement of Lutheran doctrine
1580–1660	Vincent de Paul lives: preacher, worked with the poor, religious founder
1585–1645	Mary Ward lives: English founder of Ignatian-inspired women's community
1585–1638	Cornelius Jansen lives: bishop of Ypres, originator of Jansenist theory
1586–1617	Rose of Lima lives: first canonized Latin American saint
1591–1660	Louise de Marillac lives: collaborator of St Vincent de Paul and founder of the Daughters of Charity
1594–1597	Richard Hooker's *Laws of Ecclesiastical Polity*
1599	Official Directory of Ignatius Loyola's Spiritual Exercises
1604–1664	Isaac Ambrose lives: Puritan spiritual writer
1607	Bishop Joseph Hall's The Arte of Divine Meditation
1608–1657	Jean-Jacques Olier lives: founder of the Sulpicians
1611	Bishop Bayley's *The Practice of Piety*
1615–1691	Richard Baxter lives: Puritan theologian, hymn writer, and poet
1620	Puritans found colony of Massachusetts
1621–1695	Henry Vaughan lives: Metaphysical poet and Anglican spiritual writer
1624–1691	George Fox lives: founder of the Quakers

1627–1704	Jacques-Bénigne Bossuet lives: bishop, preacher, and spiritual writer
1627	Bishop John Cosin's *A Collection of Private Devotions*
1633	George Herbert's poetic collection, *The Temple*, published
1636–1674	Thomas Traherne lives: Anglican priest, poet, and spiritual writer
1649–1660	English Commonwealth (Republic)
1650	Bishop Jeremy Taylor's *The Rule and Exercises of Holy Living*
1678	John Bunyan's *The Pilgrim's Progress*

The period from the mid-fifteenth to the end of the seventeenth century is complex. The medieval religious world broke apart and gave birth to the early modern era. The Renaissance opened up new ways of knowledge. The political landscape of Europe changed as the nation state was born. The feudal system finally collapsed. A crisis of religious authority began with the Great Schism and continued throughout the fifteenth century. New lay spiritual movements appeared alongside calls for Church reform. Out of all this grew the Reformation. At the same time, a relatively self-contained Europe opened up to new worlds with the so-called discovery of the Americas by Columbus in 1492. Despite the fall of Muslim Granada in the same year, Christian Europe confronted Islam through the medium of the Ottoman Turks after the fall of Constantinople (1453) and throughout the sixteenth century.

Nowadays, historians talk less about a "Reformation" and a "Counter-Reformation" and more about Protestant and Catholic Reformations. This reminds us that the reform movement predates Martin Luther, and that both Catholic and Protestant Christianity inherited this impulse. When did the Reformation begin and end? The institutional view starts with Luther and concludes with the end of the wars of religion in 1648. However, from the grassroots perspective, the impact of the Reformation only became definitive by about 1600 and was not complete until about 1700. During this period, a third kind of spirituality emerged alongside the monastic and mystical types. This can be called the "active-practical" type which emphasized finding God in everyday life and the practical service of other people – creating a spiritual climate favorable to lay Christians.

Seeds of Reform: The Devotio Moderna _and_ Christian Humanism

Two important strands of late-medieval spirituality fed into the Reformation: the _devotio moderna_ and Christian humanism. The _devotio moderna_ ("modern devotion") flourished in Flanders and the Netherlands from the late fourteenth century onwards. This movement represented urban middle class values and attracted educated laypeople and reform-minded clergy. The spirituality was an interesting mixture with an emphasis on education while being somewhat anti-intellectual. Equally, although the _devotio_ owed something to Flemish mysticism, it preferred quiet piety to mystical enthusiasm.

An originator of the movement was Gerard Groote of Deventer (1340–1384) who underwent conversion as a young man and became critical of clerical materialism. As a preaching deacon in Utrecht, he espoused a disciplined Christ-centered piety and supported moderate Church reform. Groote knew the mystic John Ruusbroec and translated some of his works into Latin. He produced writings addressed to laity and created a vernacular Book of Hours which was widely used. He shared with Christian humanists a high view of education to encourage a virtuous life. Groote emphasized scripture as the basis of person-centered educational method, the importance of individual moral formation, and the inculcation of a strong sense of community. The Brothers of the Common Life (founded by Groote and his priest-friend Florens Radewijns) were groups of clergy and laymen who lived in community inspired by the early Christian community but without a rule or vows. Later, groups of women, Sisters of the Common Life, emerged. The Brothers became involved in Groote's educational philosophy, though rarely ran schools. They acted as school governors and administered parallel boarding hostels offering spiritual guidance and tutoring. In addition, the _devotio_ inspired reform in religious life – especially new contemplative-pastoral communities of Canons and Canonesses of St Augustine, the most famous of which was the Windesheim Congregation.

The _devotio moderna_ produced a literary culture, and many texts were disseminated, for example, by Ruusbroec, Suso, Tauler, and Ludolph of Saxony (1300–1378), whose _Life of Christ_ (a composite text based on the gospels) had a significant influence on Ignatius Loyola, the sixteenth-century author of the _Spiritual Exercises_. The _devotio moderna_ also promoted methodical approaches to prayer – for example, meditation manuals by Radewijns and Gerard van Zutphen. The most famous work of the movement was the *Imitation of Christ* attributed to Thomas à Kempis. Subsequently, the book became a popular classic in both Catholic and Protestant circles well into the twentieth century.[1] In general, the evangelical piety and lay emphasis of the movement had a significant influence on both Protestant and Catholic Reformations.

A second form of late medieval spirituality that also had a significant impact on the Reformation was Christian humanism. This offered a new ideal of the Christian life that spoke more effectively to a lay world. Outside Renaissance Italy, the most influential figure was Desiderius Erasmus (1469–1536), a priest, theologian, and reformer. His acerbic criticisms of clerical ignorance and popular superstition mask his serious evangelical spirituality. His primary concern was to revive Christian virtue, and in this spirit he composed the *Enchiridion* or *Handbook of the Christian Soldier*, editions of patristic texts, and his critical edition of the Greek New Testament. For Erasmus, true piety must give proper attention to the Bible. With his English friends John Colet, Dean of St Paul's in London, and Sir Thomas More, later Chancellor of England and Catholic martyr, Erasmus sought to cultivate "the philosophy of Christ" – a biblically and ethically based piety. Erasmus died in Basle, a Catholic in a predominantly Protestant city.[2]

Both the *devotio moderna* and Erasmian humanism underlined the desire for reform of the Church. The tragedy was that this intense desire was matched only by half-hearted efforts on the part of Church leadership. The resulting frustration led some reformers to take radical positions where a fragmentation of the Church became almost inevitable.

The Crisis of Medieval Spirituality

In broad terms, the sixteenth-century Reformations were supported by people who sought a religion of the heart in place of formalism and an over-reliance on externals. Erasmus is indicative. In broad terms, he criticized a stress on externals (a religion of "works") and advocated a spirituality that was more personal and meditative. By externals, Erasmus and his friends meant an unbalanced reliance on rituals, veneration of relics and invocation of the saints, processions and pilgrimages, Passion devotion, and the excessive practice of penances. The humanists detected at the heart of these a deeper spiritual malaise that reinforced reliance on human effort rather than on God's grace and also provoked despondency. To put it simply, the spirituality that Erasmus critiqued was driven by fear of failure and of damnation.

In different ways, the spiritual crisis of Martin Luther (icon of the Protestant Reformation) and the temptation to despair of the newly converted Ignatius Loyola (icon of the Catholic Reformation) derived from the same source. Both men experienced futility born of an inability, despite intense ascetic practice, to know for certain that they were acceptable to God. Each man sought to escape the vicious circle by exploring a different vision of the spiritual life.

Spirituality and the Lutheran Reformation

Martin Luther (1483–1546) was influenced as a youth by the Brothers of the Common Life and entered the reformed Augustinian friars becoming a professor of New Testament at Wittenberg. Luther first provoked debate about reform when he reputedly posted ninety-five theses on the door of Wittenberg Castle Church in 1517. This led to conflict with Church authority. By 1519, Luther had denied the supreme authority of the papacy, was censured in 1520, and formally excommunicated in 1521. Over the next few years, he began to translate the Bible into German (completed 1534) and further developed a "reformed" theology and programme of Church renewal. Returning to Wittenberg from exile to confront more radical reformers, he resumed his university post and only finally left the Augustinian Order in 1524, marrying the following year.

The best known of Luther's 1517 theses concerned the sale of "indulgences," that is, a way of supposedly obtaining remission of years in Purgatory on behalf of dead relatives. Apart from objecting to the sale of "spiritual goods," Luther critiqued the notion that God's forgiveness was influenced by human actions. How can we be sure of God's mercy and be freed from anxiety about meriting God's favor? Luther concluded that while human actions ("good works") were valueless as offerings to God, they could be seen as an expression of gratitude for God's freely given forgiveness.

Luther's doctrine of justification by faith derived from his reading of St Paul's letters. This placed scriptural authority over the authority of Church tradition. Luther followed this by advocating the reform of spiritual practices that contradicted theological fundamentals. The keys to authentic spirituality were, first, being clear about human sinfulness yet also about God's generous forgiveness and, second, having regular access to the means of God's grace – that is, the scriptures and the sacraments. The Eucharist moved from being a ritual action passively observed to something in which all Christians participated by hearing the scriptures in their own language and by regularly receiving Communion. Despite a revised doctrine of "real presence," Communion was a genuine participation in the life of Christ. While rejecting the veneration of relics and reliance on the intercessory power of Mary and the saints, Luther retained individual confession and defended religious art and music against the iconoclasts.

Luther rejected a two-tier view of holiness (where special lifestyles were "superior") in favor of the holiness of the everyday life of work, family, and citizenship. Thus, all Christians had a common vocation – including ministering to others (priesthood of all believers) – while the ordained retained particular *roles* rather than special status. However, Luther did not support the view that God bypassed human mediation in favor of direct contact with individual believers. Church life remained a vital source of spirituality. Books of homilies were produced to be read in church or at home. The 1522 *Little Prayer Book* offered prayers to a lay readership that reflected the liturgical year, the phases of life, and the teachings of Luther's Catechism. The 1526 German Mass made vernacular hymns or chorales central to congregational worship. Although Luther had an interest in medieval mystical teachings (such as those of Tauler), and taught a kind of mystical participation in Christ by faith, he rejected Neoplatonic mysticism with its emphasis on "ascent" away from material existence.

Luther's close colleague, Philip Melanchthon (1497–1560), was influenced by Christian humanism and was one of the most learned people of his age. Melanchthon remained closer than Luther to Catholic understandings of human cooperation with God and less concerned about the negative impact of rituals.

Lutheranism after Luther took on a variety of forms ranging from "Catholic" structures and liturgy in Sweden to more "Evangelical" Pietism in the seventeenth and eighteenth centuries. However, at the heart of Lutheran spirituality were common texts that embodied its values such as the Augsburg Confession of 1530, Luther's 1529 *Small Catechism*, and after Luther's death, at a time of greater doctrinal emphasis, *The Book of Concord* of 1580. The Lutheran strand of Protestantism dominated in Germany from where it spread to Scandinavia and around the Baltic. One of the best known examples of Lutheran spirituality in the early seventeenth century is the Christocentric, mystical piety of Johann Arndt's *True Christianity* which anticipated aspects of Pietism.[3] Needless to say, for many people the most beautiful expression of Lutheran spirituality is its rich musical tradition, with such composers as Schütz, Buxtehude, and the genius of Bach.[4]

John Calvin and Reformed Spirituality

The Frenchman John Calvin (1509–1564) originally converted to Lutheran ideas while studying at Paris where he overlapped with the future founder of the Jesuits, Ignatius Loyola. Forced to leave Paris, Calvin was persuaded to assist with the reformation in Geneva where he remained until he died, apart from a short period in Strasbourg. Unlike Luther, Calvin was influenced by humanism and was an admirer of Erasmus. He was also inspired by Martin Bucer, the leading Lutheran in Strasbourg, and was deeply read in the early Church Fathers.

Calvin is perhaps the most influential Reformation leader, and his theology was principally developed in his classic, the *Institutes of the Christian Religion* (1539, subsequently revised), as well as in scriptural commentaries and theological treatises.[5] Calvin shared with Luther a belief in human sinfulness and in the impossibility of fulfilling God's requirements by human effort. Yet, Calvin, unlike Luther, believed that the law of God was more than a matter of keeping human depravity under control. The moral teaching of the Bible also had a positive function in that there was a genuine process of spiritual growth or "sanctification" where the believer is drawn into Christ by the Holy Spirit.

Calvin's spirituality has three principal characteristics – it is in some sense mystical, it is corporate, and it is social. First, Calvin had a sense of a mystical union between the believer and Christ. On the one hand, Calvin was an austere man both personally and in his preference for simple worship and dislike of complex hierarchies. At the same time, he had a positive view of human emotions and taught a heartfelt religiosity. In some ways, he shared with apophatic medieval mysticism a degree of skepticism about the capacity of the intellect to grasp the transcendence of God. As the *Institutes* suggest, true knowledge of God consists in a union of love. God is not merely judge but also gently attracts the believer.

Second, Calvin's spirituality is corporate. He had a high view of the Church. To be converted is to be received into the common life of the community. In one sense, Calvin continued the work of the earlier Swiss reformer Ulrich Zwingli (1484–1531), but he was less individualistic and interiorized in his religiosity. He also differed from Zwingli in his theology of the Eucharist. Calvin inherited a pattern of quarterly celebrations of the Lord's Supper but struggled unsuccessfully to have weekly celebrations in Geneva. While rejecting what he took to be the excessively material language of both Catholic and Lutheran positions, Calvin taught the notion of a "virtual presence" by which the power of Christ was united to the communicant by the work of the Spirit.

Third, Calvin's spirituality engaged strongly with society. Particularly in Geneva, spirituality became a public matter. Geneva was intended to be a Christian state in which citizenship and spirituality infused each other. The role of magistrates and elders was to administer faithfully the covenant between God and Christian citizens. A moral and spiritual life touched all elements of existence – public and personal. Behind this lay a sense that the Spirit of God was at work in the world and in all human activities.

While Calvin accepted the fundamental mark of Protestant Reformation spirituality, that God initiates and accomplishes everything in the work of salvation, the notion of human cooperation with God reappeared in Calvinist spirituality in the thinking of Jacobus Arminius (1560–1609), a Dutch theologian. It was this more open, "Arminian" Calvinism that influenced the Church of England in the early seventeenth century. During the seventeenth century, some of the richest expressions of Reformed spirituality are to be found in English Puritanism which will be considered later. Meanwhile, Calvinism was prominent in large parts of Switzerland and the Netherlands and became the state religion in Scotland. It also had a significant presence in other countries, especially France where its adherents were known as Huguenots.[6]

The Radical Reformation: Anabaptist Spirituality

A third stream of reformers, the Anabaptists, is often overlooked in traditional histories of spirituality. Their name refers to the practice of adult "believers" baptism. Because they had no single founder and little in the way of formal organization, it is difficult to say precisely when Anabaptists began. However, from around 1525 (the first recorded adult baptism) groups spread up and down the Rhine from Switzerland to the Netherlands with other pockets in Austria and Moravia. The tradition survives to this day among the Amish, Mennonites, and Hutterites. Mainly because of their radical simplicity and refusal to support secular authority, the Anabaptists were severely persecuted by mainstream Protestants as well as by Catholics. Thousands were martyred during the sixteenth century. This so-called Radical Reformation has been described as the "Protestantism of the poor."

In its early period, the movement included a version of apocalypticism which, as always, involved intense fervor concerning the imminent second coming of Christ and the inauguration of a new age. This was particularly present in such figures as Thomas Müntzer and Hans Hut. Originally a follower of Martin Luther, Müntzer parted company with Luther over his belief in continued revelation and the priority of radical prophecy. Interestingly, he had a strong theological and devotional attachment to the Virgin Mary, and her Magnificat from the Gospel of Luke was one of his favorite texts. His Prague Manifesto (1521) is an explicitly apocalyptic work. He described himself as the new Daniel in reference to another favorite text, the Book of Daniel in the Hebrew scriptures. Müntzer opposed the prevailing social order (affirming that all things are in common) and participated in the Peasants War of 1524. After its failure in the following year, he was imprisoned and executed. Hans Hut echoed Müntzer in his prophetic utterances and saw the arrival of the Muslim Turks at the gates of Vienna as a sign of Christ's imminent return. Like Müntzer, in his preaching Hut drew on the Book of Daniel and also on the Book of Revelation.

The original Anabaptist tradition had four important characteristics. First, adult faith rather than infant reception into the Church implied a voluntary process based on conversion with a related sense that God turned away no one who sincerely repented. This did not sit well with Lutheranism or Calvinism. Second, the inner process of spiritual transformation led not to a purely interior spirituality but to an outward change of life based on a radical interpretation of New Testament teachings. The sharing of material goods with those less fortunate was expected. The strict discipline of Anabaptist communities meant that back sliders were "shunned" until they amended their lives. Simplicity of life also extended to worship. At times, the mutual washing of feet was practiced. The Lord's Supper was viewed as a form of covenant renewal with each other and with Christ, celebrated in homes or in common buildings rather than in formal churches. Third, and by implication, the Christian way was a journey of repentance, faith, regeneration, and a life of obedience to God. Fourth, belief that secular authority was corrupt, combined with a non-violent philosophy, led to a refusal to participate in public or military structures.

Anabaptist spirituality owed a great deal to late-medieval mystical movements. It was particularly influenced by John Tauler from whom Anabaptists drew and adapted teachings about patient and trustful abandonment to God (known as *Gelassenheit*).[7]

As a footnote, interestingly some Anabaptists moved from their rejection of infant baptism to a belief that *all* children who had not reached the age of moral responsibility were saved by Christ. Some added that all children of whatever race and religion were saved. For a few this had wider implications. Thus, Thomas Müntzer had read the Qur'an and believed that Muslims could be moved by God's spirit to true faith. He also believed that devout Jews might be more justified by their faith than thoughtless Christians. Another Anabaptist, Jacob Palaeologus, advanced the idea of an interfaith Church composed of righteous Christians, Jews, and Muslims, and a popular Strasbourg preacher, Clement Ziegler, hoped that on the last day everyone without exception – even perhaps the devil – would be saved.

Anglican Spirituality

In comparison to the continent, the English Reformation was a more political process. It stretched from the reign of King Henry VIII (1509–1547) through a Protestant ascendancy under Edward VI and a Catholic restoration under Mary to the eventual compromise settlement under Elizabeth I (1558–1603). Elizabeth's upbringing was Protestant, but her own religious position was ambiguous or at least kept carefully private. Despite pressure to adopt a radically reformed system, Elizabeth carefully maintained the historic episcopal system and Archbishop Cranmer's 1552 Prayer Book with minor changes. Religious conformity related more to Church order than to a rigid pattern of doctrine.

The spirituality of the Church of England that developed during the seventeenth century was undoubtedly shaped by the principles of the Continental reformers but also retained pre-Reformation elements and was prepared to use aspects of Catholic Reformation spirituality (e.g. the works of Francis de Sales). The authority of the Bible was central but was set alongside the authority of Church tradition (expressed pre-eminently in the common worship of the *Book of Common Prayer*) and reason, for example, in the seminal writings of Richard Hooker during Elizabeth's reign, *On the Laws of Ecclesiastical Polity*.

"Anglican" spirituality emerged as a distinctive tradition with a group of writers known as the Caroline Divines. The title reflects the fact that many of them flourished during the reigns of Charles I and Charles II. Their spiritual teaching was not systematic but appeared in sermons, collections of prayers, pastoral works, and, perhaps most famously, as poetry of the highest quality. However, above all, Anglican spirituality was passed on by the *Book of Common Prayer* – not merely a reform of the pre-Reformation Missal but also a manual of teaching intended to promote a certain spiritual attitude. Personal spirituality was shaped by living and worshipping as part of a community both ecclesial and civic. Equally the notion of "common" countered those who sought a purified community of right believers. It also suggested that spirituality concerned the common markers of human life framed by the rhythms of a calendar of feasts and fasts.

Beyond the Prayer Book, a number of other emphases stand out. Anglican spirituality was strongly Christ-centered. Jesus Christ was, of course, the revelation of God and the privileged channel of God's salvation. However, Christ was also the pattern of Christian living. An emphasis on the Cross of Christ at times suggested that God's righteous judgment was held at bay by Christ taking upon himself the sins of the world, but at other times the dominant image was God's love revealed in Christ's suffering. Other important themes were God revealed in creation, a residual Christian humanism reflected in valuing everyday human existence, as well as music and the arts.

Among Caroline writers there was a variety of genres. There were pastoral-ethical treatises such as Bishop Bayley's *The Practice of Piety* or Jeremy Taylor's *The Rule and Exercises of Holy Living*. There were books of meditation such as Bishop Joseph Hall's *The Arte of Divine Meditation* that drew on medieval as well as reformed sources and books intended to fill a "devotional gap" such as Bishop John Cosin's *A Collection of Private Devotions*. There were also collections of prayers gathered from a wide range of ancient sources such as Bishop Lancelot Andrewes' *Preces privatae* which was used daily by Cardinal Newman in the nineteenth century. Thomas Traherne's *Centuries* offered a rich spirituality of joy in God's creation and of spiritual desire. The sophisticated poetry of George Herbert, John Donne, and Henry Vaughan is perhaps the best-loved expression of the Anglican spiritual temperament.

The early-twentieth-century writer on mysticism, Baron von Hügel, characterized Anglican spirituality as un-mystical. This seems an unfair judgment when reading the sublime poetry of Herbert and Vaughan and Traherne's meditations, not to mention the mystical concerns of the eccentric William Law in his early-eighteenth-century *A Serious Call to a Devout and Holy Life*.

George Herbert

The person and writings of George Herbert may be taken as a striking example of the Anglican spiritual tradition. George Herbert (1593–1633) was a member of the aristocratic and powerful Pembroke family who led a varied life as Fellow of Trinity College, Cambridge, and University

Orator, then as a Member of Parliament before finally being ordained and becoming a country parish priest in 1630. His two great works are the prose treatise on priestly life and ministry, *The Country Parson*, and the great poetic collection, *The Temple*. Nowadays, Herbert is considered to be one of the greatest English poets. He is also a major figure in the emergence of a distinctive "Anglican" spirituality during the seventeenth century. Herbert would not have used the word "Anglican" which seems to be a nineteenth-century invention.

Herbert is said to have described the poetic collection *The Temple* to his close friend Nicholas Ferrar (founder of the quasi-monastic Little Gidding community) as "a picture of the many spiritual conflicts that have passed betwixt God and my soul before I could subject mine to the will of Jesus my Master: in which service I have now found perfect freedom." Even if the personal tone of these words is authentic, it is widely agreed that *The Temple*, published in 1633 shortly after Herbert's death, also has a conscious structure as a work of religious teaching. While many of the poems are almost certainly genuine expressions of Herbert's own experience, their purpose is not essentially autobiographical in our modern sense. For Herbert, personal experience was simply a rhetorical device by means of which God could be communicated to the reader who would then be led to greater praise and to a deeper response.

The scheme of the poems is closely ordered. They are gathered into a three-part structure, "The Church Porch," "The Church," and "The Church Militant," of which the middle part is by far the largest. This central collection is also spiritually the richest and the most dynamic. The titles of the three sections correspond to the three different meanings of "Temple" or "Church." First of all, it is a physical building within which God is somehow present. Some poems employ features of the building as a framework for teaching (e.g. "The Altar," "The Church Floor," "The Windows," "Church Monuments"). In doing this, the poems underline the importance of order and beauty in the Christian life. The "Temple" is secondly the Body of Christ, the Christian community. Thus, other poems express the Church's year or the liturgy through which the community expresses and solidifies its identity (e.g. "Evensong," "Mattins," "Lent," "Holy Communion"). Finally, the "Temple" is the individual human soul, described in St Paul as the "temple of the Holy Spirit" (1 Cor 3, 16).

This final emphasis on the individual person points to an important aspect of Herbert's teaching. *The Temple* is clearly meant to communicate to readers the Christian spiritual path. Having said this, the poems are not primarily instructional. There is something morally exhortative about "The Church Porch," the first of the three sections of

The Temple. However, this is not true of the lyrical poems in the extensive central section, "The Church." Stylistically, most of the poems are addressed to God and therefore take the form of meditation or intimate conversation. The poems seek to move the reader to make an affective response and therefore ultimately to adopt a change of life. Precisely because the poems lay bare Herbert's own spiritual life for the sake of other people, they also identify with the problems and aspirations of all Christians.

Although the prose treatise, *The Country Parson*, deserves to be redeemed as a work of spiritual literature, there can be no doubt that the poems make the greater spiritual as well as aesthetic impact on the modern reader because the painful realities of inward spiritual struggle haunt the pages.

To take merely one example, some striking writing on prayer occurs in the poem "Prayer I." This extraordinary sonnet has no main verb but a succession of metaphors. The impact relies on a cumulative effect rather than on a conclusive definition. Metaphor provides Herbert with greater imaginative scope that enables him to move beyond the limits of the expressible. Paradoxically, therefore, Herbert offers many images of prayer and yet also suggests the underlying truth that prayer, as a relationship with God, cannot ultimately be described. It is a mysterious process that enables us to touch ultimate Mystery.

> Prayer the Church's banquet, Angel's age,
> >   God's breath in man returning to his birth,
> >   The soul in paraphrase, heart in pilgrimage,
> The Christian plummet sounding heav'n and earth;
> Engine against th'Almighty, sinner's tower,
> >   Reversed thunder, Christ-side-piercing spear,
> >   The six-days world transposing in an hour,
> A kind of tune, which all things hear and fear;
> Softness and peace, and joy, and love, and bliss,
> >   Exalted Manna, gladness of the best,
> >   Heaven in ordinary, man well drest,
> The milky way, the bird of Paradise,
> >   Church-bells beyond the stars heard, the soul's blood,
> >   The land of spices; something understood.

In prayer, it is possible to be transported, even if momentarily, to another realm. "Angel's age," "the milky way," and a tune "beyond the stars" suggest that prayer touches the infinite. The poem concludes with "something understood" – a profound but elusive encounter with the mysterious otherness of God.[8]

Puritan Spirituality

A strand of Protestantism known as Puritanism flourished in seventeenth-century England and later in America, especially New England, where it translated itself into the great religious revival of the eighteenth century. Theologically Calvinist, Puritanism emphasized spiritual and moral renewal and was never at home in the mainstream of the Church of England. A number of central figures, for example, the writer Isaac Ambrose, began as Anglican priests but became "separatists." Some Puritans left England for North America as early as 1620 where they founded the colony of Massachusetts as a utopian Christian society. In England, Puritanism enjoyed a brief period of ascendancy during the Commonwealth (1649–1660). After the restoration of the monarchy and the re-establishment of the Church of England, more Puritans left England for either the continent or North America, and those that were left became a small minority in a variety of religious traditions that we now know as Congregationalist, Presbyterian, and Baptist.

Puritan spirituality was strongly biblical. Although it emphasized the depravity of humanity, caricatures of it as gloomy are somewhat unfair, despite the emphasis on a serious, disciplined moral life. Puritans also emphasized God's mercy as well as love and desire in human relationships with God, and the possibility of immediate Communion with God. As Calvinists, Puritans accepted sanctification, a spiritual process of conformity to God's will. The great spiritual classic of Puritan literature, known to Catholics and Protestants alike, is John Bunyan's *Pilgrim's Progress* which portrays the Christian life as a journey or pilgrimage through trials, temptation, and tribulation towards union with Christ.

An important medium for communicating the spiritual life was preaching – often spiritually evocative as much as expository – but there was also a strong emphasis on regular personal prayer, Bible study, and other spiritual reading, meditation (encouraged by writers such as Richard Baxter), examination of conscience, and fasting. A somewhat ascetical spirituality was offset in some people with a more contemplative stance and even mystical raptures as in Isaac Ambrose. Some elements of this were derived from the Cistercian tradition of sermons on the Song of Songs and bridal mysticism, reflected in similar writings among Puritans and directly cited by Isaac Ambrose.

Apart from John Bunyan and some of the writings of Richard Baxter, the English Puritan spirit is probably best known in the great poetry of John Milton.[9]

Early Quakers

It is difficult to know how far to define Quaker spirituality as Puritan. Later known officially as the Religious Society of Friends, the Quaker movement derived from the inspirational teachings of George Fox (1624–1691). He had sought a response to his spiritual quest among Puritans but found that no one could answer his needs. As a result, he came to a belief in "an infinite ocean of light and love" that existed within and overcame his darkness. This light was Christ. A wandering preacher with no formal education, Fox shared the Puritan emphasis on a simple, disciplined, and ethical life. However, he differed from Puritans in believing that humans were essentially good rather than sinfully depraved. He also taught the presence of the divine "Inner Light" within every person and the sense of inward peace that followed from this. This belief in an Inner Light led to a number of characteristic Quaker spiritual emphases – each person's direct experience of God (demanding personal holiness but obviating the need for sacraments), an emphasis on silent common worship (waiting on God), and a certain spiritual democracy (leading to consensus decision-making based on discernment of the voice of God's Spirit).

Although Fox's original experience was intensely interior, he also taught that the power of God eradicated human conflict. Thus, authentic inner experience leads to a desire to work for the transformation of the social order. Quaker spirituality is intensely contemplative but also strongly ethical, associated with the quest for peace and social justice. Quakers share with the Anabaptists a doctrine of non-violence. A notable example of the utopian dimension of Quaker life was the work of William Penn in Pennsylvania to create a perfectly ordered society. In England, the Quakers achieved toleration in 1687 and became notable during the Industrial Revolution for their combination of outstanding entrepreneurial skills with the social care of their workers. Quakers set up a number of planned settlements with decent housing and schooling such as Bourneville in England. During the nineteenth century, Quakers became involved in prison reform (e.g. the work of Elizabeth Fry) and in the abolition of slavery. During the twentieth century, Quakers were noted for their pacifism during two world wars and also for their work for world peace and for interfaith understanding.[10]

The Catholic Reformation

It is now common to refer to the "Catholic Reformation" rather than the "Counter-Reformation" as it was a process that did not simply respond to Protestantism but had a broader agenda. The process was only established by the end of the seventeenth century.[11] Although it may be argued that the key event in the Catholic Reformation was the Council of Trent (1545–1563), this was dominated by doctrinal and disciplinary issues which makes it difficult to derive a clear sense from the Council of the spiritual agenda of Catholic reform. Catholic Reformation spirituality had two major elements: the foundation of new religious orders and the development of new forms of lay Christian life and devotion that were interwoven with daily life.

The New Orders

The spirituality of Catholic reform expressed itself partly in religious life. A number of the older orders sought to return to their original rigor. For example, the Franciscans produced a reformed branch, the Capuchins, who led a life of extreme simplicity. After a shaky start (their vicar-general Bernardino Ochino and others left to join the Calvinists in 1542), the Capuchins eventually developed into a successful order in their own right. It also became clear that there was a need for new groups who would cater to the spiritual needs of educated, sophisticated, and influential groups of lay Christians. Several new religious orders were founded with an emphasis on intellectual formation, an appreciation of humanist values, and a greater ability than the older orders to lead active lives spreading the Christian faith. A new style of clerical religious community called "Clerks Regular" emerged. The first groups included the Theatines and the Barnabites who continued to give priority to personal asceticism and prayer. However, the most radical of the new orders and the one most associated with the spirituality of the Catholic Reformation was the Society of Jesus, founded by Ignatius Loyola in 1540.

Ignatius Loyola and Early Ignatian Spirituality

Ignatius Loyola (1491–1556) is best known as the founder of the Society of Jesus (Jesuits). However, the main values of Ignatian spirituality and its famous text, the *Spiritual Exercises*, were directed from the start to a broader spectrum of Christians. In that sense, the Jesuits were a particular expression of a spiritual tradition that was wider than the order itself.

A Basque noble from Loyola in Spain, Ignatius initially followed a conventional military and courtly career. This ended when he was wounded at the siege of Pamplona (1521). Ignatius then underwent a religious conversion while recovering at his family castle. He subsequently lived as a hermit at Manresa near Barcelona (1522–1523) where he experienced mystical insights, received spiritual guidance at the monastery of Montserrat, and learned the lessons of discernment as he slowly outgrew a tendency to excessive asceticism. The framework for his influential *Spiritual Exercises* was probably recorded at this time and further refined by subsequently guiding others. After a short visit to the Holy Land, Ignatius undertook spiritual ministry in Spain and returned to education at the universities of Alcalá and Salamanca (1524–1528). He gathered followers, men and women, and was investigated by the Inquisition. Ignatius then went to the University of Paris where he studied theology for seven years (1528–1535). There he gathered another group of companions, and they decided that ordination and forming a new religious community were the most effective ways of promoting their spiritual ideals. By 1537, Ignatius and companions were in Italy where they obtained papal approval for their new order in 1540. The *Spiritual Exercises* were formally approved in 1548. Ignatius remained in Rome as Superior of the Jesuits, supervising the rapid development of the order and writing copious letters of spiritual guidance to a varied audience. He died in 1556.

The precise influences on Ignatius' spirituality are a matter of debate. However, his own experience and his experience of guiding others are the key to the development of the *Spiritual Exercises*. Ignatius also grew up in a culture affected by centuries of crusading against the Islamic presence in Spain. This probably had an impact on his imagery. During his conversion, we know that he read Voragine's lives of the saints and Ludolph of Saxony's *Life of Christ* – a text favored by the *devotio moderna* which suggested a form of imaginative gospel contemplation that was further developed in the *Exercises*. It seems likely that the *devotio moderna* influenced Ignatius in other ways. While at Manresa he grew to love the *Imitation of Christ*. Recently, scholars have returned to the notion that Ignatius was influenced by spiritual exercises written by Abbot Cisneros of Montserrat (1455–1510) which drew on the *devotio*. While in Paris, Ignatius was attached to the Collège de Montaigu, founded by supporters of the *devotio* movement. It seems that Ignatius also had friends in Erasmian circles at Alcalá and Paris and read Erasmus's *Enchiridion* (which may be reflected in the *Exercises*). It is likely that Ignatius was less antagonistic to Erasmus than was once believed.[12]

There is a substantial body of writing associated with Ignatius: *The Constitutions of the Society of Jesus*, elements of his *Spiritual Diary* which includes records of some of his mystical illuminations, his so-called *Autobiography* – a dictated (and probably carefully moderated) work that runs only up to 1538 – and thousands of extant letters, many of them letters of spiritual guidance to a wide range of people and a rich source of insight into his spiritual wisdom. However, the most famous and still widely used work is his *Spiritual Exercises*.[13]

The *Spiritual Exercises* is one of the most influential spiritual texts of all times. Despite their Reformation origins, they are nowadays used as a medium for spiritual guidance and retreats among an ecumenical spectrum of Christians. The text is not intended to be inspirational but is a series of practical notes for a retreat-guide that suggest how to vary the process according to the needs of each person. The ideal is a month away from normal pressures but a modified form "in the midst of daily life" is allowed. Much of the text consists of advice about the structure and content of prayer periods (five per day in the month-long version), guidance about spiritual discernment, and making a choice of life and helpful hints about practical matters such as the physical environment for prayer, moderate use of penance, rules about eating, and about scruples.

The explicit aim of the *Exercises* is to assist a person to grow in spiritual freedom in order to respond to the call of Christ. There are four phases, called "Weeks," each with their specific focus, that enable the process to unfold. The originality of the *Exercises* lies not in the detailed content or methods of prayer but in the structure and dynamic. The First Week begins with the sinfulness of humanity and of the individual but in the context of a growing awareness of God's unwavering love and acceptance. The retreatant is asked to recognize that God's call is addressed to sinners, and that unworthiness is no bar to responding. The Second Week deepens a sense of being called to "be with" Christ in mission. This is developed through a series of gospel contemplations on the life and work of Christ. This Week gradually leads the retreatant to face a choice (called an "Election") highlighted by three classic meditations on the contrasting values of Christ and the world. This confrontation with "the values of Christ" leads the retreatant to consider the cost of following Christ – expressed in the Third Week scriptural meditations on Christ's suffering and death. Here, the retreatant is invited to identify with Christ's trusting surrender to God and through this to experience something of the joy and hope of Christ's resurrection – the focus of the Fourth Week. The *Exercises* end with a "Contemplation on the Love of God" which acts as a bridge back into everyday life, now transformed into a context for finding God's presence in all things.

From the *Exercises*, it is possible to detect fundamental features of Ignatian spirituality. First, God is encountered above all in the practices of everyday life which themselves become a "spiritual exercise." Second, the life and death of Jesus Christ is offered as the fundamental pattern for Christian life. Third, the God revealed in Christ offers healing, liberation, and hope. Fourth, spirituality is not so much a matter of asceticism as a matter of a deepening desire for God ("desire" is a frequent word in the text) and experience of God's acceptance in return. The theme of "finding God in all things" suggests a growing integration of contemplation and action. The notion of following the pattern of Jesus Christ focuses on an active sharing in God's mission to the world – not least in serving people in need. Finally, at the heart of everything is the gift of spiritual discernment – an increasing ability to judge wisely and to choose well in ways that are congruent with a person's deepest truth.

The word discernment means "to distinguish between things" or "to recognize something" and derives from the Greek *diakrisis*. This relates Christian discernment back to Aristotle's *Nicomachaean Ethics*, specifically his third kind of knowledge, *phronesis*, "practical wisdom" or prudent judgment, echoed in later Christian thinkers such as Thomas Aquinas. Aristotle suggests that this kind of practical wisdom grows in and through our immersion in everyday human affairs. Discernment is not merely concerned with prayer. From the fourth century CE, discernment (*diakrisis*) is a key value in early monasticism. How are we to lead a spiritual life? Echoing Aristotle, the important word is "balance" for which discernment is the guiding principle. John Cassian, in his *Conferences*, promotes balance as the virtue which avoids the excesses of other apparently spiritual values. Cassian also portrays the relational character of discernment. Discernment is deciding responsibly as a *social* act. It is also related to communal rather than purely individual wisdom.

In Ignatian spirituality, discernment implies the wisdom to recognize the difference between courses of action that are life-directing and ones that are potentially destructive and out of harmony with our relationship with God. Faced with choices we are subject to contradictory influences from inside and outside. Some of these incline us to what is life-giving or authentic (what Ignatius Loyola called "consolation"), others to what is inauthentic or flawed (what he called "desolation"). For Ignatius Loyola, discernment works in a kind of sequence. First, a contemplative cultivation of *spiritual insight* leads to, second, *a skill* to distinguish between good and bad "spirits," resulting in, third, *an ability* to determine true balance in the spiritual life and the exercise of virtue. This is what Ignatius means by "detachment." As Ignatius recognized, desire is what powers our spiritualities. For each person, certain desires have the potential to shape serious choices and therefore to give direction to our lives. Discernment enables us to be aware of the full range of desires that we experience. Throughout the *Spiritual Exercises*, Ignatius Loyola returns again and again to the subject of desire, which is always ordered towards a healthier way of choosing.

Ignatian spirituality has promoted a range of spiritual practices and approaches to prayer both within the text of the *Exercises* and also in the large extant collection of Ignatius' letters. There is no single method that can be uniquely described as "Ignatian prayer." There are at least ten mentioned in the *Exercises*, many of them originating in the *devotio moderna* tradition and, more remotely, in adaptations of monastic *lectio*. Three are particularly notable. The first, gospel contemplation, offers a structured approach to prayer with scripture and commends the use of imagination in order to enter into a scene from the gospels as the starting point for meditation. The second method, called the Examen, suggests a brief daily practice of reflection on the experience of each day – noting where we have responded to God or failed to respond. Finally, as we have already noted, in an appendix to the *Exercises* entitled three ways of prayer, there is the "prayer of the breath." This suggests the slow, rhythmic, recitation of a familiar prayer such as "Our Father" with each word linked to rhythmic breathing. This approach is unusual in Western spirituality and comes closer to Eastern Christian hesychastic practices or to meditation in the Al-Andalus Sufi tradition that would have been known in late medieval Spain.

For all its dynamism, Ignatian spirituality also encourages a strongly contemplative attitude – summarized in the distinctive idea of being "contemplative in action." Ignatius himself witnessed to a "mysticism of service." After Ignatius' death, there was a growing reserve towards con-templative-minded Jesuits, for example, Balthasar Alvarez, Teresa of Avila's spiritual director, or Louis Lallemant in the seventeenth century. The subsequent history of the tradition suggests a narrowing of perspective especially during the time of the Jesuit Superiors Mercurian (1573–1580) and Acquaviva (1580–1615). Under Mercurian, Jesuits were forbidden to use the writings of the Rhineland and Flemish mystics, and by the 1599 Official Directory for giving the *Exercises* the official line was more ascetical-methodical than contemplative. Although there were exceptions to the general rule, the dominance of ascetical interpretations of the *Exercises* significantly constrained the Ignatian tradition until a major revival in the later twentieth century.

Although Ignatius initially allowed two women to be professed as Jesuits, this radical experiment did not last, and he did not sponsor a parallel women's order. However, during the early part of the seventeenth century, an Englishwoman, Mary Ward (1585–1645), pressed hard for her new, informal Institute to be made a religious order of active, mobile women under the Jesuit *Constitutions*. Although a number of houses were founded on the continent, her revolutionary proposal was refused and the Institute suppressed. In the longer term, her vision prevailed and the Institute of the Blessed Virgin Mary was approved at the end of the century although it only officially adopted the Jesuit *Constitutions* in the late twentieth century. This was the first of a number of active women's communities founded during the eighteenth and nineteenth centuries, inspired by Ignatian spirituality.

An important theme in Ignatian spirituality is sharing in Christ's mission to the world. Consequently, the Jesuits abandoned traditional monastic structures and added a fourth vow of mobility expressed as obedience to the pope in relation to being sent anyway in the world. From the earliest days, Jesuits volunteered to work in the Americas, Africa, and Asia. The most famous early missionary was Francis Xavier, the "Apostle of the Indies," one of Ignatius' Paris companions who worked in India and Japan and died before entering China. The seventeenth century saw contrasting expressions of the Ignatian themes of mission and engagement with surrounding cultures in the martyrdom of Jesuits in Canada and the controversial work of Roberto de Nobili (1577–1656) in South India and Matteo Ricci (1552–1610) in China. These two men to some extent affirmed the values of the cultures within which they lived by adopting local dress and lifestyles. They conversed with Hindus and Confucians and suggested that the Church should use local languages and rituals in worship. The relatively open-minded attitudes of de Nobili and Ricci were not typical at this time.

Spirituality Beyond Europe

It is striking that histories of Christian spirituality have conventionally given virtually no attention to the ancient presence of Christianity outside Europe, for example, in China, India, or Africa (e.g. Ethiopia), apart from studies of ancient Egyptian monasticism. However, this movement is scarcely treated as "African" or in any way indigenous. While we know that relatively large numbers of so-called Nestorian Christians existed in the steppes of Central Asia and in China from quite early times, and that Armenian Christians also moved along Asian trade routes, we actually know very little about these communities.

When we come to the later expansion of European Christianity into Asia, Africa, and the Americas from the sixteenth century onwards, virtually nothing is known or said about the development of indigenous Christian spiritualities but only about Eurocentric "missionary" spirituality. For example, the encounters in South India between European Christians, notably the Portuguese, and the long-standing indigenous Syriac Thomas Christians in the late fifteenth and early sixteenth centuries were overall not particularly happy. On the one hand, the European incomers sought to impose their own religious structures and liturgies. They were horrified by what they saw as "Hindu" customs, styles of dress, and festivals among local Christians. On the other hand, the relatively inculturated Thomas Christians (in solidarity with local Jewish and Islamic communities) were shocked by beef-eating, image venerating, celibate Western priests and friars wearing clerical costumes.

Turning to the impact of Spanish Catholicism on Central and Latin America, some contrasting examples will suffice to illustrate the complex story of spirituality in the colonial Americas. First, in Peru, a Dominican sister, St Rose of Lima (1586–1617) was the first canonized saint of the Americas. Her parents were settlers, and her severe penitential practice represented an imported, Spanish style of spirituality rather than anything distinctively Peruvian or indigenous. Second, however, in Mexico something different emerged. Bartolomé de las Casas (c. 1484–1566), originally a Spanish settler and entrepreneur then Dominican priest and Bishop of Chiapas, became known as the "Protector of the Indians" and a leading advocate of the rights of indigenous people in the so-called New World. His opposition to slavery and the colonial oppression of local people gained him many enemies among the settlers, and he was forced to return to Spain. He later became notable in the Valladolid debates where he argued forcefully for the full and equal human status of indigenous peoples. Las Casas is often referred to as a predecessor of liberation theology. On a different note, the most famous Christian shrine and pilgrimage site of the Americas is Our Lady of Guadalupe near Mexico City. Here it is said that Juan Diego, a poor Mexican Indian, had a vision of the Virgin Mary in 1531 followed by the miraculous appearance of a picture of the Virgin on his cloak. The town of Tepeyac was subsequently renamed Guadalupe after the famous Marian shrine in Spain, and in general the official cult was largely Europeanized. However, what is fascinating is that Tepeyac had been the site of the great temple of Tonantzin, "Mother of the Gods." The recipient of the vision was one of the oppressed locals, the image of the virgin on Juan Diego's cloak was strikingly indigenous, and overall there are resonances of the local cult of the goddess Tonantzin.[14] In broader terms, anthropologists have noted that the "pure" faith of the Spanish invaders rapidly mixed with local beliefs in a dynamic syncretism which missionaries ultimately could not control. The combining of pre-Christian sacred sites with shrines to Christian saints or the Virgin Mary was quite widespread.[15]

Carmelite Mysticism

Apart from Ignatian spirituality, the most striking spiritual movement of the Catholic Reformation was the reform of the Carmelite Order in Spain and its mystical teachings. The writings of Teresa of Avila (1515–1582) and John of the Cross (1542–1591) are among the greatest classics of Western mystical literature. Both were strongly influenced by the Song of Songs and the tradition of spiritual marriage. Only after the death of John did the Teresian reform movement become a separate religious order known as the Discalced (or barefoot) Carmelites.

Teresa of Avila was the initiator of the Spanish Carmelite reform movement in which John of the Cross came to share and which sought to return the order to its contemplative and semi-eremitical origins. She came from a wealthy, partly Jewish family and was renowned for her charm and independent temperament. She entered the moderate Carmelite convent in Avila in 1535 but after some years of intense prayer followed by visionary experiences was drawn to a life of stricter observance. Eventually, she became involved more or less full time in encouraging the reform and founding new houses and having met the young friar John of the Cross, she arranged for him to assist her. Teresa wrote a number of works in warm and engaging language such as her *Life*, *The Way of Perfection*, and others. In her great classic, *The Interior Castle*, she vividly describes the spiritual journey in terms of progression through the different rooms or mansions of the "castle" of the soul, clustered in groups corresponding to the threefold way, until the pilgrimage culminates in rooms 5–7 in which takes place a transforming union leading to spiritual marriage. In one sense, her mysticism is orthodox, Christ-centered and Trinitarian. Yet, her Jewish ancestry is nowadays more readily acknowledged, and the possible influence of Jewish mystical writings (e.g. *Zohar*) on her *The Interior Castle* would now be more freely proposed. While a visionary, Teresa was also an active and down-to-earth person with a strong emphasis on the Christian life as one of faithfulness to prayer and daily work and of charity to other people.

John of the Cross, in contrast to Teresa, came from a poor family and initially was an apprentice craftsman. When aged seventeen, a patron paid for him to attend the Jesuit College at Medina del Campo where he received a classical education before entering the local Carmelite monastery. His encounter with Teresa of Avila changed his life, and like her he was drawn into the reform movement. John trained in theology and held several senior posts in his order but was persecuted by those who opposed reform and imprisoned on two occasions. John's writings are denser than Teresa's and include mystical poetry of the highest order and systematic commentaries on the spiritual journey such as the *Ascent of Mount Carmel, The Dark Night, The Spiritual Canticle*, and the *Living Flame of Love*. He emphasized a process of stripping away our desire for "things" that, by definition, are less than "everything" and which stand in the way of union with God who is "all," or *todo* in John's language.

> To reach satisfaction in all
> desire its possession in nothing.
> To come to possess all
> desire the possession of nothing.
>
> To arrive at being all
> desire to be nothing.
> To come to the knowledge of all
> desire the knowledge of nothing.
> To come to the pleasure you have not
> you must go by a way in which you enjoy not.
> To come to the knowledge you have not
> you must go by a way in which you know not.
> To come to the possession you have not
> you must go by a way in which you possess not.
> To come to be what you are not
> you must go by a way in which you are not....
>
> (*The Ascent of Mount Carmel*,
> Book 1, Chapter 13, 11).

In the *Ascent of Mount Carmel*, John adopts the ancient metaphor of climbing a mountain to describe the spiritual journey. In John's case, progress was away from prayer based on sense experience via various "dark nights" of sensory deprivation, spiritual darkness, and purification (which unite us to the crucified Christ) to the "summit" of transforming union – a spiritual marriage between God and the soul.

As we noted briefly in Chapter 4, the impact of Al-Andalus Sufism on the language and symbolism of John of the Cross is now accepted by some scholars although the details are still a matter for debate. For example, Luce López-Baralt points to the notion of ecstatic fire and burning flames of love in John's poem *Llama de amor viva* and the imagery of flowing water and the fountain of the soul in stanza 12 of the *Spiritual Canticle.*[16]

The writings of one seventeenth-century French Carmelite also became a bestseller and are still popular today. Brother Lawrence (1614–1691) was a lay brother in the Paris monastery of the Discalced friars for some fifty years. There he worked as a cook and sandal-maker. However, his simplicity was allied to a deep wisdom that drew many people to him for spiritual guidance including Archbishop Fénelon, another important figure in seventeenth-century spirituality. Lawrence's letters and other fragments were edited after his death as *The Practice of the Presence of God.* Lawrence was unfairly caught up in the Quietist controversy because of his association with Fénelon. He stressed abandonment to God's will but also the possibility of union with God through a prayerful practice of the presence of God in the midst of even the most ordinary, everyday tasks.[17]

Lay Devotion

As we have seen from our reflections on the new religious orders and their spiritualities, the spiritual development of laypeople was a major concern of Catholic reform. This new spiritual climate was disseminated through confraternities, sodalities, and the promotion of new devotions.[18] One form was the Sodalities of Our Lady guided by the Jesuits and based on elements of Ignatian spirituality such as combining prayer and action and a daily examination of conscience. Sodalities were not narrowly devotional but were intended to inculcate a broad lay spirituality that combined personal spiritual development, collective support through meetings, and a significant amount of charitable action. Although every Sodality had a priest-director, other officers were lay and elected by the membership. Networks of sodalities spread across most European towns in Catholic countries, and alongside these developed a tradition of personal spiritual guidance aimed at laypeople.

Another important activity for encouraging the growth of lay spirituality was preaching. The absence of effective preachers was identified by Church authorities as a key reason for the success of Protestantism, and so a major emphasis on preaching, both instructional and inviting personal conversion, became part of Catholic reform. One extension was the parish mission. Missions usually consisted of interventions by visiting priests, lasting several days or a week. Their aim was the renewal of Catholic practice (e.g. by exhorting people to frequent Communion) and a more general communication of key themes of belief and devotion. So, for example, the Jesuits often adapted themes from the Ignatian *Exercises* as a basis for preached missions. Missions also included other pastoral techniques such as catechism classes, special Masses, processions, and so on. Such missions also reinforced the local parish as the primary context for sustaining lay spirituality.

Apart from books of meditation and prayers, catechisms were created to match Protestant ones, for example, the 1560 German catechism of the Jesuit Peter Canisius which went through two hundred editions during the sixteenth century. In addition to adult catechisms, small ones were created for children and specialist ones for various groups or classes of people.

Traditional devotions to Mary and the saints continued to play a role. What was new was the greater emphasis on Christ-centered devotion often in the context of reinforcing belief in the presence of Christ in the Eucharist, allied to encouraging more frequent reception of Communion. A number of devotional activities focused on the Eucharist such as Confraternities of the Blessed Sacrament, Eucharistic processions, and parish-based services of adoration such as weekly Benediction or the less frequent Forty Hours. Statues of the Holy Child encouraged devotion to the infancy of Jesus (emphasizing his humanity and the virtues of innocence and self-effacement). In France during the seventeenth century, there also developed a strong devotion to the Sacred Heart – again a symbol of the humanity and compassion of Jesus. The formalization of the devotion was associated particularly with the visions of Margaret-Mary Alacocque, an enclosed nun at Paray-le-Monial in the 1670s, and it became a dominant theme in popular Catholic spirituality over the next three centuries. Yet, tantalizingly, a strikingly similar devotion to the Sacred Heart of Christ was present among English Puritans in the same period, for example, in the writings of Thomas Goodwin, one of Oliver Cromwell's chaplains.[19]

Alongside the shift towards pastoral spirituality among the new religious orders and towards a varied pattern of lay devotion came a change in architectural style. In fact, both Protestant and Catholic communities (where they did not simply inherit medieval gothic buildings) frequently materialized their spiritualities in different versions of neo-classical architecture, inspired by the Renaissance. In the case of Protestant churches, the aesthetic lines were relatively simple and uncluttered, expressing a suspicion of visual ornamentation and an emphasis on hearing the preached word. In Catholic buildings, there was also an emphasis on spaces for listening to preaching (e.g. in the great Jesuit churches of Italy or Germany), but this "auditory" spirituality also involved an attention to acoustics for complex choral music. Catholic buildings also retained – indeed, enhanced – the importance of the visual. Baroque architecture and design expressed a sense of God's glory – a spirituality of divine splendor allied to visual drama.

Seventeenth-Century French Spirituality

Seventeenth-century France saw a second outstanding wave of Catholic reform, influenced in part by elements of Ignatian spirituality and Carmelite mysticism but with flavors of its own. However, the notion of a single "French School" of spirituality is misleading. There were several distinct and even conflicting trends. The two most theoretically developed traditions were associated with Pierre de Bérulle (1575–1629) and with Francis de Sales (1567–1622) and Jeanne de Chantal (1572–1641). There was another strand associated with Vincent de Paul and Louise de Marillac and two movements that were criticized as heretical, Jansenism and Quietism.

In 1611, Bérulle founded the French Oratory inspired by the Italian Oratory of Philip Neri – communities of priests without vows, engaged in a ministry of preaching, education, and the improvement of clergy standards. He was a sophisticated theologian and aristocrat who acted as a court chaplain and eventually became a cardinal. Bérulle and his Oratory concentrated on the reform of the diocesan priesthood and also developed a school system that paralleled the Jesuits by whom he had been educated. His influence set the tone for French spirituality over the following centuries. Bérulle developed a Christ-centered, incarnational spirituality. In a mixture of Dionysian mysticism and Trinitarian theology, he taught that the Christian was drawn into the glory of God-as-Trinity through Christ. By God-in-Christ's "humiliation" in, first, becoming human and, second, in suffering death, humanity was granted access to God's life. The appropriate human response was abasement, even obliteration of self before God's majesty. This developed into a notion of "spiritual servitude" to God's will. The corollary was a strict Augustinian view of human nature as fundamentally sinful that some commentators think comes close to Jansenism.

Among several prominent figures, the most notable "disciple" of Bérulle was Jean-Jacques Olier (1608–1657) who founded the Society of St Sulpice (or Sulpicians), a voluntary company of priests who ran seminaries and improved the spiritual formation of parish clergy. In contrast to Bérulle's more austere theology, Olier gave attention to personal experience of Jesus Christ and to the role of the Holy Spirit in uniting us to Christ. He encouraged frequent Communion and clashed with Jansenist rigorists. His teaching on prayer was affective rather than mental, but his mystical sensibilities were abandoned by his disciples in favor of a more moralistic spirituality until the spiritual renewal provoked by the Second Vatican Council in the 1960s.[20] Other important figures in the same broad school were John Eudes, the founder of the Congregation of Jesus and Mary, Louis Grignion de Montfort who developed a strongly Marian devotion, and John Baptist de la Salle, the cathedral canon who developed a spirituality of Christian education and founded the famous order of teaching brothers, the Brothers of the Christian Schools (popularly known as De La Salle Brothers).

On a different note, Francis de Sales in his *Introduction to the Devout Life* wrote one of the most popular spiritual classics of all time. Its influence spread beyond the confines of the Roman Catholic Church. Arguably, his approach had a more significant impact than Bérulle. A Savoy aristocrat, Francis originally trained as a lawyer before becoming a priest. Although he became Bishop of Geneva (1602), he was never able to reside in that resolutely Calvinist city. He encouraged Catholic reform by means of popular preaching, by reforming the clergy, and by developing an effective lay spirituality. Francis developed a deep friendship with Jeanne (or Jane) de Chantal, a widowed Baroness, who went on to found the Order of the Visitation. Together they developed a form of spirituality suitable for men and women in every context, not least the everyday world. While appreciative of the contemplative tradition, Salesian spirituality also emphasized service of neighbor, particularly people in need. Francis encouraged spiritual direction for laypeople rather than simply for clergy. Influenced by Ignatian spirituality but with its own distinctive features, Salesian spirituality emphasized God in creation and God's love for all humanity and desire to forgive anyone who sought reconciliation. An important theme was "the heart" – the heart of Christ mediating God to human hearts. The spiritual life was to be conformed to the ways of Jesus' heart. The attraction of the spirituality of Francis and Jane lay in a warmth that avoided excessive sentimentality. Also, despite their notion of humility, the approach was a long way from the austerity of Bérulle's "servitude."

The mid-nineteenth century saw a major revival of Salesian spirituality, notably a new family of male and female religious communities with lay associates known as "Salesians" founded by the Italian Don Bosco, with a strong concern for work with disadvantaged youth. Other smaller religious communities of men and women in the Salesian spirit also appeared at this time.[21]

The Vincentian spiritual tradition is associated with Vincent de Paul (or Depaul, 1580–1660) and Louise de Marillac (1591–1660). De Paul came from a poor background from which he escaped to be ordained and become a royal chaplain. A series of challenging experiences led him to empathize with the sufferings of the poor and to dedicate his life to them, to orphans, slaves, and victims of war. In this he was influenced by Francis de Sales. His was a socially engaged rather than theologically sophisticated spirituality. At the heart of it lay union with God through serving Christ in the poor. The medium for spreading the Vincentian spirit were a community of priests, the Congregation of the Mission (or Vincentians), and the community of women founded with Louise known as the Daughters of Charity. Though in effect an active religious order, the sisters avoided enclosure by making annual promises and worked intensively with the poor. Vincent's vision was also expressed in the development of lay confraternities dedicated to helping the poor in their homes. These were the forerunners of the famous Society of St Vincent de Paul founded by Frédéric Ozanam in the nineteenth century and which continue to flourish worldwide today. Ozanam anticipated the teachings of Vatican II on the single call of all Christians to both holiness and mission and is a central figure in the emergence of a distinctively lay spirituality of service.[22]

Jansenism and Quietism represent two contrasting seventeenth-century approaches to the Christian life that were condemned but had a longer-term impact on spirituality. The anti-mystical and penitential elements of Jansenism were a neo-Augustinian form of spiritual rigorism based on a pessimistic view of human existence. It was named after its main theoretician, the Louvain professor and later bishop of Ypres, Cornelius Jansen (1585–1638). Jansenists taught predestination and a limited atonement and attacked the Jesuits in particular for supposed moral liberalism and people like Olier for supporting frequent Communion (because this encouraged laxity in relation to confession). From the late

1620s, the spirit of Jansenism found its most prominent supporters in the Abbé Saint-Cyran and the circle of people associated with the Cistercian convent of Port-Royal near Versailles (including Blaise Pascal who defended Jansenism in his famous *Provincial Letters*). Jansen's propositions were censured posthumously, and the nuns of Port-Royal, after initially refusing to submit, finally agreed to moderate their position. However, Jansenist attitudes continued to have a long-term impact.

Quietism was, in its strict form, associated with the teachings of the Spanish priest Miguel de Molinos and, in a more moderate form, with the circle of Madame Guyon (1648–1717). Mme Guyon, fairly or unfairly, was associated with the notion of an excessively passive understanding of contemplation and with a total surrender to the initiative of God. Her works on prayer (e.g. *A Short and Easy Method of Prayer*) influenced such prominent figures as Archbishop Fénelon and had a wide following. Guyon's teaching on prayer emphasized both affectivity and a kind of indistinct and objectless mystical contemplation. Guyon also followed in the long tradition of bridal mysticism (e.g. her *Commentary on the Canticle*). What was open to question (and what ultimately led to her condemnation) was the notion of the soul's total "annihilation" in union with God and the lack of a solid sense of the salvific role of Christ in the spiritual life.

Russian Spirituality

One of the most striking developments in the Eastern Christian world during these centuries was the foundation of the Russian Church, coinciding with a golden age in the Greek Byzantine Empire. St Anthony of Kiev (983–1073) is credited with bringing the spirituality of Mt Athos to Russia and founding the first monastery at Pechersky in Kiev from which the first Russian bishops, missionaries, and spiritual writers largely came. After a painful period during the thirteenth century marked by the Mongol invasions, monasticism and theological culture revived in Russia during the fourteenth century under St Sergius of Radonesh (1314–1392) who founded the still famous Holy Trinity monastery near Moscow. This led to a wave of new monastic foundations by St Sergius and his followers. St Sergius was both a mystic and an important social force in the birth of Russia.

Two fifteenth-century disciples of St Sergius, St Nils Sorsky (1433–1508) and St Joseph Volotsky (1440–1515), represent diverging interpretations of both monasticism and of spirituality more broadly.

The unfortunate battle between these two schools of spirituality dominated the sixteenth century. In broad terms, St Nils, trained on Mt Athos and representing the hesychast mystical movement, believed that the work of monks was primarily contemplative to be centered on the Jesus Prayer, the study of scripture and patristic theology, and by living simply. His tradition flourished especially in the northern forests, cultivating silence and largely avoiding connections with the growing political power of the princes of Moscow. This style of spirituality lay behind the powerful development of Russian iconography.

The other spiritual tradition took a very different direction. St Joseph and his followers based their spiritual life on an obligation of obedience to God and on a meticulous observance of rituals and liturgical worship. The Josephites were also active and practical rather than purely contemplative-mystical. Their monasteries were large institutions with estates and farms, and some monks became noted social and political advisors to the Muscovite princes. In the short term, the Josephite school came to dominate the Church thanks to their close connections with the political class. There was a strong emphasis on building up the state for which the Church provided a ritual framework and a clear social discipline. The more contemplative-mystical school was actively persecuted and disappeared from public view for some two hundred years, re-emerging as the key to a major spiritual revival in the late eighteenth and nineteenth centuries.[23]

Conclusion

While Jansenism and Quietism were both condemned, it seems fair to say that in some ways a moderate form of Jansenist moralism and penitential asceticism continued to influence much Roman Catholic spirituality into the twentieth century. The seventeenth century ended not only with the triumph of the spirit of Catholic reform but also with the dominance of an anti-mystical approach to spirituality. This is symbolized by the victory of Bishop Bossuet (1627–1704) over Archbishop Fénelon in France. A noted preacher, theologian, and intellectual, Bossuet in some ways reconciled the controversies of his time. However, he was a close confidante of Armand de Rancé whose extremely penitential rather than mystical interpretation of the Cistercian tradition informed his reform of the Abbey of La Trappe (hence the nickname "Trappist" for Strict Observance Cistercians). Equally, Bossuet's sympathy for moderate Jansenist viewpoints ensured that it was a moral, ascetical, and intellectual approach to spirituality that triumphed over the mystical. As a corollary, it is perhaps not surprising that, by way of compensation, a rather sentimental devotionalism increasingly flourished at the Catholic grassroots.

Notes

1   See John van Engen, ed., *Devotio Moderna: Basic Writings*, New York: Paulist Press, 1988 and also H. Blommestijn, C. Caspers, and R. Hofman, eds., *Spirituality Renewed: Studies on Significant Representatives of the Modern Devotion*, Louvain: Peeters, 2003.

2   A brief but good study of Erasmus's spirituality is the introduction to John O'Malley, SJ, ed., *Collected Works of Erasmus: Spiritualia*, Toronto: University of Toronto Press, 1989.

3   See Peter Erb, ed., *Johann Arndt: True Christianity*, New York: Paulist Press, 1979.

4   For a single volume study of Lutheran spirituality see Bradley Hanson, *Grace that Frees: The Lutheran Tradition*, London: Darton Longman & Todd and New York: Orbis Books, 2004.

5   See John Calvin, *Institutes of the Christian Religion*, Grand Rapids: Eerdmans, 1995.

6   On Calvinist spirituality, see W. Bouwsma, "The spirituality of John Calvin" in J. Raitt, ed., *Christian Spirituality: High Middle Ages and Reformation*, New York: Crossroad, 1989 and Howard Rice, *Reformed Spirituality*, Louisville: Westminster John Knox Press, 1991.

7   D. Liechty, ed., *Early Anabaptist Spirituality*, New York: Paulist Press, 1994 and C. Arnold Snyder, *Following in the Footsteps of Christ: The Anabaptist Tradition*, London: Darton Longman & Todd and New York: Orbis Books, 2004.

8   For a selection of Herbert's writings with commentary, see P. Sheldrake, ed., *Heaven in Ordinary: George Herbert & His Writings*, London: Canterbury Press, 2009. Also G. Rowell, K. Stevenson, and R. Williams, eds., *Love's Redeeming Work: The Anglican Quest for Holiness*, Oxford: Oxford University Press, 2001 and William Countryman, *The Poetic Imagination: An Anglican Spiritual Tradition*, London: Darton Longman & Todd and New York: Orbis Books, 1999.

9   R. Lovelace, E. Glenn Hinson, and C.C. Hambrick-Stowe, "Puritan spirituality: The search for a rightly reformed Church" in L. Dupré and Don Saliers, eds., *Christian spirituality: Post-reformation and Modern*, New York: Crossroad, 1989.

10   On Quaker spirituality see, Douglas Steere, ed., *Quaker Spirituality: Selected Writings*, New York: Paulist Press, 1984 and also Michael Birkel, *Silence and Witness: Quaker Spirituality*, London: Darton Longman & Todd and New York: Orbis Books, 2004.

11   Jean Delumeau, *Catholicism Between Luther and Voltaire*, London: Burns & Oates, 1977.

12   On the influences on Ignatius, see, for example, John O'Malley, *The First Jesuits*, Cambridge MA: Harvard University Press, 1993; also J. Melloni, *The Exercises of St Ignatius Loyola in the Western Tradition*, Leominster: Gracewing, 2000; and T. O'Reilly, "The *Spiritual Exercises* and the crisis of medieval piety" in *The Way Supplement* 70, Spring 1991, pp. 101–113.

13   The full texts of the "Autobiography", *Spiritual diary* and *Spiritual Exercises* plus selections of letters are available in J. Munitiz and P. Endean, eds., *Saint Ignatius of Loyola: Personal Writings*, London/New York: Penguin Books, 1996 and G. Ganss, ed., *Ignatius of Loyola: The Spiritual Exercises and selected Works*, New York: Paulist Books, 1991 – this also contains selections from the *Constitutions*. A recent study of Ignatian spirituality is D. Lonsdale, *Eyes to See, Ears to Hear: An Introduction to Ignatian Spirituality*, London: Darton Longman & Todd and New York: Orbis Books, 2000.

14   See Adrian Hastings, ed., *A World History of Christianity*, London: Cassell, 1999, especially Chapters 5, 9, and 10.

15   See Simon Coleman and John Elsner, *Pilgrimage: Past and Present in World Religions*, London: British Museum, 1995, pp. 126–128.

16   See, L. López-Baralt, *San Juan de la Cruz y el Islam: Estudios sobre las filiaciones semíticas de su literatura mística*, Madrid: Hiperion, 1990 and *The Sufi 'trobar clus' and Spanish Mysticism: A Shared Symbolism*, Lahore: Iqbal Academy, 2000. Some John of the Cross scholars suspect that Baralt reads too much into the material but nevertheless believe there may be some Islamic influences.

17   See W. McGreal, *At the Fountain of Elijah: The Carmelite Tradition*, London: Drton Longman & Todd and New York: Orbis Books, 1999; also K. Kavanaugh and O. Rodriguez, eds., *Teresa of Avila: The Interior Castle*, New York: Paulist Press, 1979; and K. Kavanaugh, ed., *John of the Cross: Selected Writings*, New York: Paulist Press, 1987.

18   On the role of devotions in the spirituality of the Catholic reform, see Keith Luria, "The Counter-Reformation and popular spirituality" in L. Dupré and D. Saliers, eds., *Christian Spirituality III: Post-Reformation and Modern*, New York: Crossroad, 1989, Chapter 4.

19   On this point see L. Bouyer, *A History of Christian Spirituality: Volume III Orthodox spirituality and Protestant and Anglican Spirituality*, London: Burns & Oates, 1969, pp. 140–142.

20   See W. Thompson, ed., *Bérulle and the French School: Selected Writings*, New York: Paulist Press, 1989.

21   See Francis de Sales, *Introduction to the Devout Life*, New York: Doubleday, 1982; also P.-M. Thibert, ed., *Francis de Sales & Jane de Chantal: Letters of Spiritual Direction*, New York: Paulist Press, 1988; and W. Wright, *Heart Speaks to Heart: The Salesian Tradition*, London: Darton Longman & Todd and Maryknoll: Orbis Books, 2004.

22   See F. Ryan and J. Rybolt, eds., *Vincent de Paul & Louise de Marillac: Rules, Conferences and Writing*, New York: Paulist Press, 1995.

23   See S. Bolshakoff, *Russian Mystics*, Kalamazoo: Cistercian Publications, 1980 and G.P. Fedotov, ed., *A Treasury of Russian Spirituality*, London: Sheed & Ward, 1981.

Chapter 6

Spirituality in an Age of Reason: 1700–1900

1675–1751	Jean-Pierre de Caussade lives: Jesuit author of *Abandonment to Divine Providence*
1675	Pia Desideria by German Pietist Philipp Jacob Spener
1687–1752	Giovanni Battista Scaramelli lives: Jesuit writer of ascetical and mystical theology
1700–1760	Count von Zinzendorf lives: German ecumenist and Pietist
1703–1791	John Wesley lives: founder of the Methodist movement
1703–1758	Jonathan Edwards lives: leading American theologian and spiritual writer, notably *Religious Affections*, 1746
1707–1788	Charles Wesley lives: brother of John and hymn writer, notably the *Collection of Hymns for the People Called Methodists*, 1780
1724–1804	Immanuel Kant lives: German philosopher
1725–1807	John Newton lives: collaborator of William Wilberforce and leading figure in English Evangelical revival
1731–1800	William Cowper lives: leading figure in Evangelical revival
1759–1833	William Wilberforce lives: Evangelical and leading figure in abolition of slavery
1759–1835	Seraphim of Sarov lives: Russian monk, mystic, and popular spiritual guide
1759–1836	Charles Simeon lives: author of Evangelical meditations, Vicar of Holy Trinity, Cambridge
1771	Arrival of Methodist leader Francis Asbury in America
1773	Papal suppression of the Jesuit Order
1774	Arrival in America of Mother Ann Lee, founder of the Shakers

Spirituality: A Brief History, Second Edition. Philip Sheldrake.
© 2013 John Wiley & Sons, Ltd. Published 2013 by John Wiley & Sons, Ltd.

1774–1821	Elizabeth Seton lives: first canonized American saint, founder of Sisters of Charity
1776–1791	American War of Independence
1779–1865	Madeleine-Sophie Barat lies: saint and founder of Religious of the Sacred Heart
1782	Publication of the *Philokalia*, hesychast texts co-edited by Nikodemos of Mount Athos and Bishop Makarios of Corinth
1786–1859	Jean-Marie Vianney lives: the Curé d'Ars
1786–1850	Edward Bickersteth lives: co-founder of Evangelical Alliance, social reformer
1792–1866	John Keble lives: leading figure in the Oxford Movement
1792–1875	Charles Finney lives: leading American preacher and leader of the Great Revival (1857–1860)
1793	*Philokalia* translated into Russian by Paisius Velichkovsky
1800–1882	John Pusey lives: Regius Professor at Oxford, leading figure in the Oxford Movement
1801–1890	John Henry Newman lives: key figure in Oxford Movement, Roman Catholic convert (1845) and Cardinal and theologian
1801–1885	Anthony Cooper lives: Earl of Shaftesbury, Evangelical and social reformer
1802–1861	Henri Lacordaire lives: French Catholic intellectual and refounder of the Dominicans
1803–1882	Ralph Waldo Emerson lives: leader of American Transcendentalism
1811	*Practical Piety* by Hannah More (1745–1833), leading woman Evangelical
1814	Jesuit Order re-established
1815–1894	Theophan the Recluse lives: leading Russian spiritual figure
1819–1888	Isaac Hecker lives: founder of Paulist Fathers, leader of "Americanism" movement condemned by the Vatican
1833	Prosper Guéranger refounds Solesmes, the influential French Benedictine abbey
1834–1892	Charles Spurgeon lives: Baptist preacher and writer
1847–1924	Stewart Headlam lives: Anglo-Catholic "slum priest" and Christian socialist
1853–1932	Charles Gore lives: Oxford academic, founder of the Community of the Resurrection (Mirfield Fathers 1892) and bishop
1858	Bernadette Soubirous experiences apparitions of the Virgin Mary at Lourdes

1861–1909	George Tyrrell lives: English Jesuit, theologian, spiritual writer, Modernist
1861–1918	Walter Rauschenbusch lives: American Baptist preacher, spiritual writer, and founder of social gospel movement
1873–1897	Thérèse of Lisieux lives: Carmelite nun and spiritual writer
1884	Anonymous Russian spiritual work, *Way of the Pilgrim*, first published
1889	Foundation of Christian Social Union
1891	*Rerum Novarum*, encyclical of Pope Leo XIII gives birth to Catholic social teaching

For the eighteenth century, it is striking that many histories of spirituality are sparse in comparison to other periods. There are few spiritual movements of great originality or lasting significance. However, it would be unfair to conclude that the eighteenth century is spiritually dead. Much was going on that would flower in the late nineteenth century (and even more in the twentieth century) in new and creative directions.

If we begin by outlining the broad social and cultural climate of eighteenth- and nineteenth-century Europe and North America, three factors stand out: the Enlightenment, the political revolutions in France and America, and the Industrial Revolution. These are the foundations of what is often described as Modernity. The pre-Modern world, in which religion dominated not only spiritually but politically, socially, and intellectually, gave way to a new world in which independent human reason came to dominate.

The origins of "modernity" actually lie in the late medieval period with philosophical Nominalism (associated with the Franciscan William of Ockham). To simplify matters considerably, this stressed a separation of faith from reason. God was ultimately unknowable and therefore could not be revealed through reason or the natural world. Theology, faith, and spirituality were on one side and human knowledge (philosophy and science) were on the other. However, this process received its greatest impetus from the mid-seventeenth century in a movement known as the Enlightenment. In a sense, Europe was exhausted by a century of religious conflict, factionalism, and, in the opinion of many, dangerous fanaticism. There was a growing sense of detachment from a long stream of tradition and authority that made space for doubt and even unbelief. So, the dominant intellectual climate retreated from the experiential into rationalism and objectivity. Religion was increasingly described in terms of moral obligations and was fearful of the irrational.

By the late eighteenth century, the great Enlightenment philosopher Immanuel Kant (1724–1804) sought a religion without revelation. It would be too simplistic to call Kant an agnostic or religious skeptic. He was certainly not an orthodox Lutheran but, by cutting the ground from under traditional metaphysics (i.e. by denying that we can have *knowledge* of realities that transcend nature) and invalidating the classic proofs for God's existence, he claimed to be making proper room for faith rather than the opposite. What drove his religious vision was neither natural theology nor mysticism but conscience which, Kant asserted, alone teaches the reality of a righteous God who will vindicate the claims of moral justice. In this perspective, religion effectively becomes ethics. However, while much religion sought to accommodate itself to the new climate, other religious movements reacted against it.

Spirituality in the Roman Catholic Tradition

In Roman Catholic circles, a suspicion of Quietism led to the triumph of a moral-ascetical approach to spirituality over an affective-mystical one. In addition, the tendency in much seventeenth-century French spirituality, even beyond Jansenist circles, to emphasize human unworthiness and abasement before God led to a preoccupation with acquiring virtues such as humility and obedience. This quest for virtue was promoted by a life of methodical, disciplined prayer.

While a number of new religious communities that survive to this day were founded in the eighteenth century (e.g. the Redemptorists and Passionists, with male and female branches and mixed ascetical-missionary lifestyles), it seems fair to say that few major spiritual writers appeared in this period. Spirituality was expressed more in action than in substantial teaching. After a golden age of writing in sixteenth-century Spanish and seventeenth-century French spiritualities, the link between spirituality and the great traditions of the past became increasingly thin. Eighteenth-century spirituality was associated more with particular devotions. However, the work of at least two figures demands attention: the Italian Jesuit Giovanni Battista Scaramelli (1687–1752) and the French Jesuit Jean-Pierre de Caussade (1675–1751).

It appears that Scaramelli, with his *Direttorio ascetico* (1752) and *Direttorio mistico* (1754), was the first person to establish the titles of "ascetical theology" and "mystical theology" in a way that became common in Roman Catholic circles, especially seminaries and religious communities. Scaramelli entered the Jesuit Order in 1706 and from 1722 was employed chiefly in giving retreats and spiritual direction. His books became classics and were designed primarily for the use of spiritual directors. However, they helped significantly in the process of stabilizing the vocabulary of Christian perfection for some two hundred years. Notably, the process and progress of the spiritual life was conceived in two stages. So, ascetical theology dealt with the form and progress of the Christian life, based on disciplined practices, as it applied to the majority. Mystical theology analyzed the more advanced stages of the spiritual life up to mystical union – applicable only to a special minority. Apart from encouraging a rather detailed, detached, and analytical (some would even say forensic) approach to the spiritual life, this specialist vocabulary encouraged an eventual isolation of the discipline of spiritual theology from the remainder of theology (not true of Scaramelli himself) and its subordination to moral theology of which it eventually became a sub-category. Interestingly, Scaramelli clearly wished spiritual directors to be well acquainted with Christian doctrine and was obviously more sympathetic to mysticism than many of his contemporaries who were nervous of Quietism. Indeed, he was forced to alter parts of his *Direttorio mistico* in response to some serious objections. It is fair to suggest that Scaramelli's dry formalism – which has been criticized in recent times – disguised more pro-mystical sensibilities.

Because Jean-Pierre de Caussade looked back to Ignatius Loyola, to the Carmelite mystics, and to Francis de Sales, some writers describe him as the end of the golden age of seventeenth-century French spirituality rather than specific to the eighteenth century. De Caussade lived a relatively obscure life as a Jesuit who from 1728 acted as chaplain and spiritual director to a community of cloistered Visitation nuns in Nancy. He was suspected of Quietism and had to withdraw for two years 1731–1733. In 1739, he left Nancy to become a superior elsewhere and ended his life as spiritual director at the Jesuit house at Toulouse. During his own lifetime, de Caussade was relatively unknown, publishing one anonymous work on prayer in the form of a dialogue expounding the teachings of Bossuet. The work by which he is widely known, and which has remained a popular spiritual classic since its publication in 1867, is *L'Abandon à la Providence divine*, variously translated in English as *Abandonment to Divine Providence* or *The Sacrament of the Present Moment*. This draws on his letters and instructions to the nuns at Nancy and encapsulates his fundamental spiritual teachings. In the book, de Caussade is not interested in exceptional states but teaches a kind of mysticism of everyday life based on self-giving (abandonment) to God revealed to each person in the ordinary circumstances of life. From this arises the notion of "the sacrament of the present moment." Prayer is one of simple attentiveness and waiting on God. De Caussade's version of "abandonment" is very different from Quietist passivity because it involves active discernment of the presence of God and an active response of self-giving based on the certainty of God's irrevocable love.[1]

Pietism

Pietism arose in Protestant Germany and flourished mainly in the late seventeenth and eighteenth centuries in response to rationalist or over-institutionalized forms of religion. While predominantly related to Lutheranism, Pietism also influenced the Reformed Church in the Netherlands, the renewal of the Moravian Brethren, John Wesley the founder of Methodism, and later Evangelical revivals in different parts of Protestantism. Pietism spread to Scandinavia and had a particularly strong impact on Norwegian Lutheranism in the nineteenth century. From there it spread to mission territories and to North America. The leading figures in the original German Pietism were Philipp Jacob Spener (1635–1705) and his friend August Francke (1663–1727).

While Pietists were for the most part a group within Protestant Churches, the Moravian Brethren (known commonly as the Moravian Church) are interesting in that Pietism defined their essential ethos. They descended from the Bohemian Brethren, a fifteenth-century evangelical reform movement. At the Reformation, the Brethren were allied at different times with both Lutherans and Calvinists. In 1721, the exiled remnant of the Brethren amalgamated with the Herrnhut community in Saxony under the influence of the ecumenically minded Count von Zinzendorf (1700–1760). John Wesley visited Herrnhut, and it was the Pietism of the Moravians that had a particular influence on early Methodism including its hymnody (which John Wesley translated) and the use of periodic Love Feasts. Moravian spirituality reflected some elements of the radical Reformation such as pacifism, discipline, and simplicity but, above all, a religion of the heart. There is an intense devotional element focused especially on Christ's humanity and sufferings. Overall, the Moravian tradition, while small in itself, played a prominent role in eighteenth-century Pietism.

Overall, Pietism was a religion of the heart and emphasized the presence of God in everyday life. The original motivation of the movement was to encourage a recovery of the experiential dimension of faith. Genuine conversion to God, inner transformation, and holiness of life expressed in good works were more vital than a mere affirmation of doctrinal orthodoxy. Pietism can really be said to have become a movement in 1675 with the publication of Spener's *Pia Desideria* (*Pious Desires*) and with the development of small groups known as *collegia pietatis* (hence the title Pietists) who met in groups outside normal worship in the parish churches. These bore some resemblance to present-day Bible study groups or even to the "basic communities" of contemporary liberation theology. They met in homes to pray, read the Bible (but with devotional attention rather than moral or doctrinal interest), and to offer mutual spiritual guidance. In the context of orthodox Lutheranism, Pietists tended to be more optimistic about the human ability to overcome sin and to grow in the spiritual life. Their main aim was to combat the lack of spiritual vitality in the Church.[2]

Wesleyan Spirituality

Wesleyan or Methodist spirituality is associated in a fundamental way with the work of the two brothers and Church of England priests John Wesley (1703–1791) and Charles Wesley (1707–1788). Although the Wesley brothers never ceased to consider themselves priests in the Church of England, they represented an Evangelical and devotional reaction against the formalism and growing rationalism prevalent in the Church of their day. Influenced in part by German Pietism, a strong current of affective devotion was apparent in the life and work especially of John Wesley. While a young Fellow of Lincoln College, Oxford, in the early 1730s, John Wesley gathered together a community of other young men known as the "Holy Club" in order to cultivate a more intense personal spirituality. Their earnestness and disciplined regime of prayer and study gained them the nickname "Methodists," and this name eventually defined the societies the Wesley brothers founded around the country as a means of spreading their spiritual reform. John Wesley himself experienced what some might call a conversion experience, others a mystical illumination, at a spiritual meeting in Aldersgate Street, London, in May 1738. Here he recorded that he felt his heart "strangely warmed" and received an intense sense of Christ's love for him personally and assurance of Christ's salvation.

Apart from German Pietism, John Wesley drew on a remarkably wide range of influences including the early Church fathers, à Kempis and the *devotio moderna*, a number of seventeenth-century Caroline Divines such as Jeremy Taylor and Joseph Hall, Puritans like Richard Baxter (the Wesleys had Puritan ancestry), and in his own time the Anglican mystic William Law. It also seems clear that Wesley read and was influenced by a number of figures in the continental Catholic Reform, especially Francis de Sales, representatives of the French mystical tradition, the Italian Theatine priest Lorenzo Scupoli (whose *The Spiritual Warfare* had a remarkable impact beyond the Roman Catholic Church), and a number of Jesuit works. However, despite occasional claims by Wesley's enemies that he was a crypto-Jesuit and more friendly suggestions about his Ignatian influences, there is no evidence that he knew the *Spiritual Exercises*, and so any Ignatian influences were from secondary sources.[3]

Apart from the cultivation of attention to personal holiness, John Wesley was increasingly fired by a desire to evangelize those people who were effectively untouched by the ministry of the Church of England and to his mind were ignorant of God's love and the call to perfection. In the context of the times, this largely meant the working classes. Wesley became famous for his missionary preaching journeys on horseback throughout all the parts of Britain and Ireland. By the late 1760s, the Methodist revival had reached North America, and in 1771, just before the war of independence, Francis Asbury was sent to America to supervise the growing movement there.

For all his interest in a certain kind of mystical sensibility and attention to personal, "experimental" faith, Wesley was suspicious of excessive Quietism or contemplative passivity. Love and service of neighbor (particularly the poor and needy), and a spirituality that combined prayer and action, were prerequisites of scriptural holiness as Wesley understood it. Wesley accepted classical Reformation teaching on justification by faith but rejected Calvinist ideas of limited atonement. The universal need for salvation drove his missionary endeavors, and he preached a universal offer of salvation that could be known with utter assurance. Perhaps drawing on both his Puritan ancestry and his experiences of continental Pietism, Wesley organized his movement into a network of "classes" which met to read the Bible, pray, and to offer mutual spiritual encouragement and correction. The fundamental framework for Wesleyan spirituality (expressed in a tract called the *Large Minutes*) had five elements: prayer both personal and collective, scriptural reading and meditation, frequent Communion, fasting on Fridays, and spiritual conversation. Collectively, apart from class meetings, there were occasional Love Feasts (learned from the Moravians), an annual renewal of commitment known as the Covenant Service and night-time prayer vigils modeled in the early Church. While there were weekly preaching services, Wesley assumed that the "people known as Methodists" would also attend the normal services in the parish church, and he had a high view of the Eucharist, theologically and in terms of encouraging frequent Communion. It was only after Wesley's death that the Methodist movement definitively became separate from Anglicanism.

One of the most striking features of Wesleyan spirituality is hymnody. While hymn singing is now a common feature in most denominations, it was especially characteristic of Methodist corporate spirituality. Hymns have a particular capacity to combine the personal and collective dimensions of prayer and worship. The frequent use of hymns significantly shapes a person's or a congregation's spiritual outlook and even doctrinal standpoint. In the Methodist context, hymns were not strictly speaking liturgical in that they were not explicitly attached either to the seasons and festivals of the Church year or to particular parts of the Communion service – although a significant number of Charles Wesley's hymns are eucharistic or embody eucharistic themes. Wesleyan hymns often blended scriptural ideas or images with a personal, sometimes fairly emotional response. While John Wesley translated Moravian hymns, Charles Wesley is credited with composing over 7,000 of his own. The classic 1780 edition of Charles Wesley's hymnal, *Collection of Hymns for the Use of the People Called Methodists*, is a veritable source book of Methodist theology and spirituality in five parts, addressing every facet of Christian life and holiness such as fighting, praying, working, and suffering. In John Wesley's preface to the hymnal, he offers a good summary of what we might call "a spirituality of hymns":

> I would recommend it to every truly pious reader as a means of raising or quickening the spirit of devotion, of confirming his faith, of enlivening his hope, and of increasing his love to God and man. When poetry thus keeps its place as the handmaid of piety, it shall attain, not a poor perishable wreath, but a crown that fadeth not away.[4]

American Puritanism and the Great Awakening

In a particular sense, the emergence of a distinctive "American spirituality" will be dealt with later in relation to the period after the American Revolution (1776–1791). However, in eighteenth-century terms, it is important to note two significant spiritual movements: the Great Awakening among Puritans and the emergence of the Shakers.

A key figure in the "Great Awakening" or revival in mid-eighteenth-century America among the Dutch Reformed, Presbyterians, and Congregationalists, and its most important thinker, was Jonathan

Edwards of Massachusetts (1703–1758). He was a Congregationalist minister, Evangelical preacher, and Calvinist theologian. The Great Awakening was the first of many revivals in America and set in train a revivalist tendency in American Protestant spirituality that not only emphasized conversion but a robust individualism. Stress was laid on visible evidence of conversion. There was considerable disagreement on the relative importance of religious experience and sound doctrine. Edwards sought to bring the two elements more closely together. Educated at Yale, he became a minister at Northampton, Massachusetts, in 1727, where he served during a series of spiritual revivals until forced to step down in 1750 due to his strict interpretations of the standards for reception of Communion. He subsequently worked with Native American peoples until in 1757 he became President of College of New Jersey, later Princeton, where he soon died. Edwards preached the necessity of new birth and supported Evangelical revival as a work of the Holy Spirit but also wrote against an excessive emotionalism in revivals by defending the role of the will and the intellect. He was a theologically conservative Calvinist and also a capable philosopher and ethicist.

Perhaps Edwards' most important work concerned how to discern the presence and work of the Holy Spirit. On the one hand, he wished to affirm the validity of what were called "holy affections" (i.e. emotions, passions, and inward experience), but, on the other, he argued against reducing spirituality to a false emotionalism. In his classic book, *Religious Affections* (1746), Edwards suggested key signs to guide individuals in discernment of the true presence of the Spirit in inward experience. The central criteria are as follows. First, there is a genuine increase in sensitivity to what is spiritual. Second, there is an increase in disinterested love of God. Third, the affections manifest an enlightened mind. Fourth, there is a positive conviction of God's reality and an attitude of humility before God. Fifth, there is transformation away from a life of sin. Sixth, the results are meekness, quietness, forgiveness, and mercy. Seventh, joy in, and fear of, God are held in balance. Eighth, there is an increase of spiritual desire and longing. Ninth, there is a transformation of outward behavior in conformity with a Christian attitude to the world.[5]

Shaker Spirituality

The Shakers, Shaking Quakers, or, officially, The United Society of Believers in Christ's Second Appearing, originated in England but moved to North America and are generally understood as an American spiritual tradition. The origins of the Shakers lie in ecstatic and millenarian Quaker circles in Manchester, England. Ann Lee (1736–1784), an illiterate factory worker, entered this circle around 1758 and emerged as a leader. She was a visionary who began proclaiming celibacy as the road to the Kingdom of God, and gradually a simple communal lifestyle emerged along with a Spirit-filled worship that included ecstatic dancing. After imprisonment for disrupting church services, and a vision of her union with Christ, Mother Ann as she came to be known moved to America in 1774 with a few disciples. They settled near Albany in what is now New York State and suffered for their pacifist beliefs during the War of Independence. After a missionary journey by Ann Lee in New York and New England, a number of scattered communities were founded. Later on, in the nineteenth century, Shaker communities also spread to the Midwest and to Kentucky, although by the end of the century their numerical decline led to a retreat back to the East Coast. As celibates they relied on intentional commitment for new members, but as, unlike monastic life, they had no deeper hinterland of church membership beyond the celibate communities themselves, commitment was through conversion. Initially such conversions came largely via various revival movements in the nineteenth century, but as revivalism increasingly turned into renewal *within* mainstream Protestant groups, the supply of conversions to Shaker communities dried up. There now remains only one Shaker community at Sabbathday Lake, Maine, but at the end of the twentieth century, there has been a revival of interest in the values and spirituality of the Shakers, and the growing influence of the small community is out of proportion to its numbers.

The fundamental spiritual perspective of the Shaker tradition is a mystical experience of union in Christ. This is not simply personal but collective in that this union embraces all who share the gift. The Shaker experience began with the expectation of the second coming of Christ, but the apocalyptic expectations of the Shakers were transformed in unusual directions. First, they had no detailed sense of what the transformation brought about in the second coming would actually involve. Therefore, preparation for it was necessarily inward rather than in concrete actions. Following their Quaker origins, the first Shakers believed they were called by God's Spirit to seek a greater light and that an increase in Inner Light implied the pursuit of spiritual perfection. The inner work of preparation for Christ's second coming was manifested in signs such as wordless song, glossolalia, ecstatic dancing, and so on. Instead of emphasizing sin and the corruption of human nature, Shakers proclaimed a much more optimistic belief in the ultimate perfectibility of human nature. Along with their rejection of the doctrine of humanity's irrevocable sinfulness, Shakers also rejected any form of worship which reflected a never-ending recapitulation of sin and forgiveness. Paradoxically, however, they did practice individual auricular confession to an elder as a spiritual discipline. Eventually in the nineteenth century, Shaker worship became less spontaneously charismatic and moved in the direction of more formalized spiritual exercises such as sacred dancing. The extraordinary craftsmanship of the Shakers, not least their furniture, also expressed the way in which they saw work as a form of worship.

It has sometimes been suggested that Shakers believed that Ann Lee was uniquely a new incarnation of Christ or a female Christ, but this is wholly misleading. Mother Ann was seen as the medium through which all were reborn, but it is in the combined experiences of Mother Ann and all the others together that Christ is come. Hence, if Christ is alive, it is in the *union* of believers – hence the title of the Society. However, the Shakers did develop an inclusive sense of God's reality in which male and female aspects are present. The identity of Christ is shared in and through the tangible life of the community. That is why Shaker life became celibate. Celibacy was the central image of the new life-in-Christ, the New Creation. Celibacy is understood as living Resurrection life now. Equally, it implies embracing *all* people without exception rather than limiting the deepest commitment only to partner and family. A process of entry and stages of "formation" prior to final commitment not unlike monastic life was gradually introduced. The corollary of Shaker celibacy and inclusive community is a commitment to absolute peace towards all, equality (not least of men and women long before it became common in wider society), and to a radical common sharing of goods. It is not surprising that the twentieth-century monk, spiritual writer, and pacifist Thomas Merton found great affinities between the Shaker way and his own Cistercian life and values.[6]

Orthodox Spirituality

A significant development in Eastern Orthodox spirituality took place in the late eighteenth century, that is, the compilation of the *Philokalia*, and this had a significant impact on the nature of Russian spirituality in the nineteenth century.

The *Philokalia* (i.e. "the love of beautiful things") is a collection of texts on prayer drawn from the Eastern tradition from the fourth to the fifteenth centuries (with Western material from John Cassian) and edited by two

Greek monk-theologians, Nikodemos of Mount Athos (1749–1809) and Bishop Makarios of Corinth (1731–1805) as part of a spiritual renewal of the Church in Greece. This was first published in Venice in 1782 and both preserved and disseminated the hesychastic tradition of prayer. There are guidelines for the Orthodox version of the classic stages of spiritual development combined with teaching about contemplative prayer through the practice of inward stillness or *hesychia*.

Nikodemos was a highly educated author of many works who settled on Mount Athos in 1775. Makarios was a prominent traditionalist bishop. Both were overtly opposed to Western influences and promoted a spiritual renewal based on the classic Byzantine tradition. However, despite his professed anti-Catholicism, Nikodemos helped to popularize Western spirituality within Orthodoxy through his *Spiritual Exercises*, which rely closely on writings of the Italian Jesuit J-P. Pinamonti (1632–1703), and his popular *Unseen Warfare* was more or less a translation of Scupoli's *Spiritual Combat*.

The spirituality of the *Philokalia* stresses the hesychast values of inwardness, stillness, and vigilance but is not individualistic in that it also emphasizes the sacramental life including, controversially, frequent Communion. The purpose of the spiritual life is *theosis* or deification through prayer, especially the so-called Jesus Prayer.[7]

The text was widely copied not least in Russia where the first Slavonic translation was produced by Paisius Velichkovsky (1722–1794) in St Petersburg in 1793. This was the version carried by the anonymous wandering pilgrim in the famous *The Way of the Pilgrim*.[8] Another translation by Theophan the Recluse (1815–1894) influenced the novels of Dostoevsky. The Jesus Prayer became the normal form of contemplative prayer in Russian monasteries during the nineteenth century. Equally importantly, it was the form of prayer adopted by devout laypeople, but always under the guidance of a spiritual director. So, while the Westernization of Russia from the mid-eighteenth century onwards saw the Church lose hold of the aristocracy and the intelligentsia, the mass of ordinary Russians were still largely devout right up to the 1917 Revolution.

In *The Way of the Pilgrim*, the pilgrim is taught the hesychast tradition of prayer by his *staretz*, or spiritual director. The appearance of monks who acted as spiritual guides (*startzy*) to laypeople and the process of "spiritual direction" (*starchestvo*) really increased exponentially after the translation of the *Philokalia*. The nineteenth century, while a time of pre-revolutionary turbulence and great social upheaval, was also a monastic golden age. This was not a simple question of cultural or religious conservatism because monastic figures were often people with a profound concern for "this world" and for humanity and showed a striking compassion. The best *startzy* were completely identified with the humble and poor. Spiritual guidance was based on traditional monastic wisdom as well as good psychological insight and plain common sense. A good *staretz* was not necessarily exceptionally austere or learned but had surrendered completely to the demands of the gospel and to charity. Many had reputations for humility, meekness, openness to everyone, and for patient, compassionate love.

The most remarkable groups were gathered around the monastery of Optino, one of the most famous monastic communities in nineteenth-century Russia. The three greatest *startzy* were Leonid Nagolkin, Macarius Ivanov, who was particularly noted from breaking down the traditional barriers between monasticism and lay Christians, and Ambrose Grenkov. The anonymous author of *The Way of the Pilgrim* also belonged to this circle. Between them, the monks of Optino directed a number of eminent people not least skeptics and intellectuals such as Gogol, Dostoevsky, Tolstoy, and Soloviev. Dostoevsky used Father Ambrose as the model for the *staretz* Zosima in the novel *Brothers Karamazov*.[9]

A second important monastic group was at Sarov. Its greatest representative was St Seraphim of Sarov (1759–1833) – a profound mystic and the most popular saint in modern Russia. Seraphim entered Sarov monastery in 1779. After monastic training and ordination, he lived for many years as a hermit in the forest in intense ascetical practice. He regularly received visitors, monks, and laypeople, women as well as men, for spiritual conversation. Eventually Seraphim returned to live in the monastery, initially in relative solitude but in his later years in a state of extraordinary availability to others. He left his "Instructions," and his sayings were recorded by friends. The *Talks with Motovilov* on the purpose of the Christian life became a classic. During these conversations, the phenomenon of transfiguration took place (i.e. both people were surrounded by intense light). For Seraphim, the goal of the Christian life was the acquisition of the Holy Spirit. We receive this when baptized but lose it through sin and then regain it through the sacraments (especially regular Communion), true faith, and Christ-like living. Those who attain the highest degree of the grace of the Spirit are transfigured. Seraphim taught a positive spirituality – a mysticism of light, joy, and resurrection rather than a dark spirituality of sin, Cross, and spiritual torment. At the heart of his spirituality was the notion of the Holy Spirit permanently dwelling within each person. He embraced all people and all creation in a unity within the love of God.[10]

Post-Revolutionary Catholicism

As we have seen, Roman Catholic spirituality during the eighteenth century suffered from both elements of Jansenism and also a related suspicion of interiority and mysticism. The authority of the Roman Catholic Church on the Continent was further undermined by the intellectual skepticism of people such as Voltaire in France and by attempts to curb the temporal authority of the papacy by the Austrian Emperor and in the Kingdoms of Spain and Portugal. The independence of a number of religious orders was attacked. Most famously, the Society of Jesus was suppressed from 1773 to 1814 (except in Russia and Prussia where the papal writ did not run). The already weak position of the Church was further undermined by the massive upheaval of the French Revolution and subsequent wars across Western Europe which led to the wholesale suppression of monasteries and religious communities, the closure of schools, universities, and other Church-run institutions, and even the execution of hundreds of priests and members of religious communities.

Although the liberal and democratic traditions that found their origin in the American and French Revolutions had a largely positive impact in the long term, it was understandable that Catholic spirituality during the nineteenth century was deeply affected by an emphasis on reconstruction. This placed more value on Church institutions and on the restoration of authority than on either the development of new forms of spiritual wisdom or on a constructive engagement with the new social and cultural climate. A large number of new religious congregations were founded, especially for women. Indeed, the nineteenth century saw the greatest expansion of religious life since the Reformation. Most groups were dedicated to some form of educational or nursing apostolate (e.g. the Religious of the Sacred Heart in France founded by Madeleine-Sophie Barat, the Daughters of the Cross in Liège, and the Little Sisters of the Poor). The Dominican Order was re-established in France by Henri Lacordaire (1802–1861) and the Benedictines by Dom Prosper Guéranger. Lacordaire had originally belonged to a group of young intellectuals (such as de Lammenais) who sought to "translate" traditional Catholicism into modern guise by engaging sympathetically with post-Enlightenment thought and with the new climate of political progress. None of this found favor with a restored papacy that was nervous of liberalism after its Revolutionary experiences. Eventually Lacordaire moved in a more conservative direction and like Guéranger (who refounded Solesmes as the center of a major monastic and liturgical revival) tended to support greater uniformity and what might be called the "Romanization" of their religious orders. Overall, during the century, Roman Catholic spirituality (with exceptions) tended to be restorationist and defensive rather than innovative.

Popular piety increased in prominence and was dominated by an emphasis on miracles and visions. There were several notable reports of apparitions of the Virgin Mary of which the ones at Lourdes (1858) to Bernadette Soubirous (1844–1879) were the origin of the major center of pilgrimage, not least for sick people, that continues to the present day. It may be argued that, as with many visionaries of earlier centuries, the reported apparitions acted as the spiritual empowerment and authorization of someone whose social (and therefore religious) status was otherwise not worthy of attention. Apart from being a young woman of only fourteen when she reported her visions, Bernadette also came from a poor family. Despite attempts to discredit Bernadette's sanity, motives, and her surrounding influences, her visionary accounts actually come across as clear and unpretentious. She subsequently worked with the sick at a local hospital and eventually joined a branch of the Sisters of Charity, living at the motherhouse at Nevers where her notebooks reveal a deep spirituality of self-donation to God and to others.

Apart from a major figure in England, John Henry Newman, who will be considered under the Oxford Movement, two of the more interesting European spiritual personalities of the century were Jean Marie Vianney and Thérèse of Lisieux. Jean Vianney, or the Curé d'Ars (1786–1859), was not a spiritual writer but expressed in his life and pastoral practice an attractive combination of vigor and profound spiritual insight combined with humility and simplicity. He came from a peasant family near Lyons and trained for the priesthood under a Jansenist-inspired parish priest at Écully where he became curate. In 1818, he moved to the village of Ars where he remained for over forty years. Early Jansenist influences remained to some degree, perhaps in a fear for his own salvation and undoubtedly in his belief that the overwhelming duty of a priest was to reconcile sinful people to God in the sacrament of confession. He attracted vast queues of people drawn by his reputation for extraordinary insight and foreknowledge as well as for kindness and was available for counsel for up to sixteen hours a day. This, combined with a reputation for healings and other miracles, gave birth to a popular cult that led to his canonization in 1925.

The enclosed Carmelite nun, Thérèse of Lisieux (1873–1897), is now thought to have suffered after her death from the heavy editing of her spiritual autobiography and letters. A certain version of Thérèse was promoted by her community in the publication of the *Story of a Soul* which became an international bestseller and a kind of icon of Catholicism up to Vatican II. In recent decades, a more complex Thérèse has been significantly retrieved to reveal a figure of spiritual substance behind some of her rather cloying language.[11] Thérèse Martin lost her mother when she was four and was raised by her father and two eldest sisters, both of whom entered the Lisieux Carmel near where they lived in Northern France. Thérèse followed her two sisters into the monastery in 1888 aged only fifteen after a stubborn battle against the authorities who wanted to delay her entry. She lived there for less than ten years before dying of tuberculosis. Her writings reveal a close attention to scripture, particularly the gospels and St Paul. Her spirituality is notable for the concept of "the little way" – a version of the theme of abasement or self-emptying that characterized French spirituality since the seventeenth century. However, in Thérèse this is marked by two special features: first, in the light of her reading of St Paul, a sense of utter dependence on God's grace in simple trust or "spiritual childhood" (which some have compared to Luther) and, second, a spirituality of everyday love and of finding God in the pains and pleasures of each day. Although Thérèse was familiar with the mystical writings of fellow Carmelites Teresa of Avila and John of the Cross, her "little way" offered a spirituality of small actions that influenced large numbers of people who sought a credible spiritual framework for everyday, ordinary existence. In addition, Thérèse had a remarkable sense of sharing in the active mission of the Church. At one point, she sought to volunteer for a foundation in Vietnam and also carried on an intense correspondence with several priest missionaries. Thérèse's last year and a half were marked not only by illness but by spiritual darkness, a "night of nothingness," in which she battled with the silence of God and the possibility that her faith was an illusion. However, Thérèse seems to have broken through to an intensity of mystical engagement with each moment in which all that remained was a desire to love.

The English Evangelicals

The spiritual landscape of nineteenth-century England was dominated by two major movements within the Church of England: the Evangelical revival and the Oxford Movement. The latter also overflowed in important ways into the revival of Roman Catholicism after 1850.

The Evangelical revival really dates back to the middle of the eighteenth century, partly as a reaction against the prevailing rationalism of Enlightenment thought and partly as a religious response to the social degradation of the new "Industrial Revolution." Squalid physical conditions evoked a strong sense of the need for religious salvation. Evangelicalism was inspired in part by the legacy of Puritanism from the previous century, the impact of continental Pietism, and the itinerant preaching of the Wesley brothers. In addition, people like William Cowper (1731–1800) and John Newton (1725–1807) were influenced by the late medieval *devotio moderna* as well as by seventeenth-century French Catholic writers such as Guyon, Fénelon, Bossuet, and Pascal.

The theological basis for English Evangelicalism was fundamentally Calvinist. The spirituality associated with it had a number of central characteristics. First, the centrality of the Bible was preached as the moral and spiritual touchstone of life. Through hearing the word of God, people experienced both the need for and assurance of salvation. Second, everyone needed conversion. This implied an inner transformation which in turn involved a deepening relationship with Christ. Third, the cross of Christ was at the heart of the human experience of salvation. Consequently, conversion implied giving up one's own way and following the crucified savior. Fourth, following this way necessarily led to a serious sense of moral responsibility. Fifth, prayer should accompany all aspects of life, personal, family, and social – and this involved serious Bible reading as a means of spiritual growth. Finally, conversion to Christ implied a life of action.

Compared with the work of the Quakers, the Salvation Army, or Anglo-Catholic "slum priests" later in the nineteenth century, the Evangelical movement has sometimes been accused of lacking a spirituality of social engagement. This is an unfair generalization. It is true that "action" implied an active spreading of the word of God (evangelism) expressed, for example, in the work of the Church Missionary Society throughout the British Empire. However, for many people action also implied social philanthropy. The former slave trader John Newton, later Rector of St Mary Woolnoth in the City of London, became a notable supporter of William Wilberforce's campaign to abolish slavery. In turn, Newton influenced people such as Hannah More (1745–1833), one of the most notable women in the Evangelical revival. While socially conservative and well-connected, Hannah More was a noted educationalist who established a school in Bristol, set up Sunday schools, and was active among the poor and passionately opposed to slavery. She was also a popular spiritual writer, producing especially *Practical Piety* (1811) aimed at a broad lay readership. William Wilberforce (1759–1833) was the leading champion of the abolition of slavery as a result of his Evangelical conversion. Wilberforce witnessed to the direct connection between spirituality and social action by beginning each working day with two hours of prayer and Bible reading. Wilberforce became the political leader of the Evangelical movement, and on his death this role was taken on by Anthony Cooper, the Earl of Shaftesbury (1801–1885), a leading Conservative parliamentarian and one of the greatest social reformers of the nineteenth century. His overwhelming concern was the improvement of living and working conditions for the urban working classes. He was also a noted factory reformer – particularly in reference to child and female labor.

For all that the Evangelical movement preached the importance of prayer, it produced relatively few treatises on the subject. Hannah Moore wrote *Spirit of Prayer* and perhaps the most substantial equivalent to a Catholic treatise was *A Treatise on Prayer* by Edward Bickersteth (1786–1850), a lawyer turned priest who was a collaborator of the Earl of Shaftesbury in factory reform and one of the founders of the Evangelical Alliance that survives to this day. Charles Simeon (1759–1836) also wrote *Evangelical Meditations* and was in many ways the de facto leader of the Evangelical movement during his years as Vicar of Holy Trinity Church, Cambridge. Simeon was noted particularly as a preacher but, like Newton and others, was also concerned for social justice. Simeon preached that all people have the image of God within which, while marred by sin, implants a deep desire that (following Augustine) can only be satisfied in God. This infinite longing points us towards unlimited fullness. As well as this spirituality of desire, Simeon preached a religion of joy rather than dour seriousness.

In England, many of the leading figures of the nineteenth-century Evangelical movement came from wealthy or well-educated backgrounds and were loyal members of the established Church of England. A notable exception on both counts was Charles Spurgeon (1834–1892), the great Baptist preacher who spent over thirty years as Minister of London's Metropolitan Tabernacle, still a vast neoclassical "cathedral" in the Baptist tradition. Spurgeon's spirituality was expressed largely in sermons (some three and a half thousand of them survive) to congregations as large as five to six thousand people! He was a thorough-going Calvinist who sought to convince the mind as well as move the heart. In line with his orthodox Calvinism, Spurgeon preached the spiritual significance of the sacrament of the Lord's Supper and, unusually, insisted on a weekly celebration. Although he spoke of a spiritual rather than corporeal presence, one of his sermons on Communion adopts physical imagery in inviting the congregation to put their fingers into the print of Christ's nails.[12]

The Oxford Movement

The Oxford Movement, which led to the eventual formation of a strong Anglican Catholic tradition, was, like the Evangelical movement, another reaction to the dominance of rationalism in Church circles and of religious skepticism and apathy in surrounding culture. The leading figures were four young academics at the University of Oxford, John Keble, Richard Froude, Edward Pusey, and John Henry Newman. Their overall project was to recover what they saw as the patristic and pre-Reformation heritage of the Church of England. This project was promoted in a series of pamphlets, *Tracts for the Times* (hence the alternative title, Tractarian, for the movement). The movement was not simply reactionary or defensive but sought what its members saw as authentic Christianity. This embraced the restoration of a Catholic sensibility to the Church of England and, among some members at least, a concern for social improvements in the rapidly expanding industrial cities.

The Oxford Movement (or Tractarianism), and its successor Anglo-Catholicism, stressed a number of key values and spiritual principles. First, there was a strong sacramental emphasis (especially the Eucharist and frequent reception) linked to a "high" doctrine of the Church. Second, there was an emphasis on the visible aids to devotion in art, decoration, church architecture, and so on. Third, the underlying spiritual theology drew not simply on the seventeenth-century Carolines but also, and more importantly, on the writings of the Early Church (patristics) and on mystical writers. There was an emphasis on an integrated spirituality of body, heart, and mind, on inner transformation, and on the potential for union with God in Christ rather than the Calvinist stress on God's distance and a spirituality based largely on obedience to divine law. The sacramentality of Tractarianism also emphasized God's presence in creation and an incarnational theology. The Tractarians sought holiness through a properly ordered liturgy and Church disciplines such as fasting (partly to counter the supposed "emotionalism" and subjectivity of the Evangelicals) combined with rich ceremonial to emphasize the "mystical" ethos of worship. There was also an extraordinary expansion of church construction characterized by the birth of a new style of religious architecture, Neo-Gothic. This was to some extent a nostalgic and romantic return to supposed medievalism, but, in its dark and mysterious design, it also promoted the recovery of a more mystical understanding of sacred place. Towards the end of the nineteenth century, Anglo-Catholic spirituality had embraced many continental Roman Catholic disciplines (such as individual confession and the examination of conscience) along with meditation manuals and elements of devotion to Mary and to the Blessed Sacrament.

The departure of Newman, the greatest intellect of the Movement, to join the Roman Catholic Church in 1845 (followed by others such as Henry Manning and Frederick Faber) was a considerable blow. However, the "Anglo-Catholic" movement within the Church of England survived, flourished, and eventually inspired a number of major developments in the wider Church of England such as a more developed doctrine of the Church, the centrality of the Eucharist and the reintroduction of some ritual practices, the growing popularity of retreats and spiritual direction, and the restoration of religious life from the middle of the nineteenth century onwards. This gave rise to distinctively Anglican male communities such as the Community of the Resurrection (Mirfield Fathers), the Society of the Sacred Mission (Kelham Fathers), and the Society of St John the Evangelist (Cowley Fathers), as well as in Franciscan and Benedictine re-foundations. A much larger group of women religious emerged, both active and contemplative, that also included a number of Franciscan and Benedictine monasteries and such notable indigenous communities as the Community of St Mary the Virgin at Wantage, the Sisters of the Church, the Sisters of the Love of God, the Order of the Holy Paraclete, and the Society of St Margaret. Many of these groups spread from England to other parts of the Anglican Communion where other indigenous religious orders also emerged.[13]

It is also notable that the strongly incarnational emphasis of the Anglo-Catholic movement gave rise to a significant tradition of social theology and spirituality both on an intellectual level and among so-called slum priests, for example, in the East End of London. Two priests, Stewart Headlam (1847–1924) and Charles Gore (1853–1932), may be taken as examples. Headlam saw the Christian doctrine of the incarnation as having direct social and political consequences. His views persistently caused problems throughout his life as a priest, and he was forced to move from parish to parish where he always remained an assistant. While curate at the Anglo-Catholic St Matthew's Church, Bethnal Green in East London, he founded the Guild of St Matthew in 1877 to promote the study of social and political questions in the light of Christian doctrine. This rapidly became a broadly based focus for clergy and laypeople who shared both Headlam's strong sacramental theology and his social vision. Ultimately his Christian socialism led him into an active political life. By contrast, Charles Gore remained within the mainstream of the Church of England. An Oxford academic theologian, Gore became the first Principal of Pusey House which was based on the principles of Dr Pusey, one of the founders of the Oxford Movement. However, Gore's understanding of Catholic theology and spirituality took him in more radical directions. In 1889, he helped found the Christian Social Union and also edited a collection of essays *Lux Mundi* (further developed in his 1891 Bampton Lectures) which, among other things, sought to bring Christianity into dialogue with contemporary political and ethical questions. In 1892, Gore also founded and became the first superior of a fraternity of celibate priests under a rule, the Community of the Resurrection. This later moved to Yorkshire and became popularly known as the Mirfield Fathers. From 1902 to 1919, Gore was in turn Bishop of Worcester, Birmingham, and Oxford before retiring to London.[14]

John Henry Newman

John Henry Newman (1801–1890) had a profound impact on the theology and spirituality, first, of the Church of England and then of Roman Catholicism. When he became a Roman Catholic, he joined the Oratorians and eventually founded a new Oratory in Birmingham in 1849. He would not be generally thought of as a spiritual writer, yet in important ways he established an important basis for the development of a new sense of what Catholic spirituality could mean, based substantially on early Church and scriptural scholarship. Although the English bishops were suspicious of his ideas about the potential for Catholic contributions to intellectual life and his relatively progressive thinking about Church disciplines and theology, he was nevertheless created cardinal in 1879. His influence increased after his death and lay behind some of the directions taken by the Second Vatican Council in the early 1960s – for example, the importance of individual conscience, the collegiality of bishops, and the consultation of laypeople in the Church. On a more personal level, his spiritual and intellectual autobiography, *Apologia pro vita sua* (1864), had a great impact as did his poem *The Dream of Gerontius* which was not only the basis for Edward Elgar's great musical masterpiece but parts of it were used for rich and substantial hymns such as "Praise to the Holiest in the height" and "Firmly I believe and truly." Another poem, turned hymn, "Lead kindly Light" expresses a more personal note of spiritual and emotional struggle.[15]

A Distinctive "American Spirituality"

As we have already seen, the early foundations of North American Christian spirituality obviously lay in European imports. However, after the American Revolution and the birth of the United States of America (1776–1781), something distinctively "American" is easier to discern.[16] Several fundamental tenets of the Revolution had a long-term impact on American spirituality – freedom of religion and the radical separation of Church and State. This made pluralism and voluntary religion the fundamental backdrop. One result was that American religion is marked not simply by a bewildering number of Churches and sects but also by a rich diversity of styles. Another result was a stress on personal experience of God as normative and authoritative.

One notable feature of nineteenth-century America was the ever receding "American frontier" and the mentality it created. Not only did it provoke the growth of missionary endeavor but it also reinforced a varied, experience-based, and rather individualistic approach to spirituality. The frontier mentality, with its rough and ready lifestyle – not to mention a stark symbolism of living on the margins where the forces of good and evil confront each other – provided fertile ground for numerous evangelistic revivals. These were based on emotional preaching and a call to repentance, conversion, and sobriety. The rugged individualism of the frontier combined with post-Revolutionary democratic attitudes to shape an American style of spirituality that valued egalitarianism as well as pluralism.

Revivalism was not limited to the Western frontier but was a natural development of Evangelical spirituality. Charles Finney (1792–1875), a lawyer who experienced a dramatic conversion "in the Holy Spirit" and became a Presbyterian preacher, set the tone for a tradition of powerful revivalist preachers that continued into the twentieth century with figures such as Billy Graham. Finney's meetings helped to spark the Great Revival (1857–1860) which led to numerous conversions. Finney himself was also one of the early exponents of a more socially prophetic Evangelical spirituality as he vocally attacked slavery and preached social reform more generally.

Even in the more cultivated circles of New England, the emphasis on experience blended with elements of Enlightenment thinking (such a powerful intellectual force during the Revolution) and literary-poetic sensibilities to give birth to American Transcendentalism. This non-dogmatic, somewhat romantic movement was expressed in the nature mysticism of Henry Thoreau and the openness to world religions of the movement's greatest figure, Ralph Waldo Emerson (1803–1882). Many people consider Emerson's influence on American approaches to spirituality to be considerable even up to this day. He distanced himself from classical Christianity with his famous 1838 Harvard lecture in which he proclaimed that Jesus was a great teacher but not divine. His reading of the Hindu scriptures led him to a position of non-dualism and to espouse the unity of the human soul with the surrounding world. Other influential themes included his emphasis on individuality, human freedom, and self-reliance.

After the cataclysmic trauma of the American Civil War (1861–1865), American spirituality took on a much stronger social consciousness in the face of the abolition of slavery, the expansion of cities, and the American Industrial Revolution. The weakness of a purely private religion and individualistic piety had been exposed, and a kind of social awakening took place. Previously unquestioned assumptions about inevitable progress and the perfection of the American way of life were confronted by a spirituality that insisted on examining the underside of America. The Baptist pastor Walter Rauschenbusch (1861–1918) was one of best-known figures of the social gospel movement who worked among the urban poor of New York. He sought to hold together classic revivalism, with its emphasis on personal testimony and conversion, and social concern. He anticipated an important theme in twentieth-century spiritualities of liberation by asserting that true social change would only be substantial if nourished by a deep religious life. Rauschenbusch's most popular work was *Prayers for the Social Awakening* (1910). His own deep commitment to personal prayer and spirituality led him to found the "Little Society of Jesus" in 1887 with two friends Leighton Williams and Nathaniel Schmidt. They were influenced by what they saw as the zeal and enthusiasm of the Jesuit Order and sought to emulate its cohesion without compromising individual initiative. The aim was a voluntary association, based on a Jesus-centered spirituality that combined Protestant doctrine with Catholic devotion. The "Little Society" eventually became the Brotherhood of the Kingdom with both social and spiritual values.[17]

African American experience and therefore spirituality was inevitably very different from that of other Americans. Africans had come to the British American colonies and then to the United States of America in a variety of ways – sometimes directly from Africa, sometimes after periods in the Caribbean islands – the overwhelming majority as slaves or indentured workers. The encounter with Christian religion was largely through the medium of their oppressors. Their acceptance of Christian faith blended with traditional African emphases such as a perception of the world as sacred and full of the presence of the holy and religion as an essentially collective reality. What resulted was a faith forged in oppression, exile, and dehumanization and with a consequent emphasis on freedom. God was the one who liberates the people from bondage. The paradoxical side of the Christian gospels appealed strongly – Christ reveals strength through weakness, and in suffering there is redemption and eventual glory. Apart from a strong oral tradition of repeating and glossing Bible stories, one of the most original forms of African American spirituality is the body of song known as "spirituals." These resonate with deep emotions – especially suffering, the desire for liberation, and yet also profound hope. Spirituals are the largest body of American folksong – some originating with work songs in the plantations, others in worship services. Not surprisingly, the Cross and suffering of Jesus Christ is a prominent image as in the lament, "Were you there when they crucified my Lord?" But there were also songs of hope and liberation such as "Steal away, steal away, steal away to Jesus."[18]

Roman Catholic spirituality received a boost from the Revolutionary period as the exiled Catholics of Maryland found the freedom brought by the new Republic congenial. Earlier persecution had pushed their spirituality in a more domestic, interiorized, and personal direction. In that sense, the separation of Church and State after the Revolution came naturally to them. People like the Jesuit John Carroll (1735–1815), the first American bishop, and the Anglican convert Elizabeth Seton (1774–1821), the first canonized American saint and, after the death of her husband, founder of an indigenous version of Sisters of Charity, promoted a very Christ-centered piety that owed much to the writings of Ignatius Loyola and Francis de Sales. Elizabeth Seton also embraced the "pioneering spirit" as she worked tirelessly in the face of many hardships on the Western frontier. However, on the whole, the immediately post-Revolutionary Roman Catholics were people of the Enlightenment who were happy to keep the spiritual side of their lives in the home and at church and to participate in public life merely as fellow citizens. Later in the nineteenth century, the Roman Catholic community expanded beyond the relatively privileged Maryland base to embrace waves of European immigration. For immigrant Catholics, the Church became their natural community at all levels, a solidarity that united believers and gave them a distinctive identity in an alien land. Spirituality became heavily devotional in an extraordinary variety of ways, depending on the parts of Europe from which people came. This existed alongside the "official" Eucharistic piety promoted by a clergy trained in

French-influenced seminaries. An alternative perspective was suggested by Isaac Hecker (1819–1888), a convert from Methodism, who founded the Paulist Fathers. Although he worked with immigrants, Hecker was an integrationist in that he sought to drag Roman Catholic spirituality out of the ghetto and into the world. Hecker rejected the world-denying tendencies of Catholic devotionalism and placed his emphasis on a "democratic" spirituality of finding God in everyday realities and of Christian holiness shaped *in* the world. As a good American democrat, Hecker did not question the constitutional separation of Church and State but sought to move Roman Catholicism in the direction of engaging with American culture on the basis of a voluntary relationship. Hecker's so-called Americanism was condemned by Rome, and this step reinforced a dichotomy between spirituality and public life that continued to beset American Catholicism into the 1960s.[19]

Conclusion

Western Christian spirituality during the nineteenth century was marked partly by an imperceptible shift of energy from Europe towards the New World. This applies both to Protestant and Roman Catholic variants. It was also marked by a major missionary expansion in Africa and parts of Asia (to follow that in Latin America from the sixteenth century), often in association with the advance of European colonialism and imperialism. During the twentieth century, the sheer numerical strength of North American Christianity, as well as its energy and eclecticism, would have an immense impact on global Christianity and on its spiritual atmosphere. Equally, what was sown in the nineteenth century by European and to a lesser extent by American missionary movements would flower in the twentieth century into the gradual birth of truly local African, Asian, and Latin American Churches and related spiritualities.

The Enlightenment, the French and American Revolutions, and their values had an immense impact on Christian spirituality in the nineteenth century either by way of direct influence or by way of conservative reaction. The ambivalence of the Church to this new, modern world was particularly illustrated in Roman Catholic circles. Although Pope Leo XIII had condemned "Americanism," he also wrote with great sensitivity and thoughtfulness about social reform. A number of intellectuals such as the English Jesuit George Tyrell, Maurice Blondel, Alfred Loisy, and the writer on mysticism Baron von Hügel (known collectively as Modernists) sought to bring theology and spirituality into dialogue with modern developments. However, Modernism was condemned by Pope Pius X in 1907. Another factor was the immense social upheaval of the industrialization of Western Europe and North America which set in train the rapid expansion of cities. Inevitably, this too colored the way spirituality changed in emphasis and background.

Finally, three key nineteenth-century intellectual developments had begun to have an impact on all forms of Christianity and on Christian spirituality by the end of the nineteenth century. These were evolutionary theory, Marxist social analysis, and the birth of modern psychology. All of them, in different ways, shifted the dominant and long-held understanding of what it was to be human, in both individual and collective terms, and therefore of how we think about spirituality.

Notes

1 J.-P. de Caussade, *The Sacrament of the Present Moment*, London: Fount, 1981.

2 See P. Erb, ed., *The Pietists: Selected Writings*, New York: Paulist Press, 1983.

3 On this question see P. Sheldrake, "The influence of the Ignatian tradition" in *The Way Supplement*, 68, Summer 1990 (*Ignatian Spirituality in Ecumenical Context*), pp. 74–85.

4 On the spirituality of the Wesleys see F. Whaling, ed., *John and Charles Wesley: Selected Writings and Hymns*, New York: Paulist Press, 1981.

5 See J.E. Smith, ed., *Jonathan Edwards: Religious Affections*, New Haven: Yale University Press, 1959.

6 See R.E. Whitson, ed., *The Shakers: Two Centuries of Spiritual Reflection*, New York: Paulist Press, 1983. For Merton's reflections on the Shakers and their former Kentucky village of Pleasant Hill near his monastery, see T. Merton, *Seeking Paradise: The Spirit of the Shakers*, New York: Orbis Books, 2003.

7 The main English translation is G. Palmer, P. Sherrard, and K. Ware, eds., *The Philokalia: The Complete Text*, 5 vols., London/Boston: Faber & Faber, 1979–2003.

8 See A. Pentkovsky, ed., *The Pilgrim's Tale*, New York: Paulist Press, 1999.

9 On Russian spirituality, see S. Bolshakoff, *Russian Mystics*, Kalamazoo: Cistercian Publications, 1980.

10 For texts related to Seraphim, including the conversation with Motovilov, see G.P. Fedotov ed., *A Treasury of Russian Spirituality*, London: Sheed & Ward, 1981, pp. 242–279.

11 For recent revisionist studies of Thérèse, see J.F. Six, *Light of the Night: The Last Eighteen Months in the Life of Thérèse of Lisieux*, London: SCM Press, 1996; and by way of contrast also C. Fitzgerald, "The mission of Thérèse of Lisieux" in *The Way Supplement*, 89, Summer 1997, pp. 74–96.

12   See I. Randall, *What a Friend We Have in Jesus: The Evangelical Tradition*, London: Darton Longman & Todd and New York: Orbis Books, 2005.

13   O. Chadwick, *The Spirit of the Oxford Movement*, Cambridge: Cambridge University Press, 1990 and G.W. Herring, *What Was the Oxford Movement?* London: Continuum, 2002.

14   See G. Rowell, K. Stevenson, and R. Williams, eds., *Love's Redeeming Work: The Anglican Quest for Holiness*, Oxford: Oxford University Press, 2001, Part 3.

15   On Newman's spirituality, see I. Kerr, ed., *John Henry Newman: Selected Sermons*, New York: Paulist Press, 1994.

16   On spirituality in the United States of America overall, see the illuminating overview of fundamental themes and values by V. Lesniak, "North American spirituality," in P. Sheldrake, ed., *The New SCM Dictionary of Christian Spirituality*, London: SCM Press, 2005 – published in the United States of America as *The New Westminster Dictionary of Christian Spirituality*, Louisville: Westminster-John Knox Press, 2005. See also the volumes of texts in the Sources of American Spirituality Series published by Paulist Press.

17   See W.S. Hudson, ed., *Walter Rauschenbusch: Selected Writings*, New York: Paulist Press, 1984.

18   See F.W. Bridges, *Resurrection Song: African American Spirituality*, New York: Orbis Books, 2001.

19   On Roman Catholic spirituality in the United States of America, see J. Chinnici, *Living Stones: The History and Structure of Catholic Spiritual Life in the United States*, New York: Macmillan, 1989.

Chapter 7

Modernity to Postmodernity:
1900–2000

1858–1916	Charles de Foucauld lives: hermit in North Africa
1870–1922	William Seymour lives: leader of American Pentecostal movement
1875–1941	Evelyn Underhill lives: writer on Christian mysticism (notably *Mysticism* 1911)
1881–1955	Pierre Teilhard de Chardin lives: Jesuit scientist and mystic
1891–1945	Elizabeth Skobtsova (Mother Maria) lives: Russian nun, mystic, and martyr
1897–1980	Dorothy Day lives: American social activist and founder of Catholic Worker Movement
1899–1981	Howard Thurman lives: American theologian and civil rights activist
1902	William James writes *The Varieties of Religious Experience*
1903–1958	Vladimir Lossky lives: author of *The Mystical Theology of the Eastern Church*
1906–1945	Dietrich Bonhoeffer lives: German pastor, theologian, martyr
1906–1993	Bede Griffiths lives: Benedictine monk and leading inter-religious figure in India
1909	Death of Father John of Kronstadt, Russian spiritual figure
1909–1943	Simone Weil lives: French philosopher, religious writer, social activist, Jewish-Christian mystic
1915–1968	Thomas Merton lives: Cistercian monk, spiritual writer, social and political activist
1928–	Gustavo Gutiérrez born in Peru: a leading liberation theologian and spiritual writer

Spirituality: A Brief History, Second Edition. Philip Sheldrake.
© 2013 John Wiley & Sons, Ltd. Published 2013 by John Wiley & Sons, Ltd.

1931	*Quadragesimo Anno*, encyclical of Pope Pius XI, further developing Catholic social teaching
1940	Foundation of ecumenical monastery of Taizé by Roger Schutz (1915–2005)
1960s	Charismatic Movement spreads to Roman Catholic, Anglican, and traditional Protestant Churches
1961–1964	Second Vatican Council
1980s/1990s	Growth of Christian feminist theological and spirituality writings

The twentieth century was a period of immense change, culturally, socially, and religiously. Many commentators speak of a transition from "modernity" to "postmodernity." What does this mean? In general terms, "modernity" implies the dominance of a worldview born during the Enlightenment and consolidated by the technological advances of the Industrial Revolution. "Modernity" implies confidence in the power of human reason to address any question. With this went an ordered view of the world, a belief in the inevitability of human progress, and a spirit of optimism. At the beginning of the twentieth century, this "modern" sense of a rational and stable world seemed impregnable. Yet the seeds of radical change were already present by the end of the nineteenth century. For example, evolutionary theory suggested that human existence could no longer be separated from the remainder of nature's processes. The theories of Marx in a broad sense challenged fixed notions of "society." The birth of psychology revealed that human motivation is complex and called into question the objectivity of human reason.

During the twentieth century, two world wars, mid-century totalitarianism, the Holocaust, Hiroshima, and the birth of the atomic age all revealed that human technology was capable of catastrophic destruction and was not purely benign. Politically, the century saw the death of European empires, the relatively rapid rise and fall of the Soviet Union, the end of colonialism in Asia and Africa, and optimistic attempts to create international organizations for peace or political and economic cooperation such as the United Nations and the European Union. The century also witnessed the development of rapid international travel and a communications revolution (radio, television, and latterly information technology). A tide of social change also swept the Northern Hemisphere regarding the equality of women and the status of social and ethnic minorities, for example, in the Civil Rights Movement in the United States of America. Perhaps the twentieth century was not uniquely violent or more subject to changes than any other, but what was unique was the effect of global communications and new technologies. Events had worldwide immediacy and impact, information exchange became virtually instantaneous, and change consequently happened with a rapidity that was previously unimaginable.

"Postmodernity" therefore defines a culture where the simple answers and optimism of a previous age are impossible. By the close of the twentieth century, previously fixed systems of thought and behavior had fragmented, and the world was understood as radically plural. People had become increasingly suspicious of normative interpretations of truth. In Western societies as well as globally, cultural, religious, and ethnic diversity was increasingly identified as the fundamental reality of human existence.

The Impact on Spirituality

How can we describe and interpret spirituality during the twentieth century? Needless to say, the major social, political, and cultural changes had a serious impact on Christianity. Overall, three elements stand out. First, in Europe in particular, institutional religion noticeably declined – the victim of a wider loss of faith in traditional authoritative institutions. Second, the previous hard boundaries both within Christianity and between Christianity and other faiths began to erode. The ecumenical movement was born in the early twentieth century and by the end of the century had extended to a wider inter-religious dialogue. Third, Christianity became truly global. No longer were Europe and North America the sole arbiters of the Christian world. The center of gravity shifted slowly but surely to the global South.

In terms specifically of spirituality, it is too early to make an authoritative assessment. It is impossible to predict what themes and values will be enduring, what individuals will be seen as spiritual giants in a hundred years' time, what movements or teachings will have established themselves as "traditions," and what written texts or other artifacts will become "classics." At this point, it is possible only to select a few people and movements that somehow capture the climate of Christian spirituality during the century and its great variety.

The Prophetic-Critical Type

Two major spiritual themes seem especially prominent: the quest for the mystical and prophetic-political approaches to spirituality. A number of people and movements seek in different ways to bring these two strands together into a creative tension. Indeed, a fourth style of Christian spirituality emerges during the twentieth century – what may be called the "critical-prophetic type." The first cluster of people to be explored – Charles de Foucauld, Evelyn Underhill, Dietrich Bonhoeffer, Simone Weil, Dorothy Day, Thomas Merton, and Gustavo Gutiérrez – all, in their different ways, illustrate this type. For many of them, the advocacy of a socially critical spirituality led to conflict or some form of marginalization from religious or civil authority.

Charles de Foucauld (1858–1916)

Although Charles de Foucauld's life bridges parts of two centuries, he will be considered in a twentieth-century context because it was in the period after 1901 that he made his lasting impact on Christian spirituality. A member of an aristocratic family, the first part of de Foucauld's adult life was a hedonistic affair. He lost his religious faith, spent money wildly, lived the life of a dandy, became a soldier and was posted to Algeria, and then resigned his commission when asked to give up his mistress. The relationship soon ended, and de Foucauld went off to Morocco in disguise and explored for some eighteen months what was then a closed country. On his return to France in 1886, he was not only awarded a gold medal by the French Geographical Society for his Morocco report but also underwent a religious reconversion under the influence of the eccentric but outstanding spiritual guide, Abbé Huvelin.

De Foucauld had already developed strong feelings about desert solitude, and to this was now added an equally powerful devotion to the person of Jesus and to the eucharist. Initially, de Foucauld tried to be a Cistercian monk in France and then Syria but after a few years indicated that he sought something even more spiritually demanding and was allowed to leave. From 1897, he lived happily as a hermit and gardener attached to a convent of Poor Clare nuns in Nazareth. After being ordained in France, he then moved back to the Sahara desert in North Africa in 1901. First, he settled at Beni Abbes and then moved to Tamanrasett in southern Algeria where he lived among the Tuareg people, not seeking to convert them but learning their language, writing a dictionary, studying their culture, and seeking to serve their needs. He essentially lived a solitary contemplative life based on eucharistic devotion and a form of meditative scriptural prayer that comes close to the traditional monastic practice of *lectio divina*. He conceived the idea of founding a new religious community, but this did not come about fully in his lifetime. Tragically he was killed by Bedouin tribesmen in 1916 during an uprising against French colonial power. Charles de Foucauld was beatified by Pope Benedict XVI in 2005.

After his death, Frère Charles de Jésus, as he became known, was the inspiration for a new spiritual movement and eventually for the foundation of a number of different religious communities, most notably the Little Brothers and Sisters of Jesus. After the Second World War, these small semi-monastic groups developed a distinctive profile by moving in groups of four or five into the poorest parts of Western cities as well as into areas of the developing world. Like Charles de Foucauld, the Little Brothers and Sisters neither proselytize nor undertake explicit social action but see their life in terms of solidarity – a contemplative hospitable presence among and on behalf of their neighbors. They generally support themselves by working in ordinary jobs, beginning and ending each day with periods of common prayer and silence.[1]

Evelyn Underhill (1875–1941)

It may seem strange to select Evelyn Underhill as the first representative of growing fascination with mysticism as there were certainly more scholarly writers and some of Underhill's views would now be questioned. However, she remains the most widely read writer on mysticism in English, and her motivation was to promote a more "democratic" understanding of mysticism and to spread knowledge of the subject to a wider public. In fact, apart from her interest in mysticism Underhill touches upon a number of other important elements of twentieth-century spirituality. She was noted for her ecumenical relations (and also had a prodigious knowledge of mysticism in other world religions). She was a pioneering figure in developing the retreat movement in England and was perhaps the first woman to attain a prominent place in Anglicanism – indeed it has been said that she helped to keep spirituality alive in the Church of England between the world wars. She also had a life-long sympathy for Socialism, maintained a strong sense of the social and ethical dimensions of spirituality, and by her death was a committed pacifist.

Evelyn Underhill was born into a prosperous London family with little attachment to institutional religion. Although she was baptized in the Church of England, her growing interest in mysticism from 1907 coincided with an attraction to Roman Catholicism which was undermined by the condemnations of Modernism. In fact, Underhill only became a regularly practicing Anglican Christian in 1921, the same year she began to receive spiritual direction from the Roman Catholic lay intellectual, Baron von Hügel, who had an immense impact on her by pushing her more towards the Christian mainstream. Over the years, she also had close spiritual relationships with the great Anglican spiritual director Reginald Somerset Ward and with Abbot John Chapman of Downside. From the early 1920s until the late 1930s, Underhill conducted an extensive ministry of spiritual direction, not least by letter, and also became significantly involved in the retreat movement, especially at the retreat house of Pleshey in Essex. Many of her retreat addresses were published. Her approach both to direction and retreats was practical and down to earth.

Underhill's most substantial and still popular book on mysticism was *Mysticism*, originally published in 1911 but which went through several editions, and changes of perspective, during her lifetime. Originally she was somewhat preoccupied with esoteric religion and with Neoplatonic suspicions of the material world. By 1930, this had changed to an interest in psychology, a closer relationship between mysticism and her concern for social awareness, and a greater integration of mysticism with the corporate life of the Christian Church. Her treatment of specific Christian mystics in the book was based on significant textual scholarship, and by the 1930 edition her treatment of Christian mystics was more nuanced and broadly based.

In 1921, Underhill gave the Upton Lectures in Philosophy of Religion, the first woman to be invited to give theology lectures at Oxford. These appeared in 1922 as *The Life of the Spirit and the Life of Today*. Here she expresses a sense that inward transformation and outward action are to be integrated for a more complete spirituality. Growth in spirituality or mystical consciousness no longer implies leaving the everyday world but rather a change of stance towards the world and a different way of being and acting in the world. The lectures also show her growing interest in psychology but at the same time, and integrated with it, a more doctrinally rich approach to mysticism, especially in reference to the Trinity.

In her 1925 work, *The Mystics of the Church*, Underhill gave particular attention to the contribution mysticism makes to the life of the Church as well as to the great variety of types of Christian mystics. One of her last books, and in the minds of some commentators one of her finest, was titled *Worship* (1936). Apart from showing how far she had come in appreciating corporate and liturgical worship, Underhill here expressed a far more explicitly Christian approach to our relationship with God as well as an ecumenical sensitivity to the different denominational forms.

For all that Underhill suggested that the particular "genius" of Christian mysticism and spirituality was its link with action in the world, she also affirmed that Christian social action without proper attention to prayer and the mystical dimension led to an ethical piety without depth.

What is interesting about Underhill is that while she appeared to share the American philosopher-psychologist William James' lack of sympathy with more speculative and intellectual forms of mysticism as expressed in his highly influential *The Varieties of Religious Experience* (1902), she parted company with him in several ways. While interested in the mysticism of other world religions, Underhill did not describe mysticism as a category of pure experience or "pure consciousness" prior to, or radically separate from, institutional religious forms such as the Church or from interpretation produced by belief systems. Not only did she explore what was distinctive and particular about *Christian* mysticism but was clear that mysticism is practical in purpose and is never self-seeking.[2]

Dietrich Bonhoeffer (1906–1945)

Dietrich Bonhoeffer was a prominent German Lutheran theologian of the mid-twentieth century who died as a political martyr under the Nazis. Bonhoeffer may stand for the growing engagement between spirituality and theology during the twentieth century (of which other notable examples would be the Roman Catholics Karl Rahner and Hans Urs von Balthasar, the Protestants Jürgen Moltmann and Wolfhart Pannenburg, and the Anglican Rowan Williams). However, above all, Bonhoeffer is a striking example of the critical-prophetic type of spirituality.

Born in Breslau, Bonhoeffer came from a prominent intellectual and artistic family. He studied theology at Tübingen and Berlin. He was especially critical of attitudes in the German Church that he believed compromised Martin Luther's fundamental theological and spiritual insights. Probably his best-known book is *The Cost of Discipleship* where he suggests that Luther's teaching had declined into what he calls "cheap grace." That is to say that salvation by God's "grace alone" had become detached from the costly obligation of discipleship which implies what he called "the strictest following of Christ." In the context of his times, this was a prophetic critique of a politically uninvolved Christianity.

For Bonhoeffer, costly discipleship implied both a disciplined life of prayer and community and an engagement with surrounding political realities. Although an instinctive pacifist, Bonhoeffer was actively involved in anti-Nazi activities and openly critical of the public compromises made by the leadership of the Protestant Church. In prophetic contrast to the surrender of the official Church, Bonhoeffer was the inspiration behind an alternative community of those who resisted Nazi control of the state Church. After he returned from a visit to England in 1935, Bonhoeffer led an unofficial seminary at Finkenwalde where he also formed a quasi-religious community, inspired by his experiences of Anglican religious communities such as Mirfield.

Bonhoeffer had begun to practice daily scriptural meditation from about 1932. It is instructive that he called his first attempts *Exerzitien* which for Protestants of that era had clear connotations of Ignatius Loyola. While controversial, Bonhoeffer appears to have believed that an important spiritual tool had been lost by Lutherans and needed to be revived. Bonhoeffer's library from this period survives and includes his copy of the Ignatian *Spiritual Exercises*. Some of this experience found its way into his book *Life Together*, written for the Finkenwalde community, in its teaching on disciplined and regular Bible reading and meditation as the basis for community life.

While Bonhoeffer had the opportunity to settle in the United States of America where he went to teach in 1939, he voluntarily returned to Germany before the war started in order, as he said to friends, to share in the trials of German Christians. Finally arrested by the Gestapo in 1943, Bonhoeffer spent the last two years of his life in prison from where he wrote many letters – not least letters of spiritual guidance to his students – which were eventually edited and published and have become a spiritual classic. In them, his plea for a "religionless Christianity" was a further prophetic stage in his opposition to the way in which the compromises of public religion had, in his estimation, replaced the demands of a costly commitment to a living God.

In someone like Bonhoeffer, the mystic becomes the political martyr. The contemporary German theologian Jürgen Moltmann, in reference to Bonhoeffer, comments:

> The place of mystical experience is in very truth the cell – the prison cell. The "witness to the truth of Christ" is despised, scoffed at, persecuted, dishonoured and rejected. In his own fate he experiences the fate of Christ. His fate conforms to Christ's fate. That is what the mystics called *conformitas crucis*, the conformity of the cross…Eckhart's remark that suffering is the shortest way to the birth of God in the soul applies, not to any imagined suffering, but to the very real sufferings endured by "the witness to the truth."[3]

Bonhoeffer was eventually executed in 1945 just before the war's end at Flossenbürg concentration camp.[4]

Simone Weil (1909–1943)

Simone Weil is a paradoxical figure to include in a history of Christian spirituality because although she was strongly attracted to Christianity, she existed on its margins and was never baptized. Indeed, marginality or living on the edge became for Weil a significant element of her prophetic witness. Born into an agnostic French Jewish family, Simone originally studied and taught philosophy and became active during the 1930s in a variety of social and political causes. She wrote for socialist and communist periodicals, worked in factories, and served the Republican side in the Spanish Civil War. Strangely, given her background, Simone went through a series of intense religious experiences which led her to a strong commitment to Christ and a great sympathy for Roman Catholic Christianity. One of the most significant moments in Weil's spiritual journey seems to have been provoked by her introduction to the poetry of the seventeenth-century Anglican poet George Herbert while spending Easter at the Abbey of Solesmes in 1938. The poem "Love bade me welcome" had such a powerful impact on her that she then used it regularly for meditation during her stay. On one occasion, the poem then seems to have been the medium for a powerful mystical experience of the immediate presence of Christ. Weil escaped from Vichy France to the United States of America in 1942 and then found her way to London where she worked for the Free French and even sought to be parachuted into France to fight with the Resistance. She eventually died of a combination of tuberculosis and starvation in a Kent hospital in 1943.

Weil's complex and idiosyncratic thought became available posthumously through the publications of her notebooks and such works as *The Need for Roots* and *Waiting on God* – which became something of a spiritual classic. Her religious vision is deep and intense – to the degree that some people refer to her as a mystic. Apart from the Christian scriptures and the Christian mystics (not least Eckhart and John of the Cross), Weil also read widely in Greek philosophy (especially Plato), Neoplatonism, Kant, and Indian philosophy (she learned Sanskrit to read the *Bhagavad Gita* in the original). Some commentators have questioned what sometimes appear to be her negative attitudes to the created world and to the self/the body. However, her thinking and writing (largely gathered from fragments and notes) is exploratory rather than systematic, and so it is difficult to arrive at definitive judgments.

One important theme is a kind of "spirituality of attention." In an essay "On the right use of school studies with a view to the love of God" (in *Waiting on God*), she described intellectual work as a kind of spiritual exercise. The core value of study is that it cultivates our capacity for attention. Attention is the key both to prayer and to our ability to be present to and available to our suffering neighbor. Later, in *Waiting on God* she writes of prayer: "Prayer consists of attention... [the] orientation of all the attention of which the soul is capable towards God." The spiritual quality of attention is underlined: "The attitude that brings about salvation is not like any form of activity...It is the waiting or attentive and faithful immobility that lasts indefinitely and cannot be shaken."

Weil also had a complex and paradoxical idea of "the self." We exist as creatures by means of God's self-bestowal but we exist only to realize that we *are not*, in and of ourselves. We are simply made up of God's love seeking a response. We therefore become fully who we are only by handing ourselves over – to God and to others. So, for Weil the abandonment of the self is liberating – from illusions, self-images, and constructed social roles. This is a strongly counter-Enlightenment view – to become is to give up trying to be a self-contained autonomous subject. For Weil, the discovery of the true self is really the discovery of our place in the self-giving of the Trinity. In her Trinitarian view of the creation of the true self, the Holy Spirit is a seed that falls into every soul so that Christ is born in the soul. A corollary of this view of the self is a positive spirituality of sacrifice. Weil felt herself to be called to self-sacrifice for others – a kind of sharing in Christ's cross. This was expressed in her perpetual search for a practice of solidarity with a suffering world. This was what in the end led her, despite serious illness, to refuse to eat anything more than was allowed to her fellow Jews who had been left in France. In that sense she died of a self-imposed hunger ration undertaken as a token of solidarity. For Weil, Christianity was not meant to be a remedy for suffering and affliction but rather offered a supernatural *use* for suffering.

Underlying her life was ultimately a belief that in a rootless, spirit-bereft, atheist, modern world, there was the need for a new kind of saintliness, expressed in terms of total self-giving, solidarity, and the struggle for justice. This was underpinned by a spirituality of attentiveness to God and waiting in patience on God.[5]

Dorothy Day (1897–1980)

Dorothy Day was one of the most influential figures in the English-speaking world in promoting a spirituality of social justice. Born in Brooklyn to non-religious parents, Day after university initially committed herself to radical thought and mixed in both Communist and anarchist-sindicalist circles. She became a labor activist and a journalist and was arrested at times for her beliefs. Day lived in New York with her partner with whom she had a child. It was during her pregnancy that she converted to Roman Catholicism. This and the baptism of her child led to the break-up of her relationship. Day became convinced that Christianity answered the shortcomings she had increasingly felt in her revolutionary circles. In particular, while radical politics had identified the nature of alienation in modern society, the teachings of Christianity about disinterested love and inclusive community pointed the way to a solution. She soon met a French expatriate philosopher, Peter Maurin, who became her spiritual mentor. He guided her reading and offered her a vision of pacifism and close identification with the poor. Together they began the Catholic Worker Movement in New York in 1933 during the Depression.

The spirituality of prophetic social witness and pacifism was promoted by a newspaper, *The Catholic Worker*, which fearlessly documented workers' struggles and proclaimed a social gospel. The basis of Catholic Worker spirituality as conceived by Day and Maurin offered an alternative to secular Marxism in its communitarian and personalist philosophy. Based on Matthew 25, Christ was to be experienced as present in all those in need. Every human being, without exception, had a unique and equal dignity. The heart of Christian living was radical community, but this was not a community "set apart" or purified by detachment from surrounding reality. It was a community called upon to undertake prophetic action on behalf of the oppressed. Indeed, for Day, there could be no authentic Christian spirituality that did not have social justice as its core.

The active spirituality of the movement was expressed in the foundation of houses of hospitality which offered a haven for all kinds of marginalized people. The members of the movement embrace voluntary poverty and live in the houses of hospitality which currently number about a hundred and fifty across the United States of America, mostly in poor urban areas, though some are rural farming communities. The rule of life centers on the Eucharist and common prayer. The Movement has an entirely lay membership and no official Church authorization. Day was particularly inspired by the regular reading of scripture but also by the Rule of St Benedict, the teaching of Francis of Assisi on voluntary poverty, and the "little way" of Thérèse of Lisieux. While not radically revolutionary in tone, the Catholic Worker Movement was a discomforting reality for many Church people and attracted opposition. For one thing, members of the movement not only served the poor but undertook direct action against injustice where needed. Day herself continued through the Second World War, the Cold War, and Vietnam to advocate pacifism and to undertake acts of civil disobedience for which she was often arrested. Although for much of her life Day was a controversial figure, by the time of her death in 1980 she was widely admired, and more recently her canonization has been promoted.[6]

Thomas Merton (1915–1968)

Thomas Merton has been described as the greatest Roman Catholic spiritual writer of the twentieth century. He was born of mixed New Zealand and American parentage in France and had a somewhat insecure and unhappy childhood. His mother died when he was six, and his artist father rather neglected him and died when Thomas was fifteen. Thomas Merton was educated at an English boarding school, at Cambridge, and then at Columbia University, New York, and, perhaps not surprisingly, led a self-centered and even hedonistic life. He had a child while at Cambridge, but the story is that both mother and child were killed in the London Blitz during the Second World War. Consequently, the background motivations for his intense religious conversion to Roman Catholicism and entry into one of the strictest monastic orders, the reformed Cistercians (Trappists), in 1941 are complex. He remained a monk of Gethsemani Abbey in Kentucky (as Father Louis) until his premature death in an accident during a visit to Asia in 1968 in pursuit of Christian-Buddhist dialogue.

Thomas Merton is variously remembered for his contribution to reintegrating spirituality with theology, for his attempts to rearticulate contemplative-monastic life and the Christian mystical tradition for a contemporary audience, for his literary talent as essayist, poet, and diarist, for his ecumenical friendships (especially with Anglicans) and his special contribution to Christian-Buddhist dialogue, and for his later commitment to issues of social justice and world peace. Perhaps Merton's friend, the great Benedictine scholar Dom Jean Leclercq, is closest to the truth when he suggested that Merton's extraordinary popularity is linked to his iconic role in a time of massive cultural and religious transition. In a sense, Merton is a paradigm of the late-twentieth-century spiritual quest. He was a searcher and a wanderer who, in his monastic cell, journeyed not simply inwards but from an initially narrowly Catholic, Church-centered, and world-rejecting spirituality in his autobiography, *The Seven Storey Mountain* (1948), to highly committed observations on the public world in *Conjectures of a Guilty Bystander* (1966).

Merton's chosen medium for writing was above all autobiography even when the focus was not really him but contemplation, monastic life, inter-religious dialogue, or social engagement. The reader of Merton is always a companion on his inner and outer journey. In many respects, his apparent preoccupation with the journey from an inauthentic to an authentic self epitomizes the twentieth-century concern with finding the true self. Merton remained committed to his original option for a counter-cultural lifestyle but reinterpreted this in terms of a growing conviction that, in the face of the prevailing individualistic culture, the true self exists only in communion with, in solidarity with what is "other." The authentic self is to be vulnerable, no longer protected behind walls of separation and spiritual superiority. This growing insight led to a second conversion experience in the town nearby his monastery, Louisville in the early 1960s. He was overwhelmed by a realization of his unity with and love for all the people on the sidewalks. This led him to a quite different sense of relationship to "the world."

> It was like waking from a dream of separateness, of spurious self-isolation in a special world, the world of renunciation and supposed holiness. The whole illusion of a separate holy existence is a dream... This sense of liberation from an illusory difference [between monastic life and ordinary people] was such a relief and such a joy to me that I almost laughed aloud.[7]

A corollary of this re-conversion was a strong sense (expressed in *Life and Holiness*, 1964) that the spiritual life is not a question of quiet withdrawal but of the contemplative awareness of a common responsibility for the future of humanity. Three things seem to have come together for Merton at this point. First, he was increasingly attracted to a life of radical solitude and eventually lived a hermit life within the monastic property. Second, without losing his concern with the contemplative-mystical tradition, he increasingly embraced a prophetic stance in his prolific writings even though it risked unpopularity with his American reading public and with those in the Church who wanted him to remain a monastic "pin-up!" He supported the

Civil Rights Movement, criticized the Cold War, opposed nuclear weapons, and joined the anti-Vietnam War lobby. Third, his long-standing interest in Asian religions, especially Buddhism, blossomed into a more active involvement in inter-religious dialogue not least with the Japanese Zen Buddhist Suzuki and at the end of his life with the Dalai Lama.[8]

Spiritualities of Liberation

Injustice and oppression are hardly new, but explicitly social justice spirituality is certainly the product of the twentieth century. The long history goes back to the late nineteenth century when, in response to rapid social and economic change, the Roman Catholic Church gave birth to a tradition of Catholic social teaching, especially with the 1891 encyclical by Leo XIII, *Rerum Novarum*, further reinforced by Pius XI in his encyclical *Quadragesimo Anno* (1931) and the writings of John XXIII in the early 1960s on "reading the signs of the times" which pointed towards social analysis at the heart of the Church's mission. This was picked up by the Second Vatican Council and its Pastoral Constitution "The Church in the Modern World" (*Gaudium et Spes*). It was a natural move from this perspective to the quest for justice addressed by the 1971 Synod of Catholic Bishops in its document *Justice in the World*. This established that justice is *the very heart* of all ministry, mission, and spirituality.

Theologies and spiritualities of liberation embrace a wide spectrum of reflection and practice based on a critique of all forms of unjust structures and the struggle to overcome them. It is characteristic of these spiritualities that they promote social justice as integral to Christian faith. This implies that an attention to justice will radically question the ways in which spirituality has been traditionally practiced. Liberation theory, in whatever form, also questions the ways in which society and the Church have created structures that undermine the full human dignity of certain categories of people. Spiritualities of liberation now exist on every continent and focus on issues of economic poverty, racial exclusions, gender inequality, and, more recently, issues of planetary environmental responsibility.

Gustavo Gutiérrez (1928–)

In a narrower sense, liberation theology and spirituality refers to a movement in Latin America in the late 1960s and developed fully in the 1970s. Despite criticisms, the heart of this liberation theology and spirituality is not Marxism but scripture, especially key themes such as God leading his people into a new Exodus and victory over death explored through the classic themes of cross and resurrection.

Gustavo Gutiérrez may be taken as a leading exponent of Latin American liberation spirituality. He was born in a poor family in Lima, Peru, and suffered severe ill-health as a child. Eventually he went to university and then trained as a priest, studying theology in Europe as well as Peru. Ordained in 1959, Gutiérrez worked part-time in the Catholic University and part-time in a poor Lima parish. This dual experience led him to bring together theological reflection with his experience of living with the poor. Gutiérrez played a leading role at the famous conference of Latin American bishops at Medellín which translated the thought of the Second Vatican Council into the Latin American situation, especially in terms of the promotion of social justice. By 1971, Gutiérrez had published his seminal *A Theology of Liberation*, which set the tone not only for his later works but also for the thinking and writing of a range of other Roman Catholic and Protestant theologians on the continent. In recent years, Gutiérrez has entered the Dominican Order.

Gutiérrez developed his thinking specifically on spirituality in *We Drink from Our Own Wells*.[9] The book establishes clearly that spirituality, theology, and social practice form a continuum. At the heart of it all is the experience of God speaking in and through the situation of the poor. Theology consists of reflection on this experience in the light of scripture and tradition, and this reflection forms the basis for *praxis*, that is, activities that aid social justice and particularly the liberation of the poor. The book has three main parts. The first explores the deficiencies of much classic spirituality (particularly its elitism and tendency to excessive interiority) and the new form of spirituality that was coming into existence in Latin America. The second part of the book describes the fundamentals of all Christian spirituality (understood as discipleship, following Jesus), and the final part of the book outlines five key features of a spirituality of liberation: conversion and solidarity, gratuitousness and efficacious love, joy (which also includes the themes of martyrdom and victory over suffering), spiritual childhood (which implies commitment to the poor), and finally community – that spirituality is a spirituality *of a people* rather than individuals in isolation.

Another of Gutiérrez' books particularly relevant to spirituality is *On Job: God-Talk and the Suffering of the Innocent*. This has been described as a breakthrough in his theology. Gutiérrez' interpretation of Job underlines clearly that prayer and contemplation are paramount in his approach to theology, and to the connections between theology and social engagement. In Gutiérrez' interpretation of Job, the difference between Job and his friends is that the latter base their reflections on abstract principles rather than on an encounter with the limitless love and compassion of God. In contrast, Job seeks his "answer" face to face – one might say "head to head!" This moves Job beyond purely social or ethical reasoning to spiritual "reasoning" – a realization that God acts out of gratuitous love. Such an insight can only come from a kind of *confrontation* with God. Contemplation and confrontation are closely linked. One thinks of the power of the imprecatory psalms. Job does not receive a simple answer to his questions but what he does receive is much deeper than what he sought. Contemplation widens perspectives. But contemplation does more. In Gutiérrez' commentary, Job's encounter with God enables him to abandon himself into God's unfathomable love, beyond an abstract notion of justice. This abandonment is not *fatalistic acceptance*. Rather it situates justice within the broader and deeper scope of God's gratuity. "Prayer and contemplation are not separate moments from practice, but an inner element of that practice."[10]

Feminist Spirituality

One of the other forms of a spirituality of liberation that has had the widest impact, particularly but by no means exclusively, in Europe and North America, is what is called "feminist spirituality." The word "feminism" appears to have been used first in the 1880s and from the start had close religious connections (e.g. challenges to male interpretations of scripture in *The Woman's Bible* which appeared 1895–1998). The first wave of feminism resulted in women in Western Europe and North America gaining the right to vote, to own property, and to take university degrees. A further stage of feminism arose from the political upheavals in Europe in the late 1960s and, directly, from the Civil Rights Movement in the United States of America in both of which women played a prominent part. By the 1970s and 1980s, feminist studies appeared as an academic discipline, offering a critical analysis of gender stereotyping and its impact on women's identities and roles. This soon began to influence Christian theology and, by extension, spirituality in ways that continue today. Notable examples of theologians who have had a particular role in developing a Christian feminist spirituality are Sandra Schneiders, Joann Wolski Conn, Rosemary Radford Ruether, Elizabeth Johnson, Catherine LaCugna, Anne Carr, and Dorothee Soelle (all in North America), Elisabeth Moltmann-Wendell in Germany, and Mary Grey and the late Grace Jantzen in the United Kingdom.

A fundamental insight of feminist spirituality is that everyone's relationship with God and approaches to prayer and other spiritual practices are deeply influenced by gender. Gender here is not limited to biological sex (male and female) but also involves how sex is constructed within a given culture, historic or contemporary. The first step in feminist spiritualities, as it is in all liberation spiritualities, is to identify fundamental ways in which people's humanity and value is undermined. So, women's identity has been restricted not merely by various social systems or cultural stereotypes but also by important elements of traditional spirituality (e.g. suspicion of the body, excessive intellectualism, bypassing sexuality, emphasis on passivity, the limiting of certain spiritual roles to ordained males, and so on). These restrictions are then legitimized by prevailing images of God as male. "Maleness," too, has been caricatured in various ways that constrain men's spirituality as well as women's. Either way, only certain understandings of holiness and ways of being spiritual are affirmed.

The next step in feminist spirituality, as with all liberationist spiritualities, is to reconstruct alternative ways of talking about God, of understanding the human relationship with God, and of practicing Christian discipleship. This reconstruction is resourced by two critical features. First, again as in all liberationist spiritualities, the validity (indeed, priority) of *experience* is affirmed as the foundation of theology. We begin to understand about God as we understand how we have been able (or not able) to relate to God, and how God's action has been powerfully at work in people's (in this case, specifically women's) lives. Thus the specific nature of women's experience and ways of relating to God become a vital source of spiritual wisdom in place of purely theoretical categories which were often based on unexamined male-clerical assumptions. In fact, of course, the great classics of spiritual wisdom (e.g. Ignatius Loyola's *Spiritual Exercises* or Teresa of Avila's *The Interior Castle*) affirm that attention to experience is the basis of discernment and therefore of progress in the spiritual life. This leads naturally to the second feature of reconstruction. Again, following a liberationist model, this involves reflection on experience in the light of scripture and tradition. However, our understanding of both has been affected by selective interpretations. So, an important step is to retrieve a more complete picture. The work of feminist scripture scholars sensitive to spirituality such as Sandra Schneiders has been an important tool.[11] In theological terms, Elizabeth Johnson has offered a sophisticated and spiritually rich re-reading of the theology of the Trinity with a clear sense of the implications for a more adequate spirituality.[12] In terms of re-readings of classic spiritual texts and traditions, the work of the late Grace Jantzen on Christian mysticism and Katherine Dyckman and colleagues on the Ignatian *Spiritual Exercises* are important examples.[13]

In recent years, especially in the United States of America, new forms of feminist spirituality have appeared applicable to African American experience (Womanist spirituality) and Latina or Hispanic experience (Mujerista spirituality). A striking exemplar of Latina/mujerista spirituality is Ada María Isasi-Díaz (1943–2012). Originally from Cuba, Isasi-Díaz came to the United States of America as a refugee in 1960 and entered the Ursuline Order in which she was a sister for some years. She trained in theology specializing in ethics and eventually became an eminent university professor. Isasi-Díaz became closely involved in the movement for the ordination of women in the Roman Catholic Church. In terms of spirituality, her feminist perspective was firmly grounded in the religious experiences, spiritual practices, and everyday struggles of Hispanic women. For her, true spirituality is not a form of disembodied interiority but is measured by our ability to be immersed in embodied relationships and in the struggle for justice.

Spiritualities of Reconciliation

In a century of global wars, post-colonialism, a greater awareness of racial tension, and a concern for social justice and liberation, it is not surprising that another significant theme in spirituality was, and still is, reconciliation. The theme is central to Christian faith and therefore to spirituality. The contemporary South African theologian John de Gruchy asserts that the doctrine of reconciliation is "the inspiration and focus of all doctrines of the Christian faith."[14] Protestantism has tended to emphasize reconciliation between God and humanity as a result of the Cross (see Rom 5, 6–11) and Catholicism has tended to emphasize how the love of God poured out upon us as a result of the divine-human reconciliation creates a new humanity in which the walls of division between people are broken down (see 2 Cor 5, 17–20 and 6, 1). In practice, both dimensions need to be held in tension.

During the twentieth century, the interest in the horizontal dimension of reconciliation between human beings has been strongly reflected in attempts to overcome ethnic, political, and religious conflicts. Just as a Christian theology and spirituality of reconciliation (making space for what is other and finding oneself *in* "the other") implies a great deal more than mere tolerance or conciliation, so the notion of peace-making, a critical dimension of the quest for reconciliation these days, implies more than the mere absence of war, violence, and disturbance. The Hebrew word *Shalom* (which dominates Christian understandings of peace) denotes a state of full spiritual and physical harmony and well-being, within the individual, between people in society, and, foundational to both, between humanity and God. Such concepts have informed Christian work for world peace, opposition to nuclear weapons, and non-violent protest against injustice and disharmony as in the witness of the Hindu Gandhi in India under the Raj and of the African American Baptist pastor Dr Martin Luther King Jr during the Civil Rights Movement in the United States of America. Martin Luther King's vision had been shaped in part by another African American, the remarkable Howard Thurman (1900–1981), the dean of chapel at Boston University whom some consider to have been a mystic. Thurman developed a spirituality of radical social action shaped by prayer and suffering and highlighting the themes of human wholeness, the ideal of community, and the unity of all living things. Understood fully, the family of liberationist spiritualities that has already been mentioned is concerned in different ways with reconciliation as part of the hard process of righting injustice.

It is also possible to think of the work of the Jesuit geologist, paleontologist, and mystic, Pierre Teilhard de Chardin (1881–1955), in terms of another kind of spirituality of reconciliation. Because of the suspicions of Church authorities both about his attempts to reconcile science and religion and about his optimistic spiritual vision, his writings became widely known only after his death. Teilhard lived between and sought to bridge two worlds – contemporary scientific culture and the world of the Church and its spiritual teaching. A Modernist thinker rather than a Postmodern one, Teilhard embraced a fundamental optimism whereby evolution became a mystical and cosmological principle. Humanity is not alienated from but embedded in the material order and, with the world, progresses both forward in an evolutionary sense and "upward" towards God. For Teilhard, the risen Christ is the focus of the forward movement of the world and humanity, the Omega Point towards which and into which we grow. As a corollary, Teilhard also sought a kind of mysticism of involvement in the world, both inanimate and animate, and taught the progressive reconciliation and unification of everything in the cosmos and everyone in Christ.[15]

However, a spirituality of reconciliation in the twentieth century has also been concerned with specifically religious issues. What follows are two examples of a spirituality of reconciliation within religious contexts. The first concerns the movement for Christian ecumenism which came into being at the start of the twentieth century, and the second concerns inter-religious dialogue born of the growing process of globalization during the twentieth century and its growing impact on the relatively closed world of Christian spirituality.

Ecumenical Spirituality: The Example of Taizé

The growth of Christian ecumenism and the quest for the healing of divisions that have lasted hundreds of years in some respects reflects a broader concern for human reconciliation, especially in the aftermath of the Second World War. Hence, the World Council of Churches (founded 1948) may be seen as a kind of religious equivalent of the virtually contemporary foundation of the United Nations. The longer history of ecumenism (dating back to the Edinburgh Missionary Conference of 1910) also reflects the growing globalization of Christianity from the beginning of the century and also the sense that common mission lay at the heart of the Church's identity and therefore of its spirituality. The Roman Catholic Church only formally entered the ecumenical movement after the Second Vatican Council in the 1960s.

One of the most striking and effective symbols of the spiritual foundations both of Christian ecumenism and of human reconciliation more broadly is the monastic Taizé Community, founded in the South of Burgundy in 1940 by the late Brother Roger Schutz (1915–2005). Brother Roger was a Reformed pastor who felt called to help refugees (not least Jews) on the border between Vichy France and German-occupied France. At Taizé, he kept open house for displaced people and began a pattern of daily prayer on the monastic model. Denounced to the Germans, he spent two years in Geneva where he was joined by several companions, including the Reformed theologian Max Thurian who was also to be prominent in the community. They returned to Taizé in 1944 and committed themselves to a mission of reconciliation, not least involving young people and initially focused on French–German relations and pan-European peace but soon developing a broader religious, social, and global perspective. Although initially pan-Protestant, the spiritual logic of the community led them to accept the first Roman Catholic member in 1969, and nowadays the community has about a hundred members from a wide range of Christian traditions.

Apart from a classic monastic commitment to sharing a common life and to a daily rhythm of common prayer (expressed in the *Rule of Taizé* 1953), the spirituality of Taizé has several central characteristics. First, the community witnesses to the possibility and pains of reconciliation in their very common life which embraces a variety of nationalities, races, and traditions. They seek to be an image of what a future reconciled Church and humanity might be like but have done so while struggling to maintain the integrity of their varied religious origins. Second, the theme of "provisionality" has been a striking one in the spiritual writings of Brother Roger. Above all this refers to a radical openness to God's ways of leading in response to Christianity's susceptibility to entrenched attitudes and fixed patterns. In practice, it has meant that the community has been prepared to experiment architecturally with its worship space and has been prepared to plant temporary small fraternities (rather than fixed foundations with all that this implies) in places of particular need around the world. Third, the small fraternities have also expressed a commitment to the poor and the struggle for social justice and reconciliation of all kinds by means of a contemplative life as well as active engagement. Finally, Taizé has committed itself to being a place of pilgrimage and spiritual exploration for young people. Through partici-pation in worship, aided by an accessible musical tradition of repetitive chant, spiritual guidance, and the facilitation of mutual exchange bet-ween young people of all races and religious traditions, the community seeks to create a climate of peace and reconciliation across the world. Tens of thousands of young people visit Taizé each year and are led to make deep connections between contemplation and social commit-ment. Tragically, Brother Roger was attacked and killed during public worship in 2005, but the community and spirit live on in the hands of a new generation of brothers.[16]

Spirituality and Inter-Religious Dialogue: Bede Griffiths

The emergence of inter-religious dialogue and reconciliation during the twentieth century was influenced by the increasing globalization of Christianity, a growing awareness of a religiously plural world, a com-mitment to respecting and expressing cultural diversity, and, in some parts of the world, the need to address the close connections between violence and religious antagonisms.

The dialogue between faiths has frequently developed a strongly experiential (especially mystical-contemplative) dimension – especially in the context of contacts between Christianity and Buddhism and between Christianity and Hinduism. In the 1960s, the Benedictine J.-M. Déchanet helped familiarize many Western Christians with the purposes and techniques of Yoga and to recover the use of the body in meditation. More recently, another Benedictine, John Main, promoted the connections between Hindu recitations of mantras and the ancient Christian monastic practice as he found it in John Cassian. Others have engaged in what may be thought of as a more sustained contemplative dialogue, for example, in Japan with Zen Buddhism promoted notably by Jesuits such as Enomiya Lassalle (who became a Zen Master), Kakichi Kadowaki, and William Johnston. In India, a similar process took place with the French diocesan priest Jules Monchanin and his French Benedictine friend Henri le Saux (later Swami Abhishiktananda) who were succeeded by the English Benedictine Bede Griffiths. As Thomas Merton witnessed to so strongly, monastic life has proved a particularly fruitful context for inter-faith encounter and for shared experiences of spiritual practice.

Needless to say, inter-religious encounters on the level of meditative or worship practice have opened up a vast new world of spiritual possibilities, have encouraged a more open-ended approach to spirituality, and have enabled Christian worship in Asia, for example, to adopt a more open and imaginative approach to cultural forms other than narrowly Western ones. However, it would be generally accepted that on its own, this experiential dimension is not sufficient. Clearly, the precise ways in which spiritual encounters can be pursued (and even some degree of fusion take place) while retaining any kind of collective integrity by specific faith traditions still demands careful theoretical dialogue.

Bede Griffiths (1906–1993) represented a small but significant group of Christians who actively sought to develop a truly Indian spirituality. An intellectual and a pupil and friend of C.S. Lewis at Oxford, Bede Griffiths became a Roman Catholic in 1933 and entered the Benedictine monastery of Prinknash. After ordination, he held various positions of responsibility in the monastery. He went to India in 1955 with the vision of founding a contemplative community rather than for missionary motives. Like others before and since, Bede Griffiths sensed from his serious study of Indian scriptures while a monk in England the vital importance of recovering the intuitive-contemplative dimensions of life against what he perceived to be the rationalism, activism, and violence of the West. After an initial few years, he remained at Kurisumala ashram in Kerala for ten years before moving in 1968 to Sacchidananda ashram at Shantivanam in Tamil Nadu which had been founded by Monchanin and Abhishiktananda. There he remained for the rest of his life apart from occasional trips to Europe and North America.

Shantivanam is one of a range of Christian communities inspired by the pattern of Hindu ashrams and adapting dress, diet, lifestyle, and worship to a thoroughly Indian model. The essence of ashram life is the gathering of disciples around a wise spiritual leader in the quest for greater experience of the depths of God through meditation and other spiritual practices. Shantivanam consists of simple huts, an open-sided chapel modeled on an Indian temple, a refectory, a library, rooms for meditation and teaching, and land for cultivation, all in woods by the banks of the sacred river Cavery. Worship is conducted in a totally Indian style with many classic Indian rituals used in the Liturgy and Hindu scriptures playing some role alongside the Christian ones. The small community is linked to the Benedictines and attracts large number of seekers and other visitors both Christian and Hindu. The community also helps support social and educational work in local villages.

Bede Griffiths had a particular approach to the relationship between Christianity and Hinduism. The classic Hindu advaidic sense of a universal harmony and unity beyond differences and distinctions (not least between human existence and the Absolute) played a strong role in his spirituality. However, at the same time Bede Griffiths remained a thoroughly orthodox Christian in that he saw deep connections between this belief in an ultimate oneness with all things in the Divine and Trinitarian theology in which ultimate oneness and unfathomable unity is balanced with distinction. Separate identity is not an illusion. Thus, for Bede Griffiths, the Trinitarian model of existence implies that the contemplative process of losing ourselves in the abyss of the One is also nonetheless to discover our true selves rather than to pass beyond separate identity.[17]

Eastern Orthodox Spirituality

Because of its breadth and diversity, it is difficult to summarize in a brief span the riches of the Eastern Orthodox spiritual tradition during the twentieth century. What follows is therefore highly selective and concentrates on two elements – the monastic renewal on Mount Athos and Russian spirituality, both pre-Revolution and post-Revolution, through the medium of a few important figures.

Mount Athos is a mountainous peninsular in Macedonia, Greece. The all-male monastic settlements there probably date back to the exodus of Christian monks from Egypt as a result of Islamic invasions during the seventh century. As we have already noted, it was here that the Orthodox contemplative tradition known as hesychasm developed, and this has continued until the present day. At the end of the nineteenth century and during the early years of the twentieth century, there was a major influx of monks from Russia which gave Athos a new impetus and fed back into its ethos the contemplative traditions of the monastery of Optino and of *The Way of the Pilgrim*. Partly as a result of the 1917 Russian Revolution, this source of vocations diminished considerably. Combined with a mid-century indifference to monastic life in Greece, this led to a decline that might well eventually have been terminal. However, in the years after the Second World War, there was an increase of interest in Orthodox spirituality in the West. This, combined with a renewal of monastic interest in Greece, led to a significant revival. A new Greek edition of the *Philokalia* appeared in the early 1960s. Nowadays, the hesychast contemplative tradition on Athos is strong once again, and recruits from all over the world, including new converts, have entered the monasteries in recent decades.

In the case of Russian spirituality, the political and social upheavals in the homeland have had a major impact. However, one important influence on lay Orthodox believers, the parish priest St John of Kronstadt (1829–1909), predates the Revolution and became one of the most loved Orthodox figures of the century. He was canonized initially by the Russian Church in exile and then in 1990 by the main Russian Orthodox Church. St John's spirituality had three important features. First, a daily Eucharist was central to his life and he was an advocate of frequent Communion for lay Christians. Second, he insisted that charity was inherent to true Christian piety and expressed this in his work for social outcasts. Finally, he left an extensive spiritual diary which laid out his practice of personal prayer.[18]

Vladimir Lossky (1903–1958) was one of the most influential lay theologians in the Russian tradition. He lived in Russia until his family was exiled in 1922 in the aftermath of the Revolution and civil war. He subsequently studied in Paris where he remained until he died. Lossky is notable particularly for building up the Russian theological institute in Paris of which he was the first Dean and for his classic work, *The Mystical Theology of the Eastern Church*. Here he argues that Eastern Christianity maintained the priority of mystical theology which was lost by the West after the Great Schism. Lossky understood *theōsis*, the process of being drawn into the life of God as the ultimate destiny of creation, to be the core of Christianity rather than religious philosophy or abstract dogmatic theology. For him, mysticism and theology were inextricably linked so that prayer and liturgy are the foundations of theology, and conversely that theology is directed at the furtherance of the Christian life.[19]

Finally, and by way of stark contrast, Mother Maria Skobtsova (1891–1945) was a Russian aristocrat, significant literary figure, eventual nun, and finally martyr during the Second World War. She was canonized in 2004. In her youth, Elizaveta (as she was originally known) was an atheist involved in radical intellectual circles who was slowly drawn back to Christianity. After the Revolution and during the subsequent civil war, she was for a time the mayor of the town of Anapa in southern Russia. By then married for the second time, she and her family eventually went into exile and arrived in Paris in 1923. There she studied theology and worked as a social worker with the poor while continuing to write poetry. By 1932, Elizaveta's marriage ended in divorce, and she took monastic vows as Mother Maria. Her "convent" home became both a center for intellectual religious discussions and an open house for the poor and needy. After the German occupation of France in 1940, Mother Maria became a member of the Resistance and with members of her family and a priest friend helped many Jews to escape. Eventually, she was arrested by the Gestapo and sent to Ravensbrück concentration camp where she sacrificed her life in place of a Jewish woman and was gassed over Easter 1945.[20]

In the later years of the twentieth century and into the present century, the Eastern Orthodox tradition has experienced its own version of globalization. Apart from significant numbers of Russians now living and working in Western Europe and North America, several of the more recent member countries of the European Union are predominantly Orthodox or have significant Orthodox populations. As a result, the Eastern Christian tradition, including its spirituality, can no longer be seen as a tropical luxuriance represented in the majority of Western countries by small and culturally marginal groups of exiles or immigrants. Eastern Christianity is destined to become part of the European religious and spiritual mainstream. This development also offers to the wider field of Christian spirituality a reminder of the importance of liturgy and mystical theology.

Making Spirituality Democratic: The Retreat Movement

A final striking feature of Western Christian spirituality during the twentieth century is the many ways in which it became more democratic – that is, how it passed increasingly out the controlling hands of religious authorities and spiritual elites such as clergy or, in the Catholic tradition, members of religious orders. Two representative examples are the growth of the retreat movement and, perhaps more controversially, the charismatic movement.

The broad notion of "retreat" can be traced back to New Testament accounts of Jesus taking his disciples apart to rest and pray. Later on, monastic life can be interpreted as a life-long retreat, or process of deepening the Christian life through silence, solitude, and contemplation. There is little evidence for the notion of organized retreats (apart from pilgrimage) before the sixteenth century when Ignatius Loyola and the early Jesuits founded the idea of formal, structured retreats in giving the *Spiritual Exercises*. Although retreat houses existed in France by the seventeenth century, and retreats began in the Anglican tradition from the mid-nineteenth century, the modern retreat movement really started under lay inspiration in the United States of America in the early twentieth century. These were mainly group retreats for relatively large numbers which were preached by experienced priests.

The broader tradition of spiritual guidance, in which one person acts as guide, mentor, or companion to another can be traced to early monasticism in the Egyptian desert. Gradually this was institutionalized in the role of Abbot or Abbess as *the* spiritual leader and in the growing role of priest-confessors during the Middle Ages. After the Council of Trent in the mid-sixteenth century, spiritual guidance and sacramental confession in the Roman Catholic Church tended to collapse into each other making the process thoroughly institutionalized and the expertise dependent on ordination.

Although non-institutional forms of spiritual guidance did exist in the early part of the twentieth century in the persons of laypeople such as the Roman Catholic Baron von Hügel and the Anglican Evelyn Underhill, this catered for a small, rather refined, educated, elite minority of Christians. The same more or less applied to individual retreats.

It was really the teachings of the Second Vatican Council on the call of all Christians to holiness, coupled with developing ecumenical contacts, that led to the renewal both of the retreat movement and of the practice of spiritual guidance within and beyond the Roman Catholic Church. The single most striking part of this was the relative democratization of both. The work of spiritual guidance is no longer assumed to be dependent on ordination or membership of a religious order. In Western spirituality, spiritual guides or retreat givers are as likely to be women as men, lay as ordained, and from a wide range of Christian traditions. The ability to act as a spiritual guide is seen as a gift of God, inspired by God's Spirit (the true guide) even though there has also been much professionalization with spiritual direction and retreat training courses now widespread, often Ignatian in inspiration, ecumenical, and increasingly lay in their participants and training personnel.

One-to-one spiritual guidance is increasingly sought by a wide range of Christians and other spiritual seekers and often involves elements of psychology in tandem with spiritual teachings. Increasing numbers of people actually seek an explicit mixture of psychotherapy and spiritual guidance. Retreats also nowadays frequently offer some personal guidance or counseling, and the range of themes, spiritual practices, or holistic experiences on offer is continually expanding. For example, there has been a resurgence of interest in monastic and contemplative wisdom and practices suited to the needs of busy people seeking a better balance in the midst of pressurized lifestyles. If the world of retreats and spiritual guidance is now open to, and indeed dominated by, the needs of everyday seekers, this is paralleled by an increasing spiritual eclecticism whereby both retreat givers and spiritual seekers cross boundaries to use wisdom from a wide range of sources, religious and other.[21]

Making Spirituality Democratic: Pentecostal and Charismatic Spirituality

In a broad sense, the charismatic movement has a long history back to the inspiration of the Holy Spirit in the Book of Acts and developed in various spiritual movements in the Middle Ages and in the early modern era (e.g. among the Shakers). However, modern charismatic spirituality really began with an Evangelical revival at Azusa Street in Los Angeles in 1906 under the inspiration of the African American ecumenist William Seymour (1870–1922). From this grew a movement that gave birth to the Pentecostal family of Churches. "Baptism in the Spirit," speaking with tongues, the gift of prophecy, and interpretation were key elements. The movement was originally multiracial though eventually separated into different groupings and appealed particularly to fairly poor or dispossessed people. The Pentecostal family of Churches is now worldwide and is the fastest growing branch of Christianity in the Southern Hemisphere. The spirituality of the movement has certain characteristics such as the active presence and work of God's Spirit in each person and in the community as a whole, an emphasis on oral and spontaneous worship, narrative witness and testimony, participatory community, a direct relationship between prayer and decisions, and a valuation of dreams and visions.

In the 1960s and 1970s, large numbers of Roman Catholics and members of the Anglican and traditional Protestant Churches were influenced by the "charismatic movement" and had the same experiences as classic Pentecostalism. Apart from the gifts of the Spirit, there was an emphasis on healing, a spirituality of praise, and on the need to spread radical spiritual renewal throughout the mainstream Churches. The charismatic movement was also a notable context for much grass-roots ecumenism.

Opponents have often accused the charismatic movement of naïve biblical literalism and of being religiously conservative and socially middle class. The reality is more complex. Overall the movement can be understood as an experientialist reaction to over-formal worship and a dry intellectual faith. It also offers access to a source of authority (the Spirit) and of assurance in a period of considerable confusion and fragmentation in Western culture. The movement strongly emphasizes the reality of God's love, and the various Spirit-filled experiences assure people that God's presence and love are immediately present, active, and powerful. The charismatic movement was emotionally liberating in style.

Specifically in the Roman Catholic context after the Second Vatican Council, the charismatic movement offered a counter-balance to the great emphasis on liturgical renewal, a genuinely lay and communal form of spirituality, and the possibility of a new devotionalism to replace older pre-Conciliar devotions that had often gone out of fashion in parishes. However, in the context of a growing spiritual democracy and of the ecumenical crossing of traditional denominational boundaries, the charismatic movement is fundamentally a popularist spiritual movement that is not dependent on ordination for authorization or for dispensing spiritual wisdom. The Spirit of God speaks where the Spirit wills, and prophecy and its interpretation is the prerogative of all Christians.[22]

Conclusion

Even this very selective portrait of spirituality in the twentieth century suggests that by the end of the period the Christian approach to and experience of spirituality was more varied, eclectic, global, ecumenical, and radically plural than at almost any point in the history of Christianity. The wider cultural context in the West continues to show a major decline in membership of traditional religious denominations. However, at the same time, there is a more broadly based quest for spiritual wisdom and practices that engage positively with contemporary values and critically with some of the problems raised by life in a fast-moving consumer society. Despite theories of irreversible secularization and the death of religion, popular until recently, the evidence globally is that this is a narrowly Western viewpoint. Even in terms of Western culture, people are now more likely to talk about "post-secularism" and a new age of spirituality even if it is difficult to predict how the Christian spiritual tradition will flourish in the new climate of spiritual pluralism.

Notes

1   See Robert Ellsberg, ed., *Charles de Foucauld: Selected Writings*, Maryknoll: Orbis Books, 1999.

2   See Evelyn Underhill, *Mysticism: The Nature and Development of Spiritual Consciousness*, Oxford/New York: Oneworld Publications, 1993 and also C. Williams, ed., *The Letters of Evelyn Underhill*, London: Darton Longman & Todd, 1991.

3   Jürgen Moltmann, *Experiences of God*, Philadelphia: Fortress Press, 1980, p. 72.

4   See Dietrich Bonhoeffer, *The Cost of Discipleship*, London: SCM Press, 1984 and also his *Letters and Papers from Prison*, New York: Macmillan, 1971. See also G.B. Kelly and F. Burton Nelson, *The Cost of Moral Leadership: The Spirituality of Dietrich Bonhoeffer*, Grand Rapids: William B. Eerdmans, 2003.

5   See Simone Weil, *Waiting for God*, New York: Harper, 1973 and also *The Need for Roots*, London: Routledge, 2001.

6   See Robert Ellsberg, ed., *Dorothy Day: Selected Writings*, Maryknoll: Orbis Books, 1992.

7   Thomas Merton, *Conjectures of a Guilty Bystander*, New York: Doubleday, 1966, pp. 140–141.

8   See Lawrence C. Cunningham, ed., *Thomas Merton: Spiritual Master. The Essential Writings*, New York: Paulist Press, 1992 and also Lawrence S. Cunningham, *Thomas Merton & the Monastic Vision*, Grand Rapids: William B. Eerdmans, 1999.

9   Gustavo Gutiérrez, *We Drink from Our Own Wells: The Spiritual Journey of a People*, Maryknoll: Orbis Books and London: SCM Press, 1984.

10 See *On Job: God-Talk and the Suffering of the Innocent*, Maryknoll: Orbis Books, 1998. On liberation spirituality more generally, see Jon Sobrino, *Spirituality of Liberation*, Maryknoll: Orbis Books, 1988.

11 See Sandra Schneiders, *The Revelatory Text: Interpreting the New Testament as Sacred Scripture*, Collegeville: The Liturgical Press, 1999.

12 See Elizabeth Johnson, *She Who Is: The Mystery of God in Feminist Theological Discourse*, New York: Crossroad, 1996.

13 Grace Jantzen, *Power, Gender and Christian Mysticism*, Cambridge: Cambridge University Press, 1995. Katherine Dyckman, Mary Garvin, and Elizabeth Liebert, *The Spiritual Exercises Reclaimed*, New York: Paulist Press, 2001.

14 John de Gruchy, *Reconciliation: Restoring Justice*, London: SCM Press, 2002, p. 44.

15 See Ursula King, ed., *Pierre Teilhard de Chardin: Selected Writings*, Maryknoll: Orbis Books, 1999.

16 See *The Rule of Taizé*, Taizé: Les Presses de Taizé, 1961; Brother Roger, *Afire with Love: Meditations on Peace and Unity*, New York: Crossroad, 1982; Brother Roger, *The Power of the Provisional*, London: Hodder & Stoughton, 1969; and Kathryn Spink, *A Universal Heart: The Life and Vision of Brother Roger of Taizé*, London: SPCK, 1986.

17 See Bede Griffiths, *A New Vision of Reality: Western Science, Eastern Mysticism and Christian Faith*, Springfield: Templegate, 1990 and also S. du Boulay, *Beyond the Darkness: A Biography of Bede Griffiths*, New York/London: Doubleday, 1998.

18 See G. Fedotov, *A Treasury of Russian Spirituality*, London: Sheed & Ward, 1981, pp. 346–416.

19 V. Lossky, *The Mystical Theology of the Eastern Church*, London: James Clark, 1991.

20 See S. Hackel, *Pearl of Great Price: The Life of Mother Maria Skobtsova*, Crestwood: St Vladimir's Seminary Press, 1981.

21 A useful overview of spiritual direction is Kenneth Leech, *Soul Friend: Spiritual Direction in the Modern World*, revised edition, London: Darton Longman & Todd, 1994.

22 See Mark Cartledge, *Encountering the Spirit: The Charismatic Tradition*, London: Darton Longman & Todd and Maryknoll: Orbis Books, 2006.

Chapter 8

Twenty-First Century Trajectories

In which directions is Christian spirituality likely to go in the future? If the twentieth century is still difficult to evaluate, trying to predict the next few decades may seem a foolish enterprise. Today's spiritual climate is complex, and also, as we shall see, some specific features of Christian spirituality are undergoing major readjustment. This final chapter will begin with a brief examination of the widespread notion that spirituality is *replacing* religion and will ask whether religious spiritualities will survive. The chapter will then examine three critical realities to which Christian spirituality must now adjust – an increasingly globalized and multicultural world, the impact of cyberspace, and inter-religious encounters. There will then be an exploration of the potential contribution of Christian spirituality to some examples of the ever-expanding range of so-called secular and professional spiritualities. Finally, we will briefly reflect on the significant contemporary focus on "spiritual practices," what this implies, and how Christian spirituality might respond.

Will Christian Spiritualities Survive?

A critical question is whether in the long term Christian spiritual traditions will survive in the face of what has been interpreted as a "subjective turn" in the West towards understandings of spirituality that are no longer associated with "religion." Nowadays, the use of the word "spirituality" is often difficult to define once it is detached from religious belonging. As we saw in Chapter 1, some commentators on contemporary Western spiritual culture suggest that spirituality is in the process of

Spirituality: A Brief History, Second Edition. Philip Sheldrake.
© 2013 John Wiley & Sons, Ltd. Published 2013 by John Wiley & Sons, Ltd.

replacing religion in an evolutionary development, because spirituality, rather than institutional religion, is a better fit with present-day needs. There are a number of problems with this way of thinking. The sharp distinction often made between "spirituality" and "religion" is too polarized and uncritical if we take into account the broader picture.

First, such an evolutionary view reflects a belief in human existence as a simple story of progress – a belief that has been discredited in the aftermath of the technologically fueled horrors of twentieth-century war, genocide, and nuclear threat, not to mention the dangerous impact of human technology on the environment. The study of history soon teaches us that assumptions about inevitable "progress" and absolute breaks with the past are highly questionable. Second, the status of religion in the present age is complex. In Europe and North America, it may be true that significant numbers of people cease to identify with institutional religion and are exploring a range of spiritual practices beyond traditional contexts. Yet, it is equally true that other people turn to conservative forms of "religion" as their answer to the uncertainties of contemporary living. The religion versus spirituality debate is also frequently culturally one-dimensional. Once we move beyond the narrow confines of Western societies, assessments of the definitive end of traditional religion in the face of an eclectic quest for spirituality are clearly inaccurate.

There are other problems about distinguishing "spirituality" from "religion." How do we define the two words? First, in the case of "spirituality," this is sometimes assumed to consist of a range of practices that are distinct from systems of belief. However, on closer examination, it seems clear that all approaches to spirituality relate to some form of belief even if this is implicit rather than explicit. Also, in practice, contemporary approaches to spirituality are freely associated with "values" (e.g. the pursuit of human "well-being" in discussions of spirituality and health-care). Yet these values tend to be treated as though they were free-standing rather than based on prior assumptions about the nature and purpose of human life. In reality, everyone has some kind of worldview or "beliefs about life." Such belief systems may derive from a mixture of factors such as childhood upbringing, later life experience, plus a range of social and cultural influences including those that originate in the historic Christian foundations of many European countries.

Second, the clear distinction between "religion" and "spirituality" depends on a caricature of a religion such as Christianity. In the popular mind, Christianity is frequently equated with the institutional Church which, in turn, is often associated with dogma, moralism, authoritarianism, hierarchy, social expectations, and an excessive concern with buildings, money, and systems. As this brief history has shown, the Christian religion is fundamentally based on a spiritual vision. Christianity throughout its history has given rise to a wide range of spiritual traditions that offer a "map" or path for the spiritual journey.

What is undoubtedly true is that Christianity is not always associated in people's minds with spirituality. The exceptions are a few figures from the past who have been promoted outside conventional religious circles and consequently achieved almost cult status such as Hildegard of Bingen, Meister Eckhart, or Thomas Merton. Institutional Christianity has not adequately presented its rich and varied spiritual traditions even to its own adherents let alone to spiritual seekers. It has concentrated too much on formal structures, rationalistic styles of doctrine, and a preoccupation with moral teaching. The future of Christian spirituality will depend a great deal on whether this situation alters and the Christian Church learns how to unlock its spiritual treasures and to focus more on promoting spiritual wisdom.

In a world of accelerated and confusing change, people increasingly seek not only practical wisdom to live by but also the possibility of deep, even mystical, experiences of interconnectedness with other people, with nature, and with the divine. However, ultimately, the immediacy of experience on its own is unsatisfying. What the four types of Christian spirituality have to offer is a "long history," an inherited memory of spiritual wisdom and of the art of discernment. The danger with a completely rootless approach to spirituality, Christian or other, is that it offers no clear principles to judge whether the way we approach a mystical text or the way we adopt a spiritual practice is likely to be life-enhancing or spiritually dangerous. As we saw at the end of Chapter 1, such criteria of judgment are vital.

A Globalized World

The first critical reality to which Christian spirituality must now adjust is that we live in an increasingly globalized world. This notion has several dimensions. First, while Christianity was born in the Middle East and one of its earliest spiritual forms, monasticism, originated mainly in Egypt (i.e. in Africa), Christian spirituality has been seen as mainly a European or Northern Hemisphere possession. This can no longer be the case. The people of Africa, Asia, and Latin America are not merely passive recipients of spiritual wisdom imported from elsewhere. The section in the last chapter on the emergence of indigenous liberation spiritualities, particularly in Latin

America, began to address this issue. However, the inculturation of spirituality in vastly different contexts is a much broader question.

In Chapter 1, we saw how Hispanic Christians in North America have developed a theory called "traditioning" which offers critical perspectives on the dynamics of how ordinary people rather than religious authorities appropriate and pass on spiritual traditions. In similar vein, we also noted the theories of the French sociologist Olivier Roy who borrows the word *formatage* or "formatting" from computer language in his analysis of how religious and spiritual traditions are "reformatted" to fit the predominant norms of the multiple cultures within which they come to exist.[1]

Recently, in this context, writing has appeared that attempts to outline distinctive characteristics of Christian spirituality in Africa, Asia, and Latin America. Thus, to take merely one example, traditional African spirituality has an unusually strong sense of parallel visible and invisible worlds. This promotes particular spiritual emphases among Christians. Spirits, both good and evil, are always close and play an active role in people's lives. Pentecostal spirituality has had a strong impact because of its emphasis on the immediacy of the supernatural realm. The Holy Spirit is seen as an accessible source of healing both of body and spirit. In the latter case, the power of God's Spirit is believed to be a potent antidote to a traditional fear of possession by evil spirits. On the positive side, if God, angels, and saints are present among us as immediate concrete realities, this also applies to ancestors for whom traditionally there is deep respect. It is believed that ancestors act not only as a perpetual extended family but also as mediators between the living and God and as our vigilant guardians. This dramatically expresses the intensely communal nature of African spirituality. In the words of a Zulu proverb, "A person becomes a person only with others." Ancestor veneration now blends with conventional Christian devotion to angels and saints. The notion of mediation leads some to portray Christ, the definitive mediator between God and humanity, as Proto-Ancestor or Elder Brother. Equally, the surrounding reality of nature is seen as an epiphany of God. Thus, African Christian approaches to spirituality have no sense of a separation between sacred and secular or material and spiritual.[2]

Cyberspace

Another very different aspect of globalization and a sense of global interconnectedness is the impact of information technology and of communication through the Internet. The Internet presents a major challenge to Christian spirituality in the twenty-first century. It offers immediacy as a key value by means of an unprecedented concentration of interpretative power. Exploration of the Internet offers relatively unrestrained access to all the knowledge currently available. However, another striking aspect is that it creates a new kind of social space, "cyberspace," for interconnection. Cyberspace makes a qualitative rather than purely quantitative change to the way we exist: it affects our relationships with each other, how we think of ourselves, and what we perceive as real.

The positive potential of cyberspace is not in doubt. For example, in terms of human community, people who are housebound may belong to a wider community than their physically circumscribed world. As a space for knowing, the Internet democratizes education by placing more material in the public domain and by offering access to texts, artwork, or music that are otherwise difficult to obtain. A common reason to access the Internet is email. This substantially increases contacts with family and friends. Communication is relatively immediate, effortless, and cheap. Through such social networks as Facebook, an increasing number of people think of themselves as part of a "virtual family" – an immense network in comparison to connections in three-dimensional space.

However, from the perspective of Christian spirituality, is virtual space really a place of human *encounter* rather than a protected existence? A recently coined word "technomonasticism" implies a new kind of community. Yet, alongside the technomonastics, there are also "lurkers" whose anonymous presences browse the Web without identifying themselves. Further, what is the impact of "cyber-travel" on the human spirit? In the past, journeys away from familiar places disturbed our cherished assumptions about the world. Does travel through virtual space have the same capacity to challenge us? We "visit" people who are thousands of miles away, but it is a journey without real movement. We are not aggravated by strange diets, heat, or health hazards.

Yet, cyberspace enables the creation of communities of interest that are otherwise unavailable. In terms of building faith communities, new options open up. On a simple level, email has given new birth to the ancient art of spiritual guidance by letter. "Retreats in daily life" are now offered via websites. The multitude of available sources raises further questions about passing on religious-spiritual traditions. "Traditions" now exist in a fast-moving, fluid, plural, and egalitarian world where boundaries are crossed at will and there are few constraints about the material, ideas, and views to which we have access. All of this questions our understanding of a religious tradition as simple, universal, and timeless.

One of the most challenging possibilities in cyberspace is the transcendence of physical limits. Cyberspace is a kind of metaphysical gateway which transports us into an "other" realm. When the Jewish and Christian traditions use the image of "face to face" to describe encounters with God, this is not purely incidental. It reveals something vital about interpersonal encounter. The Christian vision of human nature places a high degree of importance on embodiment. The doctrine of incarnation suggests that God becomes *flesh*. Human embodiment is a kind of "sacrament" of God's presence. If cyberspace bypasses fleshliness, does this create a privileged, disembodied world that lifts the initiates into a new dualism where "perfection," as with ancient Gnosticism, is found on some kind of elevated *mental* plane?

The more advanced frontiers of speculation are already talking of cyberspace as a kind of "beyond." The language is quasi-mystical. One way of interpreting the culture of cyberspace is as a form of "total presence." Such a culture offers simultaneity in which "time" is merely simulated and "place" is ubiquitous and therefore without a real center. Yet, it may be argued that the apparently all-encompassing vision offered by cyberspace cloaks another version of ultimate unknowing. As in classic apophatic mystical texts, the human subject endlessly seeks but never finally captures the ultimate. Thus, in the technological universe we remain always on the move, passing from image to image with an endless pattern of connections but also of displacements.

Cyberspace offers exciting possibilities and extraordinary speculations. However, this underlines the need for discernment – a central value in Christian spirituality. Once again, we have to be capable of discriminating between what is dehumanizing and what is enhancing, what fragments and what binds us together, what is spiritually destructive, and what will develop human well-being.[3]

Inter-Religious Encounter

The third critical reality facing a globalized Christian spirituality in the twenty-first century is inter-religious dialogue. This is born of a deeper awareness of religious plurality, a commitment to the respect for cultural diversity, and, in some parts of the world, the need to address the close connections between political violence and historic religious antagonisms.

As we saw briefly in Chapter 7, this dialogue between faiths is no longer dominated by purely intellectual debates. More recently, it has developed a strongly spiritual dimension. For example, some inter-religious groups actively seek to forge a common language of spirituality drawn from the collective wisdom of the traditions of the world religions. Even a public religious leader such as the late-twentieth-century pope, John Paul II, controversially gathered faith leaders together in Assisi in 1986 to demonstrate the possibility of being united through prayer. Inter-religious spiritual dialogue has also led to common social action. For the movement known as "engaged Buddhism," associated with the Zen master Thich Nhat Hanh, was strongly influenced by his contacts with socially critical Christians such as the monk Thomas Merton and the priest and peace activist Dan Berrigan.

Some people claim that spirituality offers a particularly powerful point of engagement between Christianity and other faiths. Behind the institutional externals, spirituality is actually the core of all the different religions. It focuses on a virtuous life, religious experience, and the process of spiritual transformation. Those with extensive experience of inter-religious encounters suggest that sharing spiritual wisdom and practice leads members of the different religions to understand their own faith in new ways. Common reflection and shared practice does not make differences of belief disappear but shifts people's perceptions about the relative importance of the theoretical differences between the religions. Spirituality is also an important expression of how people understand what it means to be human. In this way, dialogue through the medium of spirituality reinforces a sense of common humanity.

Does a dialogue of spiritualities necessarily lead to syncretism or a pan-religious integration of spiritual experience? Those who say "no" might point to their belief that a never-ending process of dialogue without any obvious final conclusion has a spiritual value in itself. For them, God is found precisely on the borders between different faiths and in the challenging movement to and fro between what is familiar and what is "other." Other people, called "universalists," wish to honor the religious revelation present in all great spiritual teachers or traditions without giving priority to any single tradition. Another contemporary movement, known as "interspirituality," inspired by the work of an American Roman Catholic, Wayne Teasdale (1945–2004), acknowledges in all the world religions a degree of commonality that may be approached through contemplative practice and mystical experience. However, Teasdale was not a simple universalist. "Interspirituality" is not merely the superficial borrowing of spiritual practices but demands a commitment to walk a spiritual path with openness. Teasdale remained a Roman Catholic Christian while being open to the wisdom of other faiths, particularly Hinduism.

Christian spirituality will increasingly have to adapt to its existence within a multi-cultural, multi-faith world. This implies living with radical pluralism and that Christian spirituality will learn even more profoundly what a non-exclusive uniqueness implies from engaging with other faith traditions rather than existing in opposition to them. Clearly, it will also be important to learn the difference between a creative exchange of gifts with other religious traditions and the kind of syncretism that involves a loss of integrity.

Christian Spirituality and Secular Spirituality

A final, and increasingly important, category of contemporary spiritualities embraces a wide range of so-called secular approaches. Of course the word "secular" was not originally the opposite of "religious." The Latin *saeculum* simply means "this age" or "the here and now," and in Catholic Christianity the word "secular" is applied to priests who work in the everyday world rather than live in monasteries. However, in contemporary usage, "secular spirituality" refers to the varied ways in which the concept of spirituality is increasingly used outside religious contexts. Christian spirituality has something distinctive to contribute to these "secular" or everyday preoccupations and in the future will need to engage more explicitly with them. Three examples will suffice. First, there are a range of professional spiritualities which seek to encourage a spiritual dimension in the way people work and how they see themselves contributing to the greater good. It is becoming clearer that work should be understood as a spiritual issue not least because it relates to questions of human purpose and meaning. The world of business and commerce is a major example. Second, there is increasing reflection on spirituality in relation to human well-being and flourishing. The increasing interest in spirituality and healthcare is a notable example. Finally, in the context of an increasingly urbanized world, a number of urban thinkers and professionals are looking at how the concept of "spirituality" might enhance the experience of urban living.

Spirituality, Business, and Economics

One clear example of a secular spirituality is the growing popularity of management and business spirituality. Articles and books on spirituality and business are common, and there are groups that seek to promote spiritual values in the workplace, such as the Foundation for Workplace Spirituality. At the heart of this turn to spirituality in the commercial world is a recovery of the idea that work is a vocation rather than purely a practical need. Some companies encourage employees and management personnel to develop spiritual values and practices and even organize joint "retreats" to build up a corporate spirit. A range of spiritual practices have appeared, drawn from different sources. There may be tai chi at the start of the day, meditation spaces provided during the lunch break, and a library of spiritual books for the staff. The business spirituality movement also encourages an ethical approach to commerce, promotes individual and corporate integrity, and seeks to develop a clear value-system.

Professional spirituality also often focuses on qualities of leadership in the workplace. Some of these are closer to psychology than spirituality, but, among other qualities, the spiritually effective leader should possess courage, creativity, an ability to be inspirational, and so to build up team spirit among the workforce. The concept of "spiritual intelligence" is also nowadays applied to effective leadership. This type of intelligence is what connects people not merely to the physical world of immediate events but also to a world of imagination, vision, and possibility. Spiritual intelligence provides the energy to move ahead wisely into the future. Some approaches to spiritually enlightened business leadership also suggest that there should be a commitment to create a corporate sense of service to humanity and to encourage an ethos that suggests that part of what commerce should do is to change the world for the better.

In this context, a number of Christian spiritual classics such as the monastic Rule of St Benedict offer valuable insights. The Rule both affirms the spiritual value of work (notably Chapter 48) and also offers guidance on spiritual leadership (especially Chapters 2 and 64). Protestant thinkers like Martin Luther and John Calvin both asserted the holiness of ordinary work and that a "worldly calling" was just as spiritual as clerical or monastic lifestyles. A recent pope, John Paul II, wrote a 1981 encyclical letter *Laborem Exercens* ("on human work"). There he suggested that human work was in imitation of God-as-creator. It also serves the wider human community by building up the common good. Pope John Paul noted that, in practice, work situations may be demeaning or dehumanizing. Consequently, it is important to inculcate a belief that work is a positive virtue and central to what it is to be human. Such a view raises critical questions about the need for justice, human dignity, decent conditions, fair wages, and true creativity in the workplace.

Associated with the interest in spirituality and work are more theoretical and broadly based attempts to introduce spirituality into thinking about economics and its role in society. One notable example is SPES, a European-centered international forum for "Spirituality in Economics and Society." The forum brings together individuals, academic centers, and values-driven organizations that are engaged in socio-economic activity and are concerned to make spirituality a public and social "good" rather than purely a private and individual "good." While the membership of the SPES network is inclusive, its foundations are Christian, particularly in the Christian humanism and personalist philosophy of the Frenchman Emmanuel Mounier (1905–1950). Mounier's work was in many respects a socially orientated Christian alternative to Marxist-based socialism and had a significant impact in the United States of America on Dorothy Day, the founder of the Catholic Worker Movement.

SPES suggests that there are two central beliefs about the nature and value of "spirituality" in relation to economics. First, spirituality must not be confined to the private or individual sphere but needs to be reconceived as a corporate value with social and public effects. Second, without opposing or rejecting "religion," spirituality needs to find an effective everyday meaning – to step beyond the narrow preoccupations of institutional faith to focus powerfully on the humanization of the world. SPES approaches spirituality in terms of making connections between people's quest for meaning (whether in relation to God or not) and everyday activities in the social and economic fields. The forum explicitly seeks to promote a spiritually based humanism to relate spirituality to a richer understanding of social ethics and to promote hope as the key virtue in working to build a better future for Europe and the world.

Three key themes have emerged for research and action in relation to spirituality and economics in the contemporary climate. First, there is the relationship between spirituality and an "economics of frugality." This seeks to respond to the major global economic crisis that arose during the first decade of the twenty-first century. This focus asks such questions as: How may we reintroduce the concept of frugality as both a private and public virtue? What might its impact be on new approaches to economic life? How does it relate to sustainability in business, to an ethics of consumption, and to social justice? Finally, what kinds of socio-spiritual practices might take the new frugality forward?

A second theme asks questions about the spiritual identity of Europe in the midst of a European crisis of identity. It suggests that spirituality needs to be a key factor in new thinking about the revitalization of the European Union. The central questions here are: What is the "soul" of Europe? How do we create a sense of spiritual identity to enable Europe to overcome its identity crisis? What is the "spiritual deficit" in the European integration process and how may this be overcome? What spiritual resources tend to be overlooked but are available to and relevant to the social and economic spheres?

Finally, research on globalization and the "common good" focuses on the concept of the common good as developed by both ancient Greek (Aristotle) and Christian philosophy (Thomas Aquinas). Here, the motto may be summarized as "the good of all is the key to the good of each." However, the ancient virtue of seeking the "common good" needs redefining in the context of globalization and its impact both on environmental problems and on increasingly sharp socio-economic divisions in the world. We will return to the theme of the "common good" later in the chapter.

Spirituality and Healthcare

Healthcare is a second significant social area where the language of spirituality is increasingly common. In the United Kingdom, there are at least three key resources on spirituality and health: a research project "Spirituality, Theology and Health" at Durham University, a Centre for Spirituality, Health and Disability at the University of Aberdeen, and the Spirituality and Psychiatry Special Interest Group of The Royal College of Psychiatrists. There is also a European Network of Research on Religion, Spirituality and Health. In North America, there are a number of centers which address this issue, among them The Center for Spirituality, Theology and Health at Duke University, North Carolina.

American definitions of spirituality and healthcare more overtly relate spirituality to religious belief. Indeed, the consensus in health research in the United States of America relates spirituality and religion to each other rather than defines them as independent. For example, a 1999 report from the American medical schools notes that spirituality is not only a factor that contributes to health but that it expresses a person's search for ultimate meaning through participation in religion and/or belief in God, family, naturalism, humanism, rationalism, and the arts. In the United Kingdom, the British Royal College of Psychiatry (RCP) "Spirituality and Psychiatry Special Interest Group" adopts a rather more neutral approach, although it is not in opposition to religion. Thus, the RCP defines spirituality as the "essentially human, personal and interpersonal dimension that integrates and transcends cultural, religious, psychological, social and emotional aspects of the person." Elsewhere, the RCP mentions varieties of religious experience and of mystical states.

More broadly, healthcare references suggest that spirituality involves "beliefs about life," including religious beliefs. Healthcare spirituality relates people to "soul" or "spirit" and also to "the sacred."

In terms of care, spirituality offers a sense of purpose and of hope. It encourages forgiveness and reconciliation as ways for moving a person towards wholeness. Spirituality broadens both how we understand healing and also the *experience* of healing. It introduces the power of love into the healing process and also offers a dimension of interpersonal healing and reconciliation. It enables people more effectively to confront fear and all that threatens the human psyche. Spirituality offers a way of responding to suffering for which there is no medical cure and helps people to understand unavoidable suffering as paradoxically a way to human growth. There have also been attempts to develop instruments to measure spirituality in terms of positive health outcomes, especially in the area of psychological health, such as peacefulness, harmony, comfort, contentment, and a sense of well-being. Sometimes this is linked explicitly to a practice of prayer. However, other medical practitioners have serious questions about this whole approach.

Overall, spirituality in healthcare is a response to the need to move beyond a purely medicalized model of illness as simply a condition linked to organic disease. Here, sickness is whatever falls below a professionally defined standard of acceptable physical or mental capacity. In this model, the definers of health or illness are the doctors. The introduction of spirituality is part of a move towards a more person-centered approach to health. A person is to be viewed as a whole rather than merely in relation to their clinical symptoms. Thus, spirituality asks "what is a 'whole' person"? There is greater emphasis on connections between the individual and the surrounding environment. Equally, "illness" is understood to have complex causes, including personal and social contexts.

Clearly the concept of spirituality also implies that we believe that there is a spiritual dimension as part of what constitutes our personal make-up. A "person" is a psycho-spiritual-physical unity. Thus, "illness" is a fragmentation of our essential unity. "Health" therefore includes our spiritual dimension. It relates to a broader notion of human orientation – towards others and towards the integration of all the human elements, body, mind, and spirit. "Well-being" takes account of the totality of our life, and "health" is certainly more than clinical "curing" and does not exclude suffering. Indeed, there is a question of what is meant by "spiritual pain" and whether all such pain is necessarily bad and to be "cured." Are we asked to *eradicate* all our problems or simply to provide contexts in which they can be addressed?

Finally, are there any helpful clues to spirituality and healthcare in the Christian approach to spirituality? "Spirituality" expresses our engagement with "the spiritual" which, in its New Testament origins, is related to "the holy." As we have seen, this connects us to "the whole" rather than to mere fragments of life and reality. In Christian terms, what encapsulates "the whole" is God. However, also in Christian terms, God is not detached from the human condition but indwells in everyone as a presence that animates and centers us. So when we talk of "the spiritual" in reference to ourselves, it refers to the core of a person, the deepest part of our identity. Many people have called this "the soul." Others, such as St Augustine, used the symbol of the heart – in his case derived from late classical Judaism where it expressed the source of motivation and intention.

A Christian vision of spirituality embraces two major areas of belief that have a potential impact on how we understand the nature and process of healthcare. The first is the reality of God as both transcendent and immanent. Clearly, in terms of a Christian contribution to healthcare in pluralist cultures, the existence or otherwise of God cannot itself be the issue. However, such a belief is closely associated with understandings of the nature of human existence that may be introduced into the conversation. For example, the "high" Christian view of creation as an expression of the sacred counters a purely instrumental view of material existence. Second, in terms specifically of human identity "in the image of God," Christianity also has a "high" view of the unique value of each person (who should not therefore be treated merely as an example of the general category, "patient").

Where does this leave us in relation to spirituality and healthcare? Positively, Christian spirituality reinforces the holistic and integrative approach present in much contemporary reflection of healthcare spirituality, spiritual health, and spiritual care. However, the Christian spiritual tradition also highlights the practical as well as theoretical inadequacy of attempts to use generalized definitions of spirituality. For example, there is a need for spirituality in healthcare contexts to be more explicit about understandings of human purpose and direction and of human identity. Medicine and healthcare are not value-free zones associated with apparently neutral chemical or mechanical skills (drug therapy and surgery). Both of these areas are based on assumptions about hoped-for outcomes, albeit sometimes unexamined ones, that effect both the motivation of practitioners and how healthcare recipients are identified and valued. The very notion of "care" implies a sense of service, founded on a particular sense of human dignity.

Once healthcare loses this sense of the value and complexity of the individual person, it ceases to be "care-full" in the proper sense.

Spirituality and the Meaning of Cities

A third example of spirituality in relation to the everyday realm and public values concerns the meaning and future of cities. The related themes of spirituality and architecture, spirituality and planning, and urban spirituality have also begun to make an appearance in recent times.

Cities represent and create a climate of values that define how we understand ourselves and gather together. In his provocative study, *The City: A Global History*, Joel Kotkin suggests that throughout history successful cities have performed three critical functions – the provision of security, the hosting of commerce, and the creation of sacred space. Historically, the latter has often been expressed by religious buildings that embody a transcendent vision for the city. However, Kotkin's point is that a city itself is, or should be, a sacred place, embodying an inspiring vision of human existence and possibility. Kotkin notes that all world religions, including Christianity, have produced models of urban meaning. However, he critiques the religions for losing touch with their own urban visions and therefore failing to contribute these to contemporary debates about the future of cities. Yet, as he comments, without some kind of shared spiritual vision it is difficult to envision a viable urban future. A successful city is, in the end, a state of mind that captures the imagination of its citizens.[4]

The world is rapidly becoming urbanized. The contemporary growth rate of cities presents a critical challenge. In 1950, 29% of the world's population lived in urban environments. By 1990, this had risen to 50%, and according to United Nations statistics is predicted to rise to around 60% by 2025 and 70% by 2050. In the first part of the twenty-first century, the "big story" is a global migration of people from countryside to city. Humanity for the first time faces a mega-urbanized world. We are also dealing increasingly with megacities, most of which are in the new economic giants – for example, Mumbai 18 million, Sao Paolo 17+ million, and Shanghai 14+ million. However, these sprawling cities are in crisis – frequently burdened by congestion, pollution, and crime.

As we confront urban futures in the twenty-first century, a key question is what cities are for. If cities are to have meaning rather than simply an unavoidable existence, there needs to be much greater reflection on their civilizing possibilities and on what stands in the way of enhancing these. The city is *the* public realm par excellence. Since the days of Plato and Aristotle, cities have been understood as powerful symbols of human community and, in particular, as paradigms of our public life. In practical terms, what does "public" imply? It is the context where we interact with strangers and where diverse people struggle to establish a common life. This is not an easy task. Yet, precisely because cities combine differences of age, ethnicity, culture, gender, and religion in unparalleled ways, they have a capacity to focus a range of physical, intellectual, and creative energies.

The Spiritual and the Spatial

In terms of enhancing the spiritual in the city, we need to think both about spatial structures and about social and urban virtues. First of all, we need urban designs that express more than a purely utilitarian understanding of human needs. Urban designs need to speak to us, like the great cathedrals of a former age, of the "condition of the world." One design question concerns awe. What makes buildings or spaces "awesome" in a constructive sense? It surely implies more than sheer amazement at innovative design or at the overwhelming presence of buildings that dominate our skyline. "Awesome" also reflects *motive* and *purpose*. Genuine reverence and awe are more likely in relation to buildings that reinforce the overall value of people and of shared public life rather than those that simply project the profiles of socio-economic elites.

A second way that physical space shapes a spiritual city concerns how we design public spaces. Some architects talk of what they call "open-minded space" – a concept with spiritual resonances. Spaces like the piazza or city square are ideally person-centered. Their function should be left open rather than predetermined by planners or politicians. Such spaces do not prioritize efficiency but invite human participation. "Open-minded space" promotes inclusivity, encourages diversity, and enables creativity and play as opposed to control and constraint. An important feature of such space is therefore "indeterminacy," the human ability to transcend imposed, static order. This leaves room for surprise and celebrates people's social personae. Traditional city squares offer a physical and spiritual centering for a city and its inhabitants.

Finally, an interesting issue concerns the continued significance of traditional sacred spaces such as the great medieval churches and cathedrals of European cities. There is plenty of evidence for a sustained interest in these buildings as more than museums. Even though many people who enter such spaces may have little sense of the original meaning of the buildings, this does not imply a total loss of spiritual focus. An increase of visitors to, for example, the great European cathedrals as well as some Europe-wide research underlines the complexity of people's motives for entering such buildings and a residual but clear sense of the sacred. This raises important questions such as: How can we enable sacred spaces to be widely accessible without losing their integrity? How can they better express a public role beyond serving religious worshipers? How might such spaces function effectively?

The Spiritual and Urban Virtues

Urban spirituality also involves our overall "conduct of life" and human interaction. This must surely include the notion of virtue. So, what might be some urban virtues for the twenty-first century? Interestingly, the meaning of social virtues such as "urbanity" and "civility" derive explicitly from city life. Some contemporary urban thinkers write about frugality while others promote the related notions of renunciation and restraint in relation to our need for a renewed sense of mutuality. Mutuality demands the surrender of absolute claims to individual choice in favor of the "common good."

The Jewish and Christian scriptures both place a great deal of emphasis on the virtue of hospitality to strangers. As we have seen throughout this book, the classic Christian spiritualities also involve a vision of how human life is intended to be and how it can be transformed. In this context, city spirituality must be robust enough to confront the destructive side of life by offering both language and practices to confront structural evils such as violence, injustice, and social exclusion. Consequently, I want to outline briefly a significant urban virtue which has already been mentioned – to seek the "common good."

What is this "common good"? In traditional terms derived from Aristotle, it is the fitting goals for a good life. A truly good life is orientated to what is shared with others because the individual good is inseparable from the good of all. During the Middle Ages, St Thomas Aquinas who based himself on Aristotle added that the good to be sought by all in common is ultimately God. Thus, seeking the common good fulfills the double commandment to love God with all one's strength and to love our neighbor as ourselves. Later, St Ignatius Loyola in the sixteenth century wrote of making "the *more universal* good" the key criterion in discernment and choice about Christian action and service. This classic understanding of the common good counters any purely utilitarian approach to general welfare. Aristotle and Aquinas both believed that the common good includes bonds of mutual loyalty and affection that build authentic community.

A leading American Catholic social ethicist, David Hollenbach, offers a challenging exposition of the continued contemporary validity of seeking "the common good" in religiously plural and socially diverse cities. This necessarily involves negotiation and, as Hollenbach admits, is not a quick fix. What matters is not immediate success but our commitment to an open-ended process of making meaning, creating values, and discovering a shared vocabulary.

> This common pursuit of a shared vision of the good life can be called intellectual solidarity...for it calls for serious thinking by citizens about what their distinctive understandings of the good imply for a society made up of people with many different traditions. It is a form of solidarity, because it can only occur in an active dialogue of mutual listening and speaking across the boundaries of religion and culture. Indeed, dialogue that seeks to understand those with different visions of the good life is already a form of solidarity even when disagreement continues to exist.[5]

Other Factors?

Beyond this selection of three critical issues, what other factors are likely to have an impact on the future trajectories of Christian spirituality? An awareness of the current fragility of our planet and ecosystems makes the development of ecologically alert spiritualities a matter of urgency. If one theme comes to dominate Christian spirituality in the next fifty years, it is likely to be this. Rather bland or romantic creation-centered spiritualities will need to give way to more robust and challenging versions of eco-spirituality that counter the irresponsibility of extreme consumerist lifestyles. Already liberationist approaches to ecology are emerging in Latin America, Africa, and Asia, and there is also the global activism of Christian eco-feminist spirituality.

It is important to underline that a concern for ecology, however radical, needs to be informed by a contemplative dimension. Christian eco-spirituality, for example, has a mystical edge as it speaks of awe and wonder, and reverence for God present in matter. There is also a growing interest in the broader connections between mysticism, social justice, and social transformation, and here contemporary Christian spirituality has exceptional riches to offer.

Another feature of the contemporary spiritual quest is the desire for some kind of intentional community. This has, if anything, become even more broadly based among both Christians and spiritual seekers than in the past. Contemporary research underlines a paradox that while the number of people joining monastic life in Western countries is decreasing, the number of people who visit or stay at monasteries is on the increase. Some new communities have emerged that are more dynamic. Many of them have attracted a wider circle of associates, often young and both men and women. One example that combines contemplative prayer and liturgy with a working life in the midst of the city are the Fraternités de Jerusalem. Other vibrant groups, while Roman Catholic in origin, are nowadays explicitly ecumenical. Examples are the mixed monastic community at Bose in northern Italy, the lay community of San Egidio in Rome which is also deeply involved in social and peace issues, and the international network of Christians known as the Focolare Movement which promotes the ideals of human unity and universal solidarity. In the Scandinavian Lutheran churches, the *Korsvei-bevegelsen* or CrossRoad Movement emerged in the early 1980s from the earlier Jesus movement and combines a devotional element, a quest for spiritual renewal and the promotion of retreats and a strong commitment to social justice and the eradication of global poverty. The Movement has developed a rule of life partly inspired by classical monastic rules, and more recently some members decided to form an intentional residential community.

Finally, there will undoubtedly be more engagement between spirituality and human creativity both artistic and scientific. On the one hand, the arts, music, and literature have, for many people, become the media for a sometimes inchoate and non-thematic exploration of spirituality and human meaning. On the other hand, the frontiers between spirituality and science offer some of the most challenging areas for reflection. Ever-expanding developments in, for example, quantum physics, genetic research, neuroscience, artificial intelligence, and cosmology do not simply raise ethical issues or philosophical-theological questions. For scientific exploration touches directly on identity and human purpose and at the same time opens up different and unexpected ways of encountering the numinous.

The Contemporary Turn to Practice

It is worth noting a further aspect of the contemporary spiritual climate. This concerns the current priority given to spiritual *practices*. There is a theoretical basis for this in the notable "turn to practice" in a range of academic fields. Academics and writers once tended to concentrate on systems of meaning, texts, and structures. Nowadays theorists in, for example, philosophy, history, cultural theory, and the study of religion give equal attention to "practices." In some respects, this expresses a wish to counter purely systematic, theoretical, or propositional approaches to knowledge. This "turn to practice" emphasizes that knowledge, language, and historical movements are aspects of interconnected human practices or action.

The current fascination with spirituality also focuses primarily on spiritual practices rather than on complex theories. Forms of meditation, physical movements such as yoga and tai chi, disciplines of frugality and abstinence (e.g. from alcohol or meat), pilgrimage to sacred sites (e.g. the *camino* to Santiago de Compostela in Northern Spain), and spiritual retreats of various forms as mentioned in Chapter 7 seem to be particularly attractive to a wide range of people.

The emphasis on practice clearly has positive features. For one thing it emphasizes the centrality of context, embodiment, and material culture. The focus on spiritual practices also reflects a democratization of spirituality which is no longer seen as defined solely by religious authorities or as the preserve of those who adopt special lifestyles such as monasticism. The emphasis on practices such as meditation potentially offers everyone access to the spiritual dimension of life. In this context, as this book shows, Christian spirituality possesses a rich variety of spiritual practices and contemplative-mystical wisdom that deserves to be better known by contemporary spiritual seekers.

However, the long history of Christian spirituality also raises questions about an emphasis on spiritual practices in isolation. First of all, Christian spiritual traditions do not merely teach certain special practices but also outline a spiritual path directed at a transformed *practice of everyday life*. The overall approach of Christian spirituality is built on certain foundations, particularly belief in a God who acts in the world and in human lives and, indeed, who has embraced the human condition in the person of Jesus Christ. As a result, Christian spirituality also has a vision of human existence and what will lead it to ultimate fulfillment. According to this vision, the spiritual life is a journey away from self-centered attachments towards freedom and a transcendent destiny which is classically described as "union with God." Finally, the history of Christian spirituality clearly promotes an understanding of human identity as inherently social rather than purely individualistic and an approach to the spiritual life that is not focused exclusively on contemplative interiority but includes the love and service of our fellow human beings.

Conclusion

It is clear from what has been discussed in this chapter that, in the midst of the complexities of today's spiritual climate, Christian spirituality is in process of major readjustment. Of course, as I have sought to indicate throughout this book, Christian spirituality has never been static or a single, simple reality. Fresh wisdom teachings and innovative traditions with particular emphases, ways of life, and practices have persistently emerged across the centuries in response to historical events and new cultural contexts. It seems unlikely that this adaptability will cease, and for this reason Christian spirituality appears to me to be destined to survive into the future, albeit in new forms. It is already adjusting to an increasingly globalized and multicultural world, to the impact of information technology, and to the challenge of dialogue with other faiths. Finally, as I have suggested, there are already examples of how Christian spirituality has the ability to make a positive contribution to the current fascination with spirituality outside explicitly religious contexts.

Notes

1   See Oliver Roy, *Secularism Confronts Islam*, New York: Columbia University Press, 2007.
2   See L. Kretzschmar, M. Karecki, and C. Kourie, "African Spirituality" and G. Gispert-Sauch, "Asia", and M. Ashley, "Latin-American Spirituality", in P. Sheldrake, ed., *The New SCM Dictionary of Christian Spirituality*, London: SCM Press, 2005 (in North America, *The New Westminster Dictionary of Christian Spirituality*, Louisville: Westminster-John Knox Press). A recent historical study of Christian spirituality contains a more global perspective. See J. Wiseman, *Spirituality and Mysticism*, Maryknoll: Orbis Books, 2006, Chapters 8, 9, and 10.
3   D. Burke et al., *Cybernauts Awake! Ethical and Spiritual Implications of Computers, Information Technology and the Internet*, London: Church House Publishing, 1999.
4   Joel Kotkin, *The City: A Global History*, New York: Random House, 2005.
5   David Hollenbach, *The Common Good and Christian Ethics*, Cambridge: Cambridge University Press, 2002, pp. 137–138.

Select Bibliography

1 World Spirituality Series

McGinn, B., Meyendorff, J., and Leclercq, J. (eds.), *Christian Spirituality I: Origins to the Twelfth Century*, New York: Crossroad Publishing, 1985.

Raitt, J. (ed.), *Christian Spirituality II: High Middle Ages and Reformation*, New York: Crossroad Publishing, 1987.

Dupré, L. and Saliers, D. (eds.), *Christian Spirituality III: Post-Reformation and Modern*, New York: Crossroad Publishing, 1989.

2 Classics of Western Spirituality Series

Armstrong, R. and Brady, I. (eds.), *Francis and Clare: The Complete Works*, New York: Paulist Press, 1982.

Babinsky, E. (ed.), *Marguerite Porete: The Mirror of Simple Souls*, Classics of Western Spirituality, New York: Paulist Press, 1993.

Clark, M.T. (ed.), *Augustine of Hippo: Selected Writings*, Classics of Western Spirituality, New York: Paulist Press, 1984.

Colledge, E. and Walsh, J. (eds.), *Julian of Norwich: Showings*, New York: Paulist Press, 1978.

Cousins, E. (ed.), *Bonaventure: The Soul's Journey into God, The Tree of Life, The Life of St. Francis*, New York: Paulist Press, 1978.

Davies, O. (ed.), *Celtic Spirituality*, Classics of Western Spirituality, New York: Paulist Press, 1999.

De Catanzaro, C.J. (ed.), *Symeon the New Theologian: The Discourses*, New York: Paulist Press, 1980.

Erb, P. (ed.), *Johann Arndt: True Christianity*, New York: Paulist Press, 1979.

Spirituality: A Brief History, Second Edition. Philip Sheldrake.
© 2013 John Wiley & Sons, Ltd. Published 2013 by John Wiley & Sons, Ltd.

Erb, P. (ed.), *The Pietists: Selected Writings*, New York: Paulist Press, 1983.

Evans, G.R. (ed.), *Bernard of Clairvaux: Selected Works*, Classics of Western Spirituality, New York: Paulist Press, 1987.

Ganss, G. (ed.), *Ignatius of Loyola: The Spiritual Exercises and Selected Works*, New York: Paulist Books, 1991.

Gendle, N. (ed.), *Gregory Palamas: The Triads*, New York: Paulist Press, 1983.

Greer, R. (ed.), *Origen: An Exhortation to Martyrdom, Prayer and Selected Works*, Classics of Western Spirituality, New York: Paulist Press, 1979.

Gregg, R.C. (ed.), *Athanasius: The Life of Antony & the Letter to Marcellinus*, Classics of Western Spirituality, New York: Paulist Press, 1980.

Hart, C. (ed.), *Hadewijch: The Complete Works*, Classics of Western Spirituality, New York: Paulist Press, 1980.

Hart, C., and Bishop, J. (eds.), *Hildegard of Bingen: Scivias*, New York: Paulist Press, 1990.

Kavanaugh, K. (ed.), *John of the Cross: Selected Writings*, New York: Paulist Press, 1987.

Kavanaugh, K. and Rodriguez, O. (eds.), *Teresa of Avila: The Interior Castle*, New York: Paulist Press, 1979.

Kerr, I. (ed.), *John Henry Newman: Selected Sermons*, New York: Paulist Press, 1994.

Liechty, D. (ed.), *Early Anabaptist Spirituality*, New York: Paulist Press, 1994.

Luibheid, C. (ed.), *John Cassian: Conferences*, Classics of Western Spirituality, New York: Paulist Press, 1985.

Luibheid, C. and Rorem, P. (eds.), *Pseudo-Dionysius: The Complete Works*, Classics of Western Spirituality, New York: Paulist Press, 1987.

Luibheid, C. and Russell, N. (eds.), *John Climacus: The Ladder of Divine Ascent*, Classics of Western Spirituality, New York: Paulist Press, 1982.

Malherbe, A.J. and Ferguson, E. (eds.), *Gregory of Nyssa: The Life of Moses*, Classics of Western Spirituality, New York: Paulist Press, 1978.

Martin, D. (ed.), *Carthusian Spirituality: The Writings of Hugh of Balma and Guigo de Ponte*, Classics of Western Spirituality, New York: Paulist Press, 1997.

McGinn, B. and Colledge, E. (eds.), *Meister Eckhart: The Essential Sermons, Commentaries, Treatises and Defense*, New York: Paulist Press, 1985.

McGinn, B. and Tobin, F. (eds.), *Meister Eckhart: Teacher and Preacher*, New York: Paulist Press, 1987.

McVey, K. (ed.), *Ephrem the Syrian: Hymns*, New York: Paulist Press, 1989.

Meyendorff, J. (ed.), *Gregory Palamas: The Triads*, Classics of Western Spirituality, New York: Paulist Press, 1983.

Noffke, S. (ed.), *Catherine of Siena: The Dialogue*, New York: Paulist Press, 1980.

Pentkovsky, A. (ed.), *The Pilgrim's Tale*, New York: Paulist Press, 1999.

Ryan, F. and Rybolt, J. (eds.), *Vincent de Paul and Louise de Marillac: Rules, Conferences and Writing*, New York: Paulist Press, 1995.

Shrady, M. (ed.), *Johannes Tauler: Sermons*, New York: Paulist Press, 1985.

Steere, D. (ed.), *Quaker Spirituality: Selected Writings*, New York: Paulist Press, 1984.

Thibert, P.-M. (ed.), *Francis de Sales, Jane de Chantal: Letters of Spiritual Direction*, New York: Paulist Press, 1988.

Thompson, W. (ed.), *Bérulle and the French School: Selected Writings*, New York: Paulist Press, 1989.

Tobin, F. (ed.), *Henry Suso: The Exemplar, with Two German Sermons*, New York: Paulist Press, 1989.

Tobin, F. (ed.), *Mechtild of Magdeburg: The Flowing Light of the Godhead*, Classics of Western Spirituality, New York: Paulist Press, 1998.

Tugwell, S. (ed.), *Early Dominicans: Selected Writings*, Classics of Western Spirituality, New York: Paulist Press, 1982.

Van Engen, J. (ed.), *Devotio Moderna: Basic Writings*, New York: Paulist Press, 1988.

Whaling, F. (ed.), *John and Charles Wesley: Selected Writings and Hymns*, New York: Paulist Press, 1981.

Whitson, R.E. (ed.), *The Shakers: Two Centuries of Spiritual Reflection*, New York: Paulist Press, 1983.

Winkworth, M. (ed.), *Gertrude of Helfta: The Herald of Divine Love*, Classics of Western Spirituality, New York: Paulist Press, 1993.

Wiseman, J. (ed.), *John Ruusbroec: The Spiritual Espousals and Other Works*, New York: Paulist Press, 1985.

3   Traditions of Christian Spirituality Series

Belisle, P.-D., *The Language of Silence: The Changing Face of Monastic Solitude*, London: Darton Longman & Todd and Maryknoll: Orbis Books, 2003.

Birkel, M., *Silence and Witness: Quaker Spirituality*, London: Darton Longman & Todd and New York: Orbis Books, 2004.

Cartledge, M., *Encountering the Spirit: The Charismatic Tradition*, London: Darton Longman & Todd and Maryknoll: Orbis Books, 2006.

Chase, S., *Contemplation and Compassion: The Victorine Tradition*, London: Darton Longman & Todd and New York: Orbis Books, 2003.

Chryssavgis, J., *Light Through Darkness: The Orthodox Tradition*, London: Darton Longman & Todd and New York: Orbis Books, 2004.

Countryman, W., *The Poetic Imagination: An Anglican Spiritual Tradition*, London: Darton Longman & Todd and New York: Orbis Books, 1999.

De Waal, E., *The Way of Simplicity: The Cistercian Tradition*, London: Darton Longman & Todd and New York: Orbis Books, 1998.

Hanson, B., *Grace that Frees: The Lutheran Tradition*, London: Darton Longman & Todd and New York: Orbis Books, 2004.

Lonsdale, D., *Eyes to See, Ears to Hear: An Introduction to Ignatian Spirituality*, London: Darton Longman & Todd and New York: Orbis Books, 2000.

Martin, T., *Our Restless Heart: The Augustinian Tradition*, London: Darton Longman & Todd and Maryknoll: Orbis Books, 2003.

McGreal, W., *At the Fountain of Elijah: The Carmelite Tradition*, London: Darton Longman & Todd and New York: Orbis Books, 1999.

McGuckin, J., *Standing in God's Holy Fire: The Byzantine Tradition*, London: Darton Longman & Todd and New York: Orbis Books, 2001.

Murk-Jansen, S., *Brides in the Desert: The Spirituality of the Beguines*, Traditions of Christian Spirituality. London: Darton Longman & Todd and New York: Orbis Books, 1998.

Nuth, J., *God's Lovers in an Age of Anxiety: The Medieval English Mystics*, London: Darton Longman & Todd and Maryknoll: Orbis Books, 2001.

O'Loughlin, T., *Journeys on the Edge: The Celtic Tradition*, London: Darton Longman & Todd and New York: Orbis Books, 2000.

Randall, I., *What a Friend We Have in Jesus: The Evangelical Tradition*, London: Darton Longman & Todd and New York: Orbis Books, 2005.

Short, W., *Poverty and Joy: The Franciscan Tradition*, London: Darton Longman & Todd and New York: Orbis Books, 1999.

Snyder, C.A., *Following in the Footsteps of Christ: The Anabaptist Tradition*, London: Darton Longman & Todd and New York: Orbis Books, 2004.

Stewart, C., *Prayer and Community: The Benedictine Tradition*, Traditions of Christian Spirituality Series, London: Darton Longman & Todd and Maryknoll: Orbis Books, 1998.

Woods, R., *Mysticism and Prophecy: The Dominican Tradition*, London: Darton Longman & Todd and New York: Orbis Books, 1998.

Wright, W., *Heart Speaks to Heart: The Salesian Tradition*, London: Darton Longman & Todd and Maryknoll: Orbis Books, 2004.

4   Further Reading

Agnew, U., Flanagan, B., and Heylin, G. (eds.), *With Wisdom Seeking God: The Academic Study of Spirituality*, Leuven: Peeters, 2008.

Bamberger, J.E. (ed.), *Evagrius Ponticus: The Praktikos. Chapters on Prayer*, Kalamazoo: Cistercian Publications, 1970.

Barnes, M. (ed.), *The Way Supplement: Spirituality and Ethics*, 88, Spring 1997.

Bartoli, M., *Clare of Assisi*, London: Darton Longman & Todd, 1993 [1989].

Barton, S., *The Spirituality of the Gospels*, London: SPCK Publishing, 1992.

Bolshakoff, S., *Russian Mystics*, Kalamazoo: Cistercian Publications, 1980.

Bonhoeffer, D., *Letters and Papers from Prison*, New York: Macmillan, 1971.

Bonhoeffer, D., *The Cost of Discipleship*, London: SCM Press, 1984.

Bridges, F. Wilson, *Resurrection Song: African American Spirituality*, New York: Orbis Books, 2001.

Brown, P., *Society and the Holy in Late Antiquity*, London: Faber, 1982.

Brown, P., *The Body and Society: Men, Women and Sexual Renunciation in Early Christianity*, London: Faber & Faber, 1991.

Brown, P., *The Making of Late Antiquity*, new edition, Cambridge, MA: Harvard University Press, 1993.

Brown, P., *Authority and the Sacred: Aspects of the Christianisation of the Roman World*, Cambridge: Cambridge University Press, 1995.

Burton-Christie, D., *The Word in the Desert*, Oxford/New York: Oxford University Press, 1993.

Bynum, C. Walker, *Jesus as Mother: Studies in the Spirituality of the High Middle Ages*, Berkeley: University of California Press, 1984.

Calvin, J., *Institutes of the Christian Religion*, Grand Rapids: Eerdmans, 1995.

Carrette, J. and King, R., *Selling Spirituality: The Silent Takeover of Religion*, London: Routledge, 2004.

Casey, M., *Sacred Reading: The Ancient Art of Lectio Divina*, Ligouri: Triumph Books, 1996.

Chinnici, J., *Living Stones: The History and Structure of Catholic Spiritual Life in the United States*, New York: Macmillan, 1989.

Church of England Board for Social Responsibility, *Cybernauts Awake! Ethical and Spiritual Implications of Computers, Information Technology and the Internet*, London: Church House Publishing, 1999.

Colledge, E. and Walsh, J. (eds.), *Guigo II: The Ladder of Monks & Twelve Meditations*, New York: Doubleday Image Books, 1978.

Coleman, S. and Elsner, J. (eds.), *Pilgrimage: Past and Present in the World Religions*, London: British Museum, 1995.

Connor, E. (ed.), *Aelred of Rievaulx: The Mirror of Charity*, Kalamazoo: Cistercian Publications, 1990.

Cunningham, L.S. (ed.), *Thomas Merton: Spiritual Master. The Essential Writings*, New York: Paulist Press, 1992.

Cunningham, L.S., *Thomas Merton and the Monastic Vision*, Grand Rapids: William B. Eerdmans, 1999.

Cunningham, L.S. and Egan, K.J., *Christian Spirituality: Themes from the Tradition*. New York: Paulist Press, 1996.

De Caussade, J.-P., *The Sacrament of the Present Moment*, London: Fount, 1981.

De Certeau, M., *The Mystic Fable: The Sixteenth and Seventeenth Centuries*, Chicago: University of Chicago Press, 1992.

De Sales, F., *Introduction to the Devout Life*, New York: Doubleday, 1982.

De Waal, E., *Seeking God: The Way of St. Benedict*, Collegeville: The Liturgical Press, 1984.

Dreyer, E. and Burrows, M. (eds.), *Minding the Spirit: The Study of Christian Spirituality*, Baltimore: Johns Hopkins University Press, 2005.

Du Boulay, S., *Beyond the Darkness: A Biography of Bede Griffiths*, New York/London: Doubleday, 1998.

Duby, G., *The Age of the Cathedrals: Art and Society 980–1420*, Chicago: University of Chicago Press, 1981.

Dunn, M., *The Emergence of Monasticism: From the Desert Fathers to the Early Middle Ages*, Oxford: Blackwell Publishing, 2003.

Dyckman, K., Garvin, M., and Liebert, E., *The Spiritual Exercises Reclaimed*, New York: Paulist Press, 2001.

Ellsberg, R. (ed.), *Dorothy Day: Selected Writings*, Maryknoll: Orbis Books, 1992.

Ellsberg, R. (ed.), *Charles de Foucauld: Selected Writings*, Maryknoll: Orbis Boos, 1999.

Espin, O. and Macy, G. (eds.), *Futuring Our Past: Explorations in the Theology of Tradition*, Maryknoll: Orbis Books, 2006.

Fedotov, G.P. (ed.), *A Treasury of Russian Spirituality*, London: Sheed & Ward, 1981.

Flanagan, K. and Jupp, P. (eds.), *A Sociology of Spirituality*, Aldershot/Burlington: Ashgate, 2007.

Frugoni, C., *A Distant City: Images of Urban Experience in the Medieval World*, Princeton: Princeton University Press, 1991.

Griffiths, B., *A New Vision of Reality: Western Science, Eastern Mysticism and Christian Faith*, Springfield: Templegate, 1990.

Gutiérrez, G., *We Drink from Our Own Wells: The Spiritual Journey of a People*, Maryknoll: Orbis Books, 1984.

Gutiérrez, G., *On Job: God-Talk and the Suffering of the Innocent*, Maryknoll: Orbis Books, 1998.

Hackel, S., *Pearl of Great Price: The Life of Mother Maria Skobtsova*, Crestwood: St. Vladimir's Seminary Press, 1981.

Harmless, W., *Desert Christians: An Introduction to the Literature of Early Monasticism*, Oxford/New York: Oxford University Press, 2004.

Hastings, A. (ed.), *A World History of Christianity*, London: Cassell, 1999.

Hausherr, I. *Spiritual Direction in the Early Christian East*, Kalamazoo: Cistercian Publications, 1990.

Herring, G.W., *What was the Oxford Movement?* London: Continuum, 2002.

Holder, A. (ed.), *The Blackwell Companion to Christian Spirituality*, Oxford: Blackwell Publishing, 2005.

Hollenbach, D., *The Common Good and Christian Ethics*, Cambridge: Cambridge University Press, 2002.

Holmes, A., *A Life Pleasing to God: The Spirituality of the Rules of St Basil*, London: Darton Longman & Todd, 2000.

Hudson, W.S. (ed.), *Walter Rauschenbusch: Selected Writings*, New York: Paulist Press, 1984.

Isasi-Díaz, A.M., *La Lucha Continues: Mujerista Theology*, Maryknoll: Orbis Books, 2004.

Jantzen, G., *Power, Gender and Christian Mysticism*, Cambridge: Cambridge University Press, 1995.

Johnson, E., *She Who Is: The Mystery of God in Feminist Theological Discourse*, New York: Crossroad, 1996.

Kardong, T.C. (ed.), *Benedict's Rule: A Translation and Commentary*, Collegeville: The Liturgical Press, 1996.

Kelly, G.B. and Nelson, F. Burton, *The Cost of Moral Leadership: The Spirituality of Dietrich Bonhoeffer*, Grand Rapids: William B. Eerdmans, 2003.

King, U. (ed.), *Pierre Teilhard de Chardin: Selected Writings*, Maryknoll: Orbis Books, 1999.

Kotkin, J., *The City: A Global History*, New York: Random House, 2005.

LaCugna, C., "Trinitarian Spirituality," in M. Downey (ed.), *New Dictionary of Catholic Spirituality*, Collegeville: The Liturgical Press, 1993.

Laker, M.E. (ed.), *Aelred of Rievaulx: Spiritual Friendship*, Kalamazoo: Cistercian Publications, 1977.

Lawless, G., *Augustine of Hippo and His Monastic Rule*, Oxford: Clarendon Press, 1987.

Lawrence, C.H., *The Friars: The Impact of the Early Mendicant Movement on Western Society*, London: Longman, 1994.

Le Goff, J., *Medieval Civilisation*, Oxford: Blackwell, 1988.

Le Goff, J., *Saint Francis of Assisi*, English translation, London: Routledge, 2004 [1999].

Leclercq, J., *The Love of Learning and the Desire for God: A Study of Monastic Culture*, 3rd edition, New York: Fordham University Press, 1982.

Leech, K., *Soul Friend: Spiritual Direction in the Modern World*, revised edition, London: Darton Longman & Todd, 1994.

Lescher, B. and Liebert, E. (eds.), *Exploring Christian Spirituality: Essays in Honor of Sandra M. Schneiders*, New York: Paulist Press, 2006.

Leyser, H., *Hermits and the New Monasticism*, London: Macmillan, 1984.

López-Baralt, L., *The Sufi 'trobar clus' and Spanish Mysticism: A Shared Symbolism*, Lahore: Iqbal Academy, 2000.

Lossky, V., *Mystical Theology of the Eastern Church*, London: James Clarke, 1991.

Louf, A., *The Cistercian Way*, Kalamazoo: Cistercian Publications, 1989.

Louth, A., *The Origins of the Christian Mystical Tradition*, Oxford: Clarendon Press, 1992.

Louth, A., *The Wilderness of God*, London: Darton Longman & Todd, 1991.

Markus, R.A., *Saeculum: History and Society in the Theology of St Augustine*, Cambridge: Cambridge University Press, 1970.

Markus, R.A., *The End of Ancient Christianity*, Cambridge: Cambridge University Press, 1998.

Matarasso, P. (ed.), *The Cistercian World: Monastic Writings of the Twelfth Century*, London/New York: Penguin Books, 1993.

McGinn, B., *The Foundations of Mysticism: Origins to the Fifth Century*, New York: Crossroad Publishing, 1991.

McGinn, B., *The Mystical Thought of Meister Eckhart*, New York: Crossroad Publishing, 2001.

Merton, T., *Conjectures of a Guilty Bystander*, New York: Doubleday, 1966.

Miles, M.R., *Practicing Christianity: Critical Perspectives for an Embodied Spirituality*, New York: Crossroad, 1988.

Munitiz, J. and Endean, P. (eds.), *Saint Ignatius of Loyola: Personal Writings*, London/New York: Penguin Books, 1996.

Murray, P. (ed.), *The Deer's Cry: A Treasury of Irish Religious Verse*, Dublin: Four Courts Press, 1986.

Newman, B., *Sister of Wisdom: St Hildegard's Theology of the Feminine*, Berkeley: University of California Press, 1989.

O'Loughlin, T., *Celtic Theology*, London/New York: Continuum, 2000,

O'Malley, J. (ed.), *Collected Works of Erasmus: Spiritualia*, Toronto: University of Toronto Press, 1989.

O'Malley, J., *The First Jesuits*, Cambridge, MA: Harvard University Press, 1993.

Palmer, G., Sherrard, P. and Ware, K. (eds.), *The Philokalia: The Complete Text*, 5 vols., London/Boston: Faber & Faber, 1979–2003.

Perrin, D., *Studying Christian Spirituality*, London/New York: Routledge, 2007.

Rice, H., *Reformed Spirituality*, Louisville: Westminster John Knox Press, 1991.

Rowell, G., Stevenson, K., and Williams, R. (eds.), *Love's Redeeming Work: The Anglican Quest for Holiness*, Oxford: Oxford University Press, 2001.

Roy, O., *Secularism Confronts Islam*, New York: Columbia University Press, 2007.

Ruggieri, G., "Faith and History," in Alberigo, G., Jossus, J.-P, and Komonchak, J.A. (eds.), *The Reception of Vatican II*, Washington, DC: Catholic University of America Press, 1987, pp. 92–95.

Schneiders, S., *The Revelatory Text: Interpreting the New Testament as Sacred Scripture*, Collegeville: The Liturgical Press, 1999.

Schneiders, S., "The Study of Christian Spirituality: Contours and Dynamics of a Discipline," in E. Dreyer and M.S. Burrows (eds.), *Minding the Spirit: The Study of Christian Spirituality*, Baltimore: Johns Hopkins University Press, 2005.

Schutz, R., *The Power of the Provisional*, London: Hodder & Stoughton, 1969.

Sheldrake, P., *Spirituality and History: Questions of Interpretation and Method*, revised edition, London: SPCK and New York: Orbis Books, 1995.

Sheldrake, P., *Living Between Worlds: Place and Journey in Celtic Spirituality*, second edition, London: Darton Longman & Todd and Cambridge, MA: Cowley, 1997.

Sheldrake, P. (ed.), *The New SCM Dictionary of Christian Spirituality*, London: SCM Press, 2005/*The New Westminster Dictionary of Christian Spirituality*, Louisville: Westminster John Knox Press, 2005.

Sheldrake, P., *Heaven in Ordinary: George Herbert and His Writings*, Norwich: Canterbury Press, 2009.

Sheldrake, P., *Explorations in Spirituality: History, Theology and Social Practice*, New York: Paulist Press, 2010.

Six, J.-F., *Light of the Night: The Last Eighteen Months in the Life of Thérèse of Lisieux*, London: SCM Press, 1996.

Smith, J.E. (ed.), *Jonathan Edwards: Religious Affections*, New Haven: Yale University Press, 1959.

Sobrino, J., *Spirituality of Liberation*, Maryknoll: Orbis Books, 1988.

Spink, K., *A Universal Heart: The Life and Vision of Brother Roger of Taizé*, London: SPCK, 1986.

Spohn, W., *Go and Do Likewise: Jesus and Ethics*, New York: Continuum, 2000.

Teresa, Frances, *Living the Incarnation: Praying with Francis and Clare of Assisi*, London: Darton Longman & Todd, 1993.

Tracy, D., *Blessed Rage for Order*, New York: Seabury Press, 1975.

Underhill, E., *Mysticism: The Nature and Development of Spiritual Consciousness*, Oxford: Oneworld Publications, 1993.

Waaijman, K., *Spirituality: Forms, Foundations, Methods*, Leuven: Peeters, 2002.

Ward, B. (ed.), *The Prayers and Meditations of St Anselm with the "Proslogion"*, London/New York: Penguin Books, 1984.

Ward, B. (ed.), *The Desert Fathers: Sayings of the Early Christian Monks*, London/New York: Penguin Books, 2003.

Weil, S., *Waiting for God*, New York: Harper, 1973.

Weil, S., *The Need for Roots*, London: Routledge, 2001.

Williams, C. (ed.), *The Letters of Evelyn Underhill*, London: Darton Longman & Todd, 1991.

Williams, R., *On Christian Theology*, Oxford: Blackwell Publishing, 2000.

Williams, R., *The Wound of Knowledge: Christian Spirituality from the New Testament to St John of the Cross*, second revised edition, London: Darton Longman & Todd, 1990.

Wiseman, J., *Spirituality and Mysticism*, Maryknoll: Orbis Books, 2006.

Wood, I., *The Missionary Life: Saints and the Evangelisation of Europe 400–1050*, London: Longman, 2001.

Select Glossary

Abandonment: A varied process of active self-giving to God, based on the certainty of God's irrevocable love, emphasizing trust, patience, or obedience.

Anthropology, theological: The theology of the human person and human identity, particularly the relationship between embodiment and "spirit" or "soul."

Apocalyptic/Apocalypticism: Based on the Apocalypse or Book of Revelation in the New Testament, movements of intense religious fervor in relation to the end of the world and the second coming of Jesus Christ.

Apophatic: The "negative way" or "negative theology," from the Greek for "denial" or "negation," that negates or denies conclusive definitions of God. God is said to be experienced through love but is never finally "known."

Ascent: A classic image for spiritual development. For example, a journey of ascending stages away from material existence towards union with God.

Ascetical theology: Reflection on the initial stage of the spiritual life, associated with the majority of people, related to overcoming disorder and passions and to the cultivation of disciplined spiritual and moral practices.

Spirituality: A Brief History, Second Edition. Philip Sheldrake.
© 2013 John Wiley & Sons, Ltd. Published 2013 by John Wiley & Sons, Ltd.

Asceticism: From the Greek for "training" or "discipline," spiritual dispossession and the cultivation of disciplined practices that enable spiritual growth.

Cataphatic (see Kataphatic)

Character: A concept in Christian ethics (or moral theology) which focuses on what we should aim to be, rather than merely to do, if we are to become fully human.

Christology: Theological reflections on the identity and nature of Jesus Christ as both human and divine.

Common good: The notion that a truly good life is orientated towards what is shared with others. The individual good is inseparable from the good of all.

Contemplation: Sometimes refers to non-discursive styles of meditative practice but, more profoundly, implies an intensification of awareness of God's presence.

Contemplative life: The cultivation of a life of contemplation, focused on attentiveness to God's presence.

Council (of Church): Gatherings of representatives of the worldwide Church to promote reform or to establish key aspects of theological orthodoxy.

Deification (theōsis): The notion that human destiny is ultimately to share in God's own life (but without merging human and divine identities) through the work of God's Spirit acting within each person.

Discernment: A form of spiritual wisdom that involves the capacity to judge wisely in reference to human desires, to choose well, and to recognize the difference between the inspiration of God and the illusory promptings of human dependencies.

Discipleship: Leading a Christian life – the fundamental New Testament image for Christian spirituality. Discipleship has two elements: conversion from sin and following the way of Jesus Christ.

Enlightenment, The: The late-seventeenth-century and eighteenth-century intellectual movement which promoted human reason rather than religion as the guiding principle of a satisfactory life.

Eschatology: From the Greek for the study of "the last things," theological or spiritual reflection on the ultimate destiny of humanity and its implications for life in the here and now.

Eucharist: The central Christian ritual of blessing and eating bread and wine to recall the Last Supper of Jesus with his disciples and to "make present" in the Christian community the reality of the risen Jesus and God's transformative power.

Gothic: A style of European art and architecture beginning in twelfth-century France and involving pointed arches, ribbed vaulting, and flying buttresses. Originally used pejoratively in reference to the barbarian "Goths" by those who preferred classical Greco-Roman architectural styles.

Grace: A theological word that refers to God's active and transformative presence in the world and human existence.

Hagiography: Literally, biographies of the saints. The genre is usually reverential and idealized with the aim of inspiring the reader to imitate the virtues of the person described.

Hesychasm: A distinctive tradition within Eastern Orthodox spirituality, from *hesychia*, the Greek for quietness. A state of stillness in prayer whereby, as a prelude to communion with God, we are freed from images and desire.

Holiness: A state of virtuous human life that powerfully reflects the nature of God to other people. Associated with the category of spiritually realized Christians recognized as "saints."

Humanism: A philosophy or worldview that focuses on the positive value of human nature and of physical or everyday realities. Originally a medieval Christian concept but from the eighteenth century a form of "secular" rationalism opposed to religion.

Iconoclasm: The destruction of religious images and symbols because they are thought to be idolatrous.

Iconography: The tradition of understanding religious art or design as a quasi-mystical channel of God's power and presence.

Illumination: An enlargement of spiritual vision and the reception of spiritual wisdom.

Illuminative way: The second stage of the classic Christian approach to spiritual development, known as "the threefold way." Associated with the "proficients" and related to a movement beyond ascetical self-discipline to a more contemplative life.

Incarnation: The Christian doctrine that God entered the human condition and was "incarnated" (literally, "enfleshed") in the person of Jesus Christ.

Kataphatic: The "affirmative way" or "positive theology." An approach to spirituality and theology that seeks to express the reality of God through images or positive terminology.

Lectio divina: Literally "spiritual reading." The ancient monastic practice of meditative reading of the scriptures.

Liturgy: Public common worship (e.g. the Eucharist) involving formal rituals performed according to an established pattern rather than spontaneously.

Martyrdom: Derived from the Greek *martus* or witness, to suffer death in witness to one's faith.

Meditation: A form of prayer involving a structured and focused practice of reflection on religious and scriptural themes or silent concentration on the presence of God.

Mendicant: From the Latin for "begging," a person whose spiritual life emphasizes the centrality of voluntary poverty and itinerancy modeled on the life of Jesus and the early disciples.

Millenarianism: A belief in the transformation of society, based on the second coming of Jesus, and leading to the establishment of a thousand-year kingdom of God on earth.

Modernism: A controversial late-nineteenth century movement within Western Christianity, especially Roman Catholicism, which sought to bring theology and spirituality into sympathetic dialogue with modern intellectual and social movements.

Modernity: The social and cultural climate that originated with the European Enlightenment and which emphasizes the priority and independence of human reason as opposed to the dominance of religion.

Monasticism: From the Greek *monachos*, "the single one." A counter-cultural spiritual movement characterized by withdrawal from everyday society in order to practice an austere, non-materialistic lifestyle and to cultivate contemplation.

Mystical theology: Originally, theological reflection on the process whereby Christians are drawn into the divine Mystery through exposure to scripture and the sacraments. Later, mystical theology referred to the study of "higher" states and ways of knowing related to a few spiritually developed individuals.

Mysticism: A deep form of spiritual knowledge or experience, often in the context of contemplative practice, associated with the quest for union with God and involving a heightened awareness of God's immediate presence.

Natural theology: Theology based on reason and experience of the everyday, "natural" world as opposed to theology derived from scriptural revelation or from classic Christian doctrines.

Neoplatonism: A school of religious philosophy based on the teachings of Plato and his followers and with a significant influence on Christian theology. The main emphasis is the divine origin of the human soul and its capacity to return to its source by rising above the material, phenomenal world.

Nominalism: A later-medieval intellectual movement that believed that only particular things exist in space-time, and that universals (e.g. the category "cow") are merely "names" or abstractions. Also, faith and revelation alone give us access to theological truth for the ways of God are not accessible via reason, analysis, or rational definition.

Perfection: In the history of Christian spirituality, an idealized state of completion associated with achieving union with God as the culmination of the spiritual journey.

Personalism: A school of philosophy that emphasizes the uniqueness of human beings in the natural world. In explicitly Christian terms, twentieth-century "personalism" countered an instrumentalized understanding of human life and affirmed that people are not be exploited but to be respected and loved.

Pietism: A spiritual movement within Continental Protestantism that emphasized individual spiritual regeneration, the spiritual renewal of the Church, the priority of holiness of life over doctrinal orthodoxy, devotional use of the Bible, and a reduction in the privileged status of clergy.

Piety: Literally, reverence or devotion. In practice, piety refers to a spiritual emphasis on devotional practices, affectivity, and the cultivation of purity of heart.

Pilgrimage: A journey to sacred places undertaken as an act of penitence or in search of spiritual transformation.

Post-secular: A contemporary theoretical concept that implies that the dominance of Western secularism has come to an end and that we have entered a period of greater spiritual sympathies.

Praxis: Activities that aid social justice and the liberation of the poor.

Prayer :   An explicit act of communication with God. The great variety of prayer styles, silent or vocal, brief or extended, complex or simple, alone or in common, act as explicit realizations of a fundamental relationship with God.

Purgative way: The first stage of spiritual development in the classic "threefold way," associated with beginners and related to repentance and the "purgation" or elimination of all that is destructive in human behavior.

Religion: A collection of belief systems, traditions, values, lifestyles, and practices derived either from divine revelation or from a philosophy of transcendence and ultimacy.

Religious life: Communitarian associations of celibate men or women who dedicate their lives to God and are committed to a spiritual lifestyle based on a historic Rule or tradition derived from a founder or founding group.

Retreats: A period of varied length, alone or in a group, spent away from everyday life for the purpose of deepening one's spiritual life and connecting with God through periods of prayer.

Rules, monastic: Normative texts which set out the spiritual principles that guide communities and act as the medium for communicating a distinctive spiritual ethos.

Sacrament: A religious ritual, formally recognized by the Christian Church, involving physical symbols such as bread and wine in the Eucharist, which is a medium for God's transformative action in human life.

Sacred: Related to what is holy or divine. What is worthy of spiritual devotion or what inspires awe and reverence.

Salvation: The redemption or deliverance of human beings from sin and its effects by the action of God.

Sanctification: Depending on the particular Christian tradition, the process of change whereby people become more holy through the work of God's Spirit in their lives, through selfless action, or through a combination of both.

Scholasticism: The dominant philosophical and theological system of learning in medieval universities based on dialectical reasoning.

Secular: From the Latin word *saeculum*, meaning "the here and now" or "the everyday." Contemporary usage tends to contrast "secular" with "religious," but the idea of a "secular realm" of legitimate this-worldly concerns was originally Christian and has positive theological resonances.

Spirituality: The deepest values and meaning by which people seek to live, based on a vision of the human spirit and what will enable it to achieve its full potential. A quest for ultimate meaning and fulfillment.

Spiritual direction: A practice of regular guidance or spiritual counseling of people who seek to grow spiritually. There are various traditions of "direction," some of which are more structured and theoretically based than others.

Spiritual theology: Theological reflection on the nature of, and pursuit of, a "spiritual life."

Syncretism: The combining and blending of practices, symbols, or beliefs from different religions even if these are apparently exclusive or even contradictory.

Threefold way (triplex via):   The historic tradition of formulating three developmental stages on the spiritual journey: the "purgative way" for beginners, the "illuminative way" for proficients, and the "unitive way" for the advanced.

Union: The experience of a habitual presence of God or a quality of immediacy in one's relationship to God.

Unitive way: The third and final stage of spiritual development in the "threefold way" implying a consistent immediacy of presence to God.

Universalism: The philosophy of honoring the religious beliefs and spiritual teachings present in all religions without giving priority to any one religion.

Virtue: A concept in Christian ethics referring to qualities that enable us to become fully human and to the power to act in accordance with our true nature.

Index

Spirituality: A Brief History, Second Edition. Philip Sheldrake.
© 2013 John Wiley & Sons, Ltd. Published 2013 by John Wiley & Sons, Ltd.